Seeking Food Rights

Nation, Inequality and Repression in Uzbekistan

NANCY ROSENBERGER
Oregon State University

WADSWORTH
CENGAGE Learning™

Australia • Brazil • Japan • Korea • Mexico • Singapore • Spain • United Kingdom • United States

WADSWORTH
CENGAGE Learning™

Seeking Food Rights: Nation, Inequality and Repression in Uzbekistan
Nancy Rosenberger

Publisher: Linda Schreiber-Ganster

Acquisitions Editor: Erin Mitchell

Editorial Assistant: Mallory Ortberg

Marketing Manager: Andrew Keay

Marketing Assistant/Associate: Dimitri Hagnere

Marketing Communications Manager: Tami Strang

Content Project Management: PreMediaGlobal

Art Director: Caryl Gorska

Manufacturing Manager: Marcia Locke

Manufacturing Buyer: Linda Hsu

Rights Acquisition Specialist, Text/Image: Tom McDonough

Production Service: PreMediaGlobal

Cover Designer: Carole Lawson

Compositor: PreMediaGlobal

For product information and technology assistance, contact us at **Cengage Learning Customer & Sales Support, 1-800-354-9706**
For permission to use material from this text or product, submit all requests online at **www.cengage.com/permissions**.
Further permissions questions can be emailed to **permissionrequest@cengage.com.**

Library of Congress Control Number: 2011920539

ISBN-13: 978-1-111-30149-1

ISBN-10: 1-111-30149-2

Wadsworth
20 Davis Drive
Belmont, CA 94002
USA

Cengage Learning is a leading provider of customized learning solutions with office locations around the globe, including Singapore, the United Kingdom, Australia, Mexico, Brazil and Japan. Locate your local office at **international.cengage.com/region**

Cengage Learning products are represented in Canada by Nelson Education, Ltd.

For your course and learning solutions, visit **www.cengage.com.**

Purchase any of our products at your local college store or at our preferred online store **www.cengagebrain.com.**

Instructors: Please visit **login.cengage.com** and log in to access instructor-specific resources.

Printed in the United States of America
1 2 3 4 5 6 7 15 14 13 12 11

Table of Contents

Preface

S*eeking Food Rights* brings my lengthy experience of anthropological teaching and research to an area that is new to me: central Asia and Uzbekistan. As a scholar of Japan and East Asia, and applied anthropologist in the United States, I followed a new opportunity to study an Islamic area of the world that has recently emerged as an independent country from the Soviet Union. I offer my observations and analysis humbly, grateful for the international agencies and Uzbek scholars whose studies and accumulated knowledge have enhanced my work. My insights derive from contrast and comparison with the 'far east' of Japan and the 'far west' of America, as seen from the geographical and cultural perspective of Uzbekistan.

I was attracted to expand my research into central Asia after I had helped to lead a workshop there in the early 2000s. An anthropologist needs the stimulus of studying new ways of life, and here was a part of the world that promised difference—little American influence, much Russian influence, and a long and unique history. Furthermore, in a period when the study of Islam is central to understanding the world, Uzbekistan claimed my attention because people there struggle to understand the various meanings of Islam in their own religious and political life.

At first, Uzbekistan seemed like the other side of the world; it was after all halfway around the globe from Oregon. But after I lived there for several months, talked with people about food, and analyzed the results, the struggles that all of us hold in common emerged much more strongly than any exotic differences. In writing about Uzbekistan with a comparative chapter about food in the United States, I was impressed that we deal with very similar questions about control over our food systems and the resulting inequalities in the quantity and kind of food that we consume. Even though the Uzbek government tries to isolate its people from global influences, I found surprising economic and social links extending across the country's borders, even to the United States. Ultimately, we bring our varied histories and political economies to the challenge we share— to build a sustainable and just food system for humans living on this earth.

I have written *Seeking Food Rights* in a dialogic and personalized style that makes it easily accessible for readers new to anthropology. The book has several purposes. First, it introduces readers to a country that is in a part of the world—just north of Afghanistan and Iran—where political and economic currents challenge us to reach a better understanding.

Peace, justice, and full stomachs in this part of the world contribute directly to the national security of Americans.

Second, *Seeking Food Rights* gives readers practice in thinking through the meaning of food rights in a certain time and place: Uzbekistan in 2005. Such an intensive investigation in one part of the world can teach us a great deal about understanding the relationships that occur in other parts of the world within a nation: its use of its land; its place in global trade; and the variations among its people as they grow, buy, cook, and eat their food in myriad households and communities.

Third, *Seeking Food Rights* alerts readers to channels for considering power differences that exist within a nation. Everyone wants to partake of foods culturally enshrined in the national cuisine and foods currently regarded as fashionable, yet people's taste must adjust to their income level, regardless of whether the result gives them an obese or lean body. Rural people sacrifice in various ways to produce food for urban people. Gender differences, well symbolized in food, highlight women's hold on power or lack of it, in households with different income levels. Ethnic differences, often understood in terms of food by the culturally dominant population, show how tolerance and prejudice coexist in one nation and how various ethnic groups are useful in nation building. Finally, institutions of power—governments and corporations—emerge as frameworks that establish the rationale for power differences, often resisted by people in organized and inchoate ways to move their lives closer to food equality.

My hope is that this book provides not only a learning experience, but also a stimulus to think more deeply about our food systems on local and global levels. *Seeking Food Rights* awakens us to the fact that how we share food in our households, communities, nations, and the world fundamentally shapes and reshapes the contours of the globe for its lands and its peoples.

ACKNOWLEDGEMENTS

I want to express my heartfelt appreciation to the people whom I interviewed and talked with in Uzbekistan. They had the courage to interact with me, despite the fact that revealing anything about one's self can be risky in these political circumstances.

I am also eternally grateful to my academic colleagues in Uzbekistan who aided and advised me with my work in myriad ways. I do not name them here because I do not want to bring political repercussions on them, but I hope that they know how much I appreciate their help.

I extend thanks to the Fulbright Commission for their support while I was in Uzbekistan, and to the Department of Anthropology at Oregon State University for assistance while analyzing and writing this research project. I also appreciate the ongoing encouragement of my departmental colleagues.

John Young, the editor of this series, has given time and effort to clarifying my prose and organization. The manuscript is better for his close attention. I am grateful for his faith in me as a researcher and writer, and for his passion for the issues raised in the project.

Last, thanks to my children who have helped me think through various aspects of this project, and who are open to exploring the world with me, sometimes at their peril. Love and thanks go to my husband Clint for his abiding support in all ways from edits to endless discussions, but most of all, for his companionship and insights as we take the journey together.

Chapter 1

Tashkent Chill

It was our first day in Central Asia, and first day in Tashkent, capital of Uzbekistan and home to 3.5 million people. The night before, we had landed on a runway surrounded by snow with Uzbek and American military planes parked nearby. They reminded me that I was welcome here as a Fulbright Scholar in part because Uzbekistan was now a jumping-off place for the United States Air Force flying into Afghanistan after 911.

On that first cold day, slipping across icy patches down a street called Broadway, a professor from the institute where I would teach, my husband, and I looked for a warm place for a cup of tea and lunch. Dr. Park had showed us substantial buildings in Tashkent—the old opera building, banks, department stores, the Parliament building—but Broadway offered only popular restaurant-tents with walls made of heavy tarp material—a bit like modern yurts. Dr. Park pulled the hanging door to one side and led us in. It was warm inside with plastic tables and chairs. "Do you want black or green tea?" he asked. We had spent time in Japan, so for us, Asia meant green tea, but I asked, "What do people drink here?"

"In winter in Tashkent, people drink black tea. I heard a story that once a man asked for black tea in summer, and they gave it to him for free because the shopkeeper said that black tea didn't really even exist in summer!" he said. We all chuckled and, of course, ordered black tea. It came sweet with lemon in a pot. Our host also ordered a hot stew called *laghmon*. "This was brought here by the Uighurs, a group that came over the mountains from western China," he said. Wow—I really am on the opposite side of the world, I thought. I shivered a bit, only in part from the cold air that was still blowing in under the walls of the tent.

By his appearance and name, it was clear that Dr. Park was Korean. The question was begging to be asked: Why was he here in Uzbekistan? "I was born here, but my parents came with their parents when they were small. Stalin shipped the Koreans living north of the Korean border by train on cattle cars to central Asia. People from all over the USSR got banished here. It was a step above concentration camps. Stalin was afraid of rebellion. At first we were not allowed to live in cities. We had to live in the country and we couldn't get any higher education."

"What a terrible thing. But here you are a PhD. You've done very well for all of that."

"Yes, I was able to go to high school. By the 1970s the policy changed, and I was able to go to university. Now many Koreans are doing very well."

The *laghmon* stew came—red soup in big bowls with mutton, potatoes, tomatoes and turnips. We were silent as we ladled it into our mouths with gusto. Warm and full, my husband and I both looked up with surprise as Dr. Park said in a low voice, "There are some things we have to be careful of here." The cold air seeped onto my feet again. "You have to be careful about what you research and how you do it while you are here. We welcome you, but if you don't do things right, you could make it harder for others."

"What do you mean?" I asked nervously.

"Well, not long ago, a person interviewed by an anthropologist went to the secret police. They said that the person was asking too many questions." Uh-oh, I thought. Asking questions is what anthropologists like me do. He continued. "They weren't what we would think of as questions that seem so private—like 'How did you decide to take up this profession?' But the person grew afraid and reported the anthropologist. The police came to me to ask about this researcher. Was she okay? I tried to explain to the policeman that this is how we do our research. We want to hear what people are thinking and doing. 'Can't you just read it in books?' he asked. I said again that this is just our form of research. We learn about people's world views from what they say."

"So what happened?" I asked.

"He never came back. But it was a warning to be careful," answered Dr. Park.

"But why was the person being interviewed so worried—worried enough to go to the police?"

Dr. Park glanced around. There was only one table of young women over by the plastic window and the waitress was lounging back by the door to the makeshift kitchen. In an even lower voice in English he said, "The government has many people spying on each other. If you say anything against the government or the president, it may not be good for you. So people are wary of anyone asking questions. They might say the wrong thing and get into trouble."

I glanced at my husband whose eyebrows were raised. Not a good situation for an anthropologist like me.

"So what are you thinking of researching while you are here?" asked Dr. Park. Good question, I thought to myself.

"Well, I had thought about interviewing women who are running non-governmental organizations, NGOs—you know, like non-profit organizations."

"Maybe that's not such a wise topic," Dr. Park said with restraint, although for him I could see that it was all too obvious. "Not long ago, the president disbanded all NGOs and made them re-register with the government. Only those that he likes got to re-register. Ones that are too much into human rights issues didn't make it."

"Okay, not a good topic," my husband and I laughed. "I have another possibility. In Oregon, I have been studying the topic of food among low-income

Statue of the national hero Amir Timur in a Tashkent park.

people. I thought maybe I could just study about food—find out what people like, where they get it, who cooks it, and so on. How would that be?"

Dr. Park smiled. "That sounds like a very good theme—very safe."

I didn't tell him that I thought you could find out some pretty dicey things just talking about food, but that wasn't the point. Dr. Park didn't care that I found out about things. He just didn't want to have to deal with government security.

"Show me your questions, and we can talk more about it. Now let's go back to your hotel, and tomorrow we can begin to look for an apartment."

We stepped out into the darkening day as boys and girls made their way home from school. Some snow still sat on the top of the head of the statue of their national hero, Amir Timur (Tamerlane in English), as he rode upon his big bronze horse in the park outside our hotel.

★ ★ ★

My husband and I were going to be here for six months, funded by my Fulbright grant. I would be teaching and doing research. Clint, my husband, would try to continue his work online translating Japanese technical documents into English. We hoped that the Japanese translation agencies would not become too nervous about sending work to be done in Uzbekistan, but Japanese also were present in this part of the world building airports and funding health projects. Volunteers from their version of the Peace Corps were here, as were volunteers from the United States Peace Corps. We hoped it would be fine.

I had been taking Russian for several years preparing for this trip. I had become interested in central Asia when I had helped to run a training session for NGO leaders from Tajikistan, the country next door, three years before. Fulbright grants were not available in Tajikistan, where there had been a war after independence from the Soviet Union in 1991, so I applied for Uzbekistan.

Both of these "-stans," or states, had been part of the Soviet Union and were still in the process of adjusting to the independence that had been suddenly thrust upon them. I had said I was ready for anything, but I realized now that the politics of Uzbekistan might have made others nervous to apply here.

Taking risks was part of the fun of being an anthropologist, as long as the risk was manageable. Most of my work had been done in Japan, however, where the government respected research, welcomed Americans, and kept the freedoms of democracy intact. After the first formalities, Japanese people, especially women, had always been quite willing to talk to me in some depth. I was not endangering myself or them. In Uzbekistan, I would have to be careful to protect everyone I knew. Hopefully, talking about food would seem to the government and interviewees alike to be an innocent topic.

Although my Fulbright was to last for six months, the Uzbek government had given me only a one-month visa a few days before I flew to England and then on to Uzbekistan. My husband, the accompanying family member, had a three-month visa! It seemed irrational, but politics had entered the equation. Americans were half welcome and half not welcome. Although the Americans now rented a military base in southern Uzbekistan, the Uzbeks did not like the way Americans had been criticizing their human rights policy and complained that Americans were not paying enough rent for the base.

The next morning when we got up, we did not want to pay $10 for a hotel breakfast, when Dr. Park had told us the day before that the typical salary in Uzbekistan was about $30 a month in 2005. As an anthropologist, I always wanted to eat where common people went, so I dragged Clint across the square to where I had seen a cafeteria sign. We entered a rather cavernous concrete room where a cafeteria line had tea and coffee, eggs, bread, and other foods. We got a tray-full and fumbled around with our *sum* (rhymes with 'room')—the Uzbek money—to pay less than a dollar. Mostly men in working clothes sat at tables in the large, drafty room. The place looked like the state-run cafeterias that served standardized Soviet food under the USSR. The idea was that everyone should eat in such places rather than at home so that both men and women could work hard for the state, and all could prosper equally under the Communist system.

We were to meet Dr. Park later that afternoon to look at an apartment. Meanwhile, we had lunch at a middle-class Turkish restaurant around the corner, including a choice of beef or mutton with vegetables bubbling on a hot metal plate. Clint said we did not have to feel guilty for having more money than most people in the country, but somehow it felt strange to be suddenly part of an upper class because we received our pay in dollars and were citizens of the politically and economically powerful United States. Going between countries, anthropologists notice the stark inequalities between countries that people in poorer countries live with every day. When you really talk to people in these countries, it is hard to lean back and enjoy your accidental riches.

★ ★ ★

Late that afternoon, Dr. Park picked us up in a taxi. He asked if we would be interested in looking at an apartment owned by the brother of a professor at the institute. It was older, but in the modern part of the city built up by the Soviets and on the border of the 'old city.' We wanted to see it, and I thought having material connections to back up social connections at the institute would not be a bad idea. We picked up the landlord and drove together to the apartment complex. The landlord was short and stout like many middle-aged Uzbek men, and he wore a small, black square hat with white embroidery on the top-back of his head. Crowded tight together in the back seat, we listened to his sales pitch about raising his family in this neighborhood: "There are some very good restaurants around here that you will like. *Palov, somsa, tabaka...*" He licked his lips. "Ah, Uzbek food is very good!" I was not yet sure about renting the apartment, but I was impressed with his enthusiasm for the food of his country.

Turning in off the main street, concrete apartment buildings of four to five stories trailed off in all directions. Between each was an area with trees, benches, bare dirt, and a few cars. As we stepped out of the taxi in front of the door of the apartment building, a soccer ball bounced across our feet, and a boy in late elementary school bounded by to retrieve it and rejoin the game. These courtyards were sometimes playgrounds, sometimes parking lots, sometimes places for neighbors to talk or meet with a food seller. We walked into a concrete stairwell with mailboxes sagging open. I guessed we would not be getting much mail here. Indeed, the mail system only worked minimally following the Soviet withdrawal. We climbed up four stories to a fake leather-covered door. The landlord unlocked it and then another door inside it and led us into what would become our apartment for the next six months. It was big by Tashkent standards with toilet, bath, two small bedrooms, a large living room, and a balcony and small kitchen at the front that had been enclosed and heated, at least minimally. Coming straight from an American house, it did not look glamorous, but after we saw other houses in Uzbekistan, it soon began to look quite cushy. For us the rent was cheap, but for the landlord, it was a handsome income to supplement the little he earned from teaching.

Our apartment building in Tashkent.

As we sat on the overstuffed, dark furniture in the living room discussing the deal, the landlord expressed his concern about the rental tax that the government would take from him. As we were to hear repeatedly, the government tried to extract money from the people any way it could. People even avoided getting bank accounts or putting money into their accounts because the government used their money for its own projects and then made people pay a bribe to get their money back!

At any rate, in order to avoid the rental tax, the landlord asked that we be his "friends" who were simply using (not renting) the apartment. If the police came to the door, we were to confirm this arrangement. No problem, we agreed. Meanwhile, the government was keeping track of its foreigners. It had to account for our whereabouts every night. Evidently a common practice was to bribe hotel employees to confirm that we were staying there rather than at the apartment. Welcome to Uzbekistan, where in the face of a greedy government, people did what they must to augment their incomes and stay afloat.

★ ★ ★

I spent my first several weeks in Uzbekistan adjusting to a new concept of time, which incidentally gave me a chance to also adjust to the food. My lectures and interviews were arranged and then cancelled. Several times, the director of the institute asked researchers and graduate students to attend a meeting with little warning. A conference arose unexpectedly. At the conference an unscheduled speaker appeared, and everyone had to attend the talk. Afterwards we had an impromptu lunch in the director's office followed with bread, soup, and *palov*— the much-loved national dish of Uzbekistan which did not become available for ordinary people until the 1930s (Zanca 2003). My colleagues explained to me that this dish was made of rice, that it originated from Persia, and that it became the inspiration for the French dish known as pilaf. It was served with a tomato and onion salad called *achiq-chuchuk* here in Tashkent. On a warm, sunny day, several graduate students took me out to a sidewalk café to sample an especially delicious version of *palov*. Tables sat on a broad sidewalk beside a huge black vat where a man fried mutton in fat and then added yellow carrots, onions, and rice to steam for a long while. At this particular café, the cook added raisins and garbanzo beans which these young people seemed to love, but which some older people thought was a citified compromise to the real thing. I actually thought it was delicious, especially if you asked for the part of the rice that was on the top, away from the thick mutton fat collected at the bottom of the vat. Older Uzbeks who were not worried about becoming overweight regarded the fat as the best part.

The great food and good company was compensation for unpredictability, but I had never felt such a lack of control over my time and activities. Anthropologists always find it difficult to get started on interviews when they first arrive in a new place, but this was extreme. I counseled myself to relax and go with the flow, but that had never been my strength. Here there was no choice.

I finally decided that time was tightly linked with an authority-centered hierarchy. One was not supposed to have control over personal time; rather, those above had the right to shape your use of time. Deans and directors cancelled classes without warning. Likewise, if the President of the country decided to declare a holiday, or if he decided to cancel one, it was so. The bonus for the teachers was that they also could cancel lectures as needed—often to go do other jobs that could earn them more money, for everyone had several jobs to survive.

My theory was supported by the daily cavalcade of the president through the city. The president's house was located outside Tashkent, but his route to his office went right along the street which I took to the Institute. Walking along the road around 10:00 AM put me in a perfect place to watch this scene. Traffic stopped at all the streets entering the main road so that the way was clear. Uniformed policemen lined the road, one at every side street and apartment entry road. Pedestrians stopped and waited. The policemen stood with their backs to the cavalcade so as not to appear threatening, while onlookers faced the street. After a few minutes, four black cars raced by. Men with machine guns and black-covered faces leaned out of the windows of the first and last SUVs. After they passed, the policemen turned around and people calmly continued walking to work. If they felt critical or resented the interruption, they dare not show it.

PUBLIC FOOD CULTURE

While waiting for classes and interviews to begin, I started studying the public food culture as best I could. We resided near a famous, old market in Tashkent called Chorsu, one of the largest in central Asia. It was located in the "old city"—the part of the city that existed before the Russians came in the late nineteenth century. It still consisted of old neighborhoods built along narrow, winding streets lined with white walls, enclosing courtyards with gardens and small houses. Chorsu was a huge market, the cheapest in the city. It had everything from raisins to live chickens, to t-shirts to velvet coats for weddings.

Chorsu Market was also the most political market in the city. Why is it considered political? It was a huge gathering place where people conversed daily, shared information, and shaped each other's opinions. Also it was near the old city and a huge mosque, both of which had been identified with political opposition against the president. Furthermore, while the president and his government were trying to increase their control over the circulation of goods and money, people in the markets were always working to subvert this aim in one way or another.

As my friend, a graduate student who had offered to show me around, and I worked our way through the gate and up the stairs into the main building of the market, we passed between people on both sides of the staircase with clothes to sell. One older woman was selling a man's white shirt still in the package. Another was holding socks in her hands and draped over her arms. Another held a small wool pink coat over her arm in a plastic bag. Several had long, black ladies' boots in their hands. A man had a pair of child's slippers slung around his shoulders. They were talking to passersby in soft voices. On the landing, a boy and a woman were looking out over the entrance of the market.

What were they doing there? My friend told me that they were looking out for the police. Then I noticed that all the women had bags on their arms or at their feet, ready to throw their clothes into the bags and disappear if the police came. They did not have a permit to sell in the market, and probably they or family members had smuggled their goods over the border from Kazakhstan to the north or even from Dubai. Custom taxes were so high—70% on non-food items since 2002—that bribing the customs guards was cheaper.

We entered a large rotunda with wooden stands from which men sold rice, beans, and spices—red pepper, saffron, cumin—from huge bags. We saw women selling milk products such as *katik*, a kind of yoghurt typically eaten for breakfast along with bread, and *kurt*, a rounded hard ball of goat's milk to carry in your pocket or take on a journey. We bought some *kurt*, but the strong goat milk taste was overwhelming. I would have to cultivate that taste. A meat section featured mutton and beef, as eating pork is against Islamic law. Outside I saw some people selling frozen chicken legs protruding from a bucket sitting on the pavement. These were often called "Bush legs" in jest because they were overflow commodities from the United States sold cheaply (and making business hard for the local chicken sellers). You could buy brand oil in little shops here and there, or you could buy oil from Kazakhstan sold in recycled bottles along the stairs. In January, vegetables were mainly limited to potatoes, carrots, and onions left over from the year before.

In one area, you could buy already-cut-up yellow carrots. Remember the yellow carrots in *palov*? With a little extra money, people could save themselves some time, but money was the problem, of course. The Uzbeks bargained hard to bring prices down, yet they also looked for quality. Rather than buy the government wheat, for example, many bakers preferred to buy the better wheat from Kazakhstan, especially for making bread in the cities. A 30% tariff on Kazakh wheat made it expensive legally, and kept the black market price high, too (Musaev et al 2010:39).

In short, the market was rich with foods and goods made in Uzbekistan because the nation pursued a strategy of self-sufficiency, but it was also a place where people sold uncertified goods when they could. Struggling consumers needed these cheaper goods; the elite wanted this variety; and the unemployed needed to sell here in the market, the main place to make a few *sum* to keep life and limb together.

The Chorsu Market snack shops had delicious *somsa*, rather like meat pies—dough wrapped around mutton, mutton fat, onions, and potatoes. Vendors baked them in small clay ovens set on a board with wheels for portability. We sat down to have a bite and warm ourselves with tea on a still cold winter day.

"Uzbek food is so delicious," sighed the graduate student. She looked quite sophisticated in her maroon wool coat and black boots, almost as out of place in this part of the city as we were. But she was proud to be Uzbek. "We have some of the best food in the world."

"I agree!" The warm *somsa*, crunchy on the outside and soft inside, practically melted in my mouth. "You don't get a lot of packaged food from outside the country, but maybe you don't need it," I ventured.

"We wish we could get more. There is some food from outside here. There are bananas that traders bring in from Dubai in the Persian Gulf. I like to use Knorr soup broth. You can buy it here and lots of places."

"Food seems to be tied up with politics a lot here."

"Everything is! The police really watch Chorsu Market because almost a year ago, a woman suicide bomber killed people here. Oh, it's almost the anniversary of the bombings of 1999—February 16. Six bombs exploded downtown near government buildings and almost killed the president. The government said that it was a radical Islamic group. People hand out pamphlets at the markets, so police really watch the markets because protests could start here. You probably shouldn't come to the market around the anniversary of the bombings."

"Oh, okay." I noted the date in my mind. "Is there any trouble now?"

"Well, the vendors are angry because the government just passed a law that only the people who grow food can sell it. Of course that is impossible. Farmers or middlemen bring the food to a big wholesale market outside of Tashkent, and then the sellers go there to pick it up."

"What's the government trying to do?"

"I don't know," she said. "I study literature, not politics." I accepted her right to say no more. But it was clear that the circulation of food was quite a political matter in Uzbekistan. I realized that, if followed to its end, food was not such an innocent topic after all.

We licked our fingers and made our way out of the market and past the big mosque nearby. She pointed out a new grocery store located across from the Chorsu Market. "The prices are much higher there, but the prices are fixed, and it might be easy for you to shop there," she suggested.

"I'll check it out. Who runs it?" I asked.

"I think Turkish businessmen run it." Places for the rich to shop and places for the poor, I thought, but as I was to find out, the latter were much more crowded than the former. My friend disappeared down the stairs to the metro and I headed down the sidewalk and turned into the pot-holed lane that led into our apartment complex. The vegetable truck was sitting along the lane as always, an older man and woman sitting inside it with not much more than potatoes and onions to sell to apartment dwellers at this time of year. Later, spring vegetables would be very welcome.

Over to my right, I noticed people slipping into a basement door at the bottom side of a four-story apartment building and coming out with hot bread. I decided to go over and see if I could buy bread there closer to home. I pushed in the old, wooden door. The steamy warmth and a smell of gas enveloped me. It was a room perhaps 7x10 with a tiny place for customers behind a small wooden fence, over which we looked into a big rounded clay oven open in the front with three young men working around it. One young man kneaded the dough; another slapped it into a round shape, stamped the center down, and sprinkled it with sesame seeds; and a third slapped the rounds up against the inner walls of the igloo-shaped oven, daringly stretching over the gas fire as he threw it up against the back wall of the oven. The loaves stuck to the wall because they were made of sticky dough, and as they baked, they swelled up and became un-sticky. At this

A baker removes the baked bread rounds from the clay oven.

point the worker held a round pan and with a long stick, nudged the bread off the wall, caught it in the pan, and shook it out on the counter where my neighbors and I bought the loaves for the equivalent of about 10 cents each. No bags and no advertising were necessary, so we were able to benefit from low overhead. I took my bread up to our apartment where Clint and I broke it into pieces and ate it instantly in a most un-Uzbek way with apricot jam.

Of course there was a proper way to eat bread in Uzbekistan, as bread was the mainstay of hearth and family. "Without bread, an Uzbek family can't live," one person told me. Whenever we sat down at a table at someone's home to eat, the first food served was the bread. The oldest host or the male head of the house would break it with their hands and pass a piece to each person. It wasn't so important that you ate it as that hosts gave it, and you received it as a symbol of the generosity and hospitality of the host (Zanca 2003). Indeed, at the very least a poor family should be able to eat and serve bread and tea. When a family member left home, the person took a bite out of a loaf of bread and hung it on the wall until returning home again to take another bite.

Furthermore, bread had political importance. Since independence in 1991, President Karimov had converted almost 40% of cultivated land into wheat (Musaev et al 2010:56). Previously the Soviet Union had used Uzbekistan as a cotton plantation to the extent that they could grow neither their own wheat nor their famous melons and grapes. Being able to grow their own wheat was symbolic of independence and national strength. Soon after becoming president, Karimov held up a round of bread during a speech and promised that he would never raise the price of bread. He did not strictly keep this promise, but his symbolic act showed that he was well aware that bread was absolutely fundamental to the social and cultural life of the nation. If it became expensive, he would have a protest on his hands.

★ ★ ★

Of course, most people wanted a lot more than bread. Bread was only the minimum requirement. Early in our stay, a professor at the institute invited us to her house on *Qurban Hayit*, an Islamic holy day called "Feast of the Sacrifice." She knew I was interested in learning about food and thought I would enjoy attending a special ceremony wherein a new bride serves tea, bread, cakes, and other special festival food to women of the family and neighborhood. A young woman about to graduate from college had just married into her husband's sister's family, who lived down the block. The professor, a stout, friendly woman in her 50s, led us down the narrow street and through a gate into the courtyard of a house. Like many Uzbek houses, the multi-generational family lived in a series of small two-to-three room buildings built around this courtyard. This family had a number of bare trees that held the promise of bearing fruit and a garden area that could produce vegetables in the summer. A low, wide platform looked lonely now against the snow, but it would become a place to sit when the weather warmed up. The professor ushered us into a room with big windows on one side of the courtyard and inside a big table laden with three big cakes—one with a small swan on the top—along with fruit and other dishes I did not yet recognize. Guests sat on chairs lined up around the walls.

The bride, Yuliya, appeared, wearing a long, bright silk dress of patterned yellows, reds and greens that I would come to recognize as *izkat*, a 'traditional' Uzbek pattern. At first she bowed to the guests several times offering "*Salaam*" (meaning "peace," a daily greeting) while her hands held out a heavy lacy veil in front of her face, the traditional humble posture of a new bride (*kelin*) entering into the husband's family. However, Yuliya was not a typical bride, as she soon took off the veil and greeted us in English. She was pleased to speak English, the language that she used to communicate with her professors at her particular university.

"You have to serve the tea in just the right way," she said smiling happily. "You have to serve it with your right hand and you have to curl your fingers under the bottom of the cup. You only fill it half full. If you fill it full, it means the guests should leave." She broke bread and served it to us, then passed us tea with her right arm stretched out, supported at her elbow with her left hand.

"You're really good at this," I said.

"I practiced," Yuliya giggled.

She pointed out the pistachios, cakes with walnuts, and *chukchuk*—a long string of dough dipped in honey and wrapped up in a circular pattern. Later the family brought out homemade noodles, cut very thin and mixed with horse meat—a dish called *norin*. In front of us bottles of Coke and Fanta sat untouched, more for status than for drinking.

The bride's grandmother-in-law came in with her sister, her daughters-in-law, and their children. Slight differences in scarves marked differences between the generations. The older women tied their scarves under their chins; the younger women tied their scarves behind their heads; and the younger girls had no scarves at all. The older woman took the lead in welcoming us and telling us how happy they were to have us in their home. She then led everyone in a lengthy prayer expressing thanks to Allah for life, family, and food, and hoping

Women gathered to receive the bride's tea and welcome her into the family and neighborhood.

for blessings to bring many children for this newly married couple. As she talked, she reached out her hands as if she were holding an open book. Everyone else followed suit, including us. At the end of the prayer, everyone swiped open palms down over their faces, and then a great din arose as everyone nodded around to others asking, "How are you?" "How are your children?" "How is your health?" No one needed to answer. They were reaching out to each other almost like clinking glasses after a toast.

Yuliya served everyone bread and tea and then disappeared, only to reappear soon afterward in another costume—a thick dark velvet coat overlaid with prominent gold threaded patterns and under it a wispy peach-colored dress. The purpose of changing costumes was to highlight her beauty and, they were frank, to display the family's wealth. The proffered tea and cakes signified her membership in the family, and her new ties to the guests who came to welcome her. Later her parents, brother, uncle, and unmarried girl cousins came to receive tea. By serving them in her new house, she acknowledged that she had left their home and joined her husband's—a patrilineal style of kinship.[1] Men usually did not participate in this event, but this was a modern family and after all, the men too had contributed money for the bride's beautiful dresses prominently on display.

Still later, three of the bride's best friends from university came to pay their respects. Yuliya saluted them by bowing and greeting them with *Salaam* from under the veil, but they laughed at each other as they bowed in return. After the bride served tea, the girls told me, "This is a terrible time for the bride really! She has to bow and say *Salaam* from under a veil and serve tea all day. It used to be three days! It's especially bad if you are already pregnant." I guessed pregnancy was the next thing in the bride's future.

The bride's friends were dressed in modern Western sweaters and skirts, and soon Yuliya herself returned in a long, pink, Western party gown. During a lull in the arrival of guests, the bride came back and sat by her friends. They were all majoring in financial management at the same polytechnic university and had a huge test the next day. The bride was not quite sure how she would pass. She and her friends expected to graduate in May and were all getting nervous about finding work and marriage partners.

"Is it important to marry by a certain age?" I asked.

"Yuliya is normal. She is 19. It starts from about 17 now. If you get to be 21 or 22, you are too old."

"People our age go to several of these celebrations in one day! Then they go home and compare which of the brides was more beautiful!"

"Will you go to more today?" I asked.

"No, we aren't normal!" they answered laughingly.

"Is that good or bad?" I queried with a smile.

"It's good. We are getting education," said one.

"I don't know. Maybe it is unfortunate," said another. "We can't get too old and marry well."

"So how will you find your marriage partners?" I asked.

"It doesn't depend on us."

"Our parents find us a husband. The boy's father's relatives come and talk with the girl's relatives and ask them to give the girl as a wife."

Yuliya was the authority as she had already gone through the whole mate-selection process. Her words emphasized that she had a degree of choice in choosing a husband. "The [future] bride must choose among the various candidates. Her parents meet the man's parents and the man, and then the two of us meet somewhere. There is the first candidate, the second candidate, and the third candidate. Which is better? I have to think. I must look at the plusses and minuses." Her shining face seemed to indicate that she was pleased with her choice from among the men offered to her.

More guests came in and we needed to leave. We will meet these three girls again later in the book, but not Yuliya. I tried to contact her, but she never returned my calls or e-mails, and her friends later said, "Ah, yes, things aren't going so well with her." I inferred that adjusting to the low status and work of a *kelin* under her mother-in-law's thumb was difficult for this well-educated young woman.

★ ★ ★

Food was obviously at the center of important rituals. When we arrived back at the professor's house, her husband and son were sacrificing a sheep. They held its head down over a special hole in the ground and dedicated the sheep to Allah and the ancestors reading the Koran as they slit its throat with a special carved knife. They made sure to kill it correctly with blood drained well so that they could offer it to Allah and then share it with relatives and neighbors for a *Hayit* feast.

It was a busy holiday in this neighborhood. Clint and I went to a neighbor's house where family members were celebrating the first *Hayit* after the death of another neighbor who had made the trip to Mecca. This person deserved special respect because he had been able to fulfill one of the most difficult of the five precepts of Islam.[2] Making the journey to Mecca was especially difficult given the economic hard times in Uzbekistan; some said that under such conditions, it is better to care for your family than to spend the money traveling to Mecca. But this family appeared to have money. Their home was large, although not new, and several cars sat in the driveway. The women ushered me inside while my husband sat outside with the men. Inside the table was spread completely with many of the same *Hayit* foods. At one end of the room hung a large portrait of the dead man, and on his head was a typical white skullcap worn by pilgrims to Mecca. The women urged me to eat a special dish made for funerals and death remembrance days like this—a brown pudding called *halvatar* made by frying flour in oil and adding sugar.

Foods connected people. Already I had encountered foods for marital union, for the hopes of marriage and having children, for separation and reuniting with family, and for a continued bond with ancestors. People loved some foods just because they were Uzbek and they had grown up eating them, but as we see below, some also consumed foods to display global awareness and sophistication.

★ ★ ★

Our friend Usman, a university student in Tashkent, had taken a bite of his family's bread, gone to the United States for a year, and returned to his home to take the next bite. He was introduced to us by a mutual friend at the Kosmonavtlar station on the metro, a dimly-lit station decorated with large paintings in ghostly blues of Soviet heroes who had ventured into outer space. The first time we met, Usman was dressed very well in a long, wool overcoat and nice shoes—a sign of respect he showed to us in a culture where respect figured in actions, gestures, language, and feelings, especially towards older and more important people. (That's us, I had to remind myself.) Tashkent experienced a terrible earthquake in 1966. Usman's grandfather died in it. Usman told us that people from all over the Soviet Union felt badly for Tashkent and sent money and workers to help with the recovery. Many Russians came at that time to participate in rebuilding the city by constructing the very concrete apartment buildings of which ours was one. The Russians also built the Metro with elaborately decorated stations.

We walked up out of the station and down past the president's official palace which was fronted by huge billboards with pictures symbolizing the independent Uzbek nation. Food was evidently important in this effort to visualize the nation and create a tradition. Uzbekistan did not exist as a nation prior to the formation of the Union of Soviet Socialist Republics (USSR), which created it as one of the republics. After independence, President Karimov and his government provided all the accoutrements of a modern nation for their citizens: they featured historical cultural heroes like Amir Timur on the bronze horse; they claimed various tribes and groups as Uzbek and encouraged schooling in Uzbek rather than Russian; and they codified Uzbek foods that had developed from various sources over centuries as the "national foods". In short, they developed what we call ethnic nationalism, in this case Uzbek nationalism, as the foundation of the nation.

Usman knew that I was interested in food, and he proved a good tour guide for my study. "Look," he said craning his head upwards and pointing, "There are two white-beards carrying round loaves of bread and standing in a field of wheat. It means a lot to us to be able to grow our own wheat. And over there do you see the woman carrying a plate of—it looks like grass? Well, those are wheat sprouts that women grow at home and then bring together and use the liquid from them to make a special pudding in the spring called *sumalak*."

"I'd like to taste it."

"Don't worry. You'll get a chance. Everyone has it in February and March." It didn't sound as if it were his favorite food, but neither did he put it down. Instead, he said,

Pride in the nation: tradition represented by elderly men, bread, and wheat; modernity represented by car and airplane made in Uzbekistan.

"Now, wouldn't you like to go get some pizza?" My husband and I laughed. Here, for better or worse, was a dual citizen of the Western world and of Uzbekistan. We followed him up a street with a park on one side and book shops on the other. He said that he shared an apartment with four other young men from his home-town. Usman was the cook. "I learned to cook from my father and brother. They are very good at making *palov*," he said. "My friends are supposed to buy the food and clean up, but sometimes I have to wash the dishes before I cook. And then they'll say, 'This is too salty.'" I noted two things to find out more about: that food could be a source of conflict as well as togetherness and that in Uzbekistan men cooked.

We soon turned back behind a fashionable department store to enter a fast food Turkish restaurant that Usman liked but rarely could afford. We ordered a pizza with cheese and minced beef. An MTV video was playing on the television mounted up in the corner of the room—Britney Spears throwing off her coat to appear in bra and corset, a guy trying to kiss her. She throws him off, only to appear naked in a bath, sink and drown, get saved by the guy, and disappear up a staircase with a baby. What a contrast to the conservative world outside the window, I thought.

"Britney Spears is really popular over here, even though she isn't very popular anymore in the United States," said Usman. Indeed, a girl in her late teens soon passed by our table in a very short skirt and striped tights, her face embellished with plenty of makeup. Even

Billboard featuring a woman carrying wheat sprouts for a spring ritual of making *simulak*.

though President Karimov seemed to be trying to keep the modern world out of Tashkent, it was seeping in. Fast food was only the tip of the iceberg.

"So are there fast food restaurants from the United States here in Tashkent?" I asked Usman.

"No, not many. I guess there is Baskin Robbins, but not much else. And it is so expensive. Most of them are Turkish." The pizza came. It had a very thin crust and little cheese. "Not bad," Clint reluctantly offered in the spirit of international friendliness. I was sure that in his mind he was comparing it to the thick-crusted Edward Abbey vegetarian from our favorite restaurant back home. Usman saved the day in his understated way. "Well, I wish I could start a pizza shop here. It would be pizza like the stuff I used to like when I was in the States."

Clint, always interested in business ventures, took him up on the idea and they imagined all the machines, techniques, and supplies that they would need to start a pizza shop.

"Only one problem," said Usman. "Number one, it's expensive to get the licenses and inspections to start a café or restaurant. There are a lot more than there used to be but still not so many here. You actually have to bribe a lot to do it. And then, if you would get a lot of customers and get famous…"

"Which of course you would with pizza like that," Clint interrupted.

"Of course!" Usman smiled broadly, and then laughed. "Well, actually, you'd get bought out. Remember I told you about the president's daughter? She buys out anyone who is doing too well."

"You're kidding. How can she do that?" I said out loud as if I were in the United States.

Usman shrugged. "She's the president's daughter," he answered more quietly. "You can see her black Jeep SUV around town with the license plate '1.'" Indeed, it did not take long before Clint began spotting it here and there around Tashkent. Usman did not look happy about the prevalence of bribes, but neither did he criticize the president. He had to be careful even though the snack bar was fairly empty.

Not many local people could afford to eat in a place like this; the price for a pizza was about fifty cents. The poverty rate in Uzbekistan had increased after independence. Measured by international standards of $4 per person per day, the poverty rate had shot up from 24% in 1988 to 63% in 1993. The economy suffered from shortages of cotton for export in the mid-1990s, so that the average monthly wage of $54 in 1994 declined to $29 by 2002. By the time we were there in 2005, declining wages left almost 30% of the population of 27 million unable to buy or grow enough food to get the 2100 calories per day that they needed to be healthy (WFP 2008:19; Musaev etal 2010:47).

But poverty was less in Tashkent, where people had glimpses of global food. The government did not allow McDonald's in, but as we were to see later in a Tashkent park, creative Uzbeks made an imitation of it. Along a sidewalk on a national holiday, we glimpsed a banner in red with golden arches. We looked closer. Above the golden arches was the name Madonna's. Anywhere else McDonald's would sue, but in Uzbekistan, cut off from the outside, this combination of two popular symbols could bring in business for local hamburgers.

An outside cafe in a Tashkent park on a holiday.

The upshot of all of this was that citizens of Uzbekistan who were happy to gain independence in 1991 were hungry by 2005 for something more. Some people were hungry for foods that had become global like pizza and hamburgers, others for bread and national foods like *palov* and *somsa*. All were hungry for freedom to open their mouths free of any national cuisine and simply say what they thought.

FOOD, NATION, UNITY, AND DIFFERENCE

This book is first about food as a human right and secondly about the question of what food as a human right means within nation-states—especially Uzbekistan and the United States.

What does it mean to have rights to food? At the most fundamental level, it is the right not to starve or be hungry, but people use the phrase "food security" to describe a broader right to food. The United Nations' Food and Agriculture Organization defined it 2001:

> Food security exists when all people have at any time a physical, social, and economic access to a sufficient quantity of safe and nutritious products corresponding to nutritious needs and individual preferences, and providing for an active and healthy life (Musaev et al 2010:10).

Note that this definition targets access—that food is available in the market, that everyone can afford it, and that social inequalities do not bar access to food. The definition includes the right to eat nutritiously according to people's food preferences. We cannot assume that people's food rights are being met if international emergency food aid supplies them with corn in a country where people eat mostly rice, or if people have mainly wheat to eat and little meat or milk.

People have the right to eat foods that give them adequate energy to learn and work, and that are appropriate to their history and contemporary habits.

The reasons why people live without the right to food security are varied. The right to food includes the right to have enough food to live without social inequalities. The right to food depends not only on adequate food production, but fair food distribution, which is often a political problem. Amartya Sen (1990) has observed that certain people have social and political entitlements to food, and those entitlements could depend on what gender you are or how you relate to your family. For example, in Ethiopia, a divorced or deserted woman used to have entitlement or access to the food raised by her mother's extended family, including her brothers and their wives. Now Ethiopian families have changed towards male dominance, and a brother and his wife do not necessarily want to feed a divorced sister and her children. Thus, divorced women and their children have lost entitlement to get food from their families' farms in times of famine. In Uzbekistan, divorced women are sometimes ostracized at the village level, and in the United States, poor unemployed people are sometimes shunned as lazy. In short, the right to obtain food is often complicated by beliefs and ideologies that lead to a lack of political will to make sure everyone gets fed.

On the international level, some people do not have food rights because food itself comes to be a pawn in global political battles. A case in point is the mid-1990s famine that occurred in North Korea. Because of their political isolation and pride as a communist country, North Korea did not ask for help even as the famine raged. At the same time, however, North Korea was building the capacity to make nuclear weapons. In countries such as Japan and the United States, one argument was that food aid should not be given unless the government stopped their nuclear weapon building and allow monitors into the country. Others argued that North Korean citizens should not be allowed to starve regardless of what the government was doing. The United States ultimately gave them food aid as did South Korea and China, but monitors could not check who received it. Much of it went to the military and high officials.

This example brings us to another important concept when talking about food rights: food sovereignty. The first part of the 2007 declaration approved in Mali at the Forum for Food Sovereignty by delegates from 80 countries, goes like this:

> Food sovereignty is the right of peoples to healthy and culturally appropriate food produced through ecologically sound and sustainable methods, and their right to define their own food and agriculture systems. It puts those who produce, distribute and consume food at the heart of food systems and policies rather than the demands of markets and corporations (Declaration 2007).

Another international example illustrates a battle over food sovereignty. Japan feels that it has lost food sovereignty. In 2007, Japan has a self-sufficiency rate of 38% in calories—the lowest in its history (Nagata 2008). They import almost all their soybeans and corn from the United States, having concentrated on industrial development—a policy supported by both the Japanese and

American governments. Now the World Trade Organization is bringing pressure on Japan to open up its rice market, a move which would benefit the United States and China, whose agricultural companies want to boost rice sales to Japan. Rice is a strong food preference in Japan, and is still grown by small, mostly part-time farmers, whom the government has supported with subsidies since the 1960s. Some Japanese believe that imported rice challenges their rights to their food preference for self-sufficiency and homegrown Japanese rice. Furthermore, if corporate agriculture takes over, it threatens the vitality of small farms and rural communities in Japan. Moreover, small organic farmers in Japan claim the right to grow rice without chemicals for the sake of protecting the environment. Just as the definition above implies, rights for increased trade and corporate markets clash with the rights of farmers to grow food for their own nation as they wish.

Food security and food sovereignty in the sense of control over food can also differ within a nation. On the national level, food can become a way to give political favors to some and keep favors from others. In North Korea, men in the military receive the best food. As we will see in Uzbekistan, those with political and economic power definitely eat better, and those of Uzbek ethnicity have better access to their food preferences than other ethnic groups. We can make the same statement about the United States—those with higher incomes have much stronger "rights" to a variety of nutritious and safe foods. Those who are of European ancestry have easier access to the ingredients they need to make the food they like than people whose ancestry and food preferences come from India or Mexico.

As I will demonstrate in this book, differential rights to food reveal important inequalities that exist within a nation. In addition to conversations and observations, in-depth interviews with 55 people who represent different groups in Uzbekistan lay the foundation for this analysis of food and inequalities. Wealth differences between Tashkent and rural areas and smaller cities are reflected in the food that people eat. Ethnic nationalism in Uzbekistan favors Uzbek foods as the best and most normal over those of other ethnicities. Food differentiates men and women from each other and underscores men's dominance. Shades of religious difference are also reflected in diet, but would not have become so important if it were not for Karimov's identification of strong religiosity with political dissidence.

This book also examines social divisions reflected by food in the United States. Although the United States is rich as a nation, it harbors sharp differences between classes, especially as shown in the amount and quality of food that lower-income people eat. The study of lower-income people in Oregon presented here shows that their food desires are not much different from higher-income Americans. However, their eating and shopping habits are different as a result of their economic status. The study of food clearly reveals who is powerful and who is not.

Despite its tendency to divide, food can be very effective as a symbol that brings a nation of people together. For example, when young Japanese people are asked about what represents "Japanese-ness" to them, they often mention food such as sushi (raw fish on rice). Japanese people eat many foods from the West and China, but food identified as Japanese continues to construct a sense of Japan as a nation, and leads people to feel that they have a "right" to that food.

Nations are not natural things. A sense of the nation needs to be constantly built and re-built in the minds and hearts of citizens. Sometimes it is everyday things that build this identity the best. For example, the fact that we always hear the news and weather mainly about the United States, not Canada or Mexico, builds the sense of a nation. The flag waving, the national anthem sung at sporting events, and learning about Abraham Lincoln in school all go into constructing our feeling of being part of the United States. What about food? Does it bring us together? Some people say that food does not unite us because regional and ethnic foods are strong, while others claim that American foods such as McDonald's and Coca Cola do more than bring us together: they make us feel that our foods are superior—the world's common denominator (Billig 1995).

Uzbekistan is not going along with the trend to adopt American food. In Uzbekistan "national foods" are symbolically important in building a sense of nation for its citizens. Uzbeks accept their foods as traditional even though the histories of different foods vary. They love to eat them, share them, and talk about them. As their tables groaned with food for their guests, the hosts urged my husband and me to eat with the sense that by eating their food, we could participate in their identity as Uzbeks. Uzbekistan lags behind many nations economically, yet food is one area of life in which they feel superior to the United States. People would often ask, "So what is the national cuisine of the United States?" And I would cock my head without an answer causing everyone to laugh. They were proud to show off their food to foreigners. Although as a nation they lacked many of the rights of more powerful nations in the global system, they claimed the right to a national cuisine that their president was only too glad to reinforce.

ENDNOTES

1. Patrilineal style of kinship means a family line centered around men—grandfather to father to son. Family name and land follow this line, and often the ideal is that these men's families share a household. In many patrilineal systems, the ideal is inheritance by the eldest son, but in Uzbekistan the youngest son inherits the land and cares for the parents in old age.

2. The five precepts or pillars of Islam are: testimony that Allah is the one and only one God and that Muhammad is his prophet; pray five times a day; give compulsory charity (*zakat*); observe Ramadan, a yearly month of fasting; visit Mecca, the birthplace of Islam, once in one's life (*Hajj*) (Ali and Leaman 2008).

Chapter 2

Creating Uzbekistan: Historical Struggles

In order to understand the debates and tensions in contemporary Uzbekistan, we have to understand the history behind them. In this chapter, I discuss important aspects of Uzbek history that are relevant today. The first is President Karimov's use of history to establish a sense of nationalism and to justify his dictatorial power in independent Uzbekistan. He reaches back to the fourteenth century to identify himself and the nation with one of the great empire-builders of the world: Amir Timur, or Tamerlane, as he is known in the West. I show how making Amir Timur the cultural hero of Uzbekistan helps Karimov to construct an ethnic Uzbek nationalism, but I also demonstrate how this Amir Timur hero worship covers up important aspects of Uzbek history.

One aspect that Karimov's version of history hides is a second theme of this chapter: the rich ethnic mixture of what is today Uzbekistan. Many different kinds of peoples, languages, and religious beliefs mixed in the cities along the Silk Road. Throughout the centuries, people of this area have identified themselves in a variety of ways, and Karimov's efforts to persuade them to identify now as Uzbek is only one chapter in a varied history.

A third theme is modernization and the debate as to how that should occur. This theme focuses on the tension between the power of the colonizer, the Soviet Union, and the resistance of the colonized, the Uzbeks. Without a doubt, the Soviets wanted to modernize its vassal states, but they insisted that communist ideology replace local traditions deemed "backwards," and that collective agriculture displace private landowners. When the Soviets came to power in 1917, a movement called Jadidism already was pushing for reform of Islam, particularly for broadening of education and women's opportunities. But the Soviets tried to wipe out Islam and landowners, which caused a strong backlash. Over time, however, Soviet modernization also improved education and government services. Today, even in independent Uzbekistan, the effects of this Soviet-imposed modernization reverberate in debates over the value of going

21

back to older ways and the need for reform in Islam, women's positions, and agriculture.

AMIR TIMUR'S RESURRECTION

When the Soviet Union fell, and independence was announced in 1991, Timur's reputation shifted in one fell swoop. A friend of mine was just taking her exams to get into university in Uzbekistan. Under the Soviet Union, she said, Amir Timur had been a villain of history, known for his exaggerated violence symbolized in gruesome piles of skulls. When his army confronted a city that did not surrender, his soldiers killed, raped, looted, and took slaves without mercy.

But Karimov had turned the tables. Now Timur was the cultural hero of the nation. My friend's teacher advised her to simply take everything that she was going to say that was bad about Timur and make it good. She did, and she passed.

And thus Timur became a valiant hero and clever leader who in the late 1300s led his troops to conquer an empire that by 1402 stretched from India to the Mediterranean Sea. His power served as a model for Karimov who ensconced him as the founder of the Uzbek nation. Timur reportedly commanded the loyalty of his thousands of soldiers by keeping them on the warpath and rewarding them handsomely with conquered goods, thus keeping them from falling into tribe-based arguments among themselves. He killed leaders and citizens in cities that resisted and put his own leaders in place. Karimov aspires to this style of power, removing local governors and any political opponents around the country, and rewarding his own group of loyalists by installing them as leaders throughout Uzbekistan.

Amir Timur's capital was Samarkand, a city in central Uzbekistan, not far from where Timur was born. It should be noted that Karimov was born in Samarkand. Clint and I travelled to Samarkand to see the huge mosques and *madrassas*, or schools, that are built there. The tiled towers glow in turquoise under the hot Uzbek sun. Although they had fallen into disrepair, grim ruins on the skyline in historic pictures, the Soviets refurbished them in order to attract the tourist dollar. It was done quickly and not entirely authentically but they are splendors of architecture. They are reminiscent of a more celebrated palace, the Taj Mahal, built in the style of Timur's empire by Timur's great-great grandson, Bobur, who founded the Moghul Empire in India.

In the time of Timur, the Silk Road, the centuries-old trading route between Europe and China, was thriving—and filling Timur's coffers with taxes. A Spaniard visiting the place in Timur's era marveled at the bazaars filled with goods brought by caravans along this road that stretched from Baghdad to the border with China: furs from Russia, silks from China, glass from Syria, and spices—nutmegs, cloves, cinnamon, and ginger—from India. The Spaniard marveled at the parks and fruit trees planted throughout the city, and he gobbled up the culinary riches of the

In Samarkand with friends at a modernized version of an old teahouse. Nancy and Clint on the left.

fertile region. He mentions the special sheep with tails so fat they weighed twenty pounds; sheep's tails are choice meat even today in Uzbekistan. Bread and rice were cheap. "Everywhere there were open squares with butchers selling meat ready-cooked, roasted or in stews, with fowl, pheasants and partridges, fruit and vegetables, including the delicious Samarkand melons, grown in such abundance that many were cured and kept for a year" (Marozzi, 2004, p. 215).

Timur solidified his military power with kinship alliances by marrying women related to his rivals. (Karimov has not married multiple times as Timur did, although he did marry a part-Russian wife which solidified his Soviet ties.) Timur's favorite and most powerful wife had been married to his childhood friend who had helped him in battle but finally got in the way of his expansion and had to be conquered. Timur had promised not to kill his friend, but after the battle he turned a blind eye while his general killed the friend. Timur took his wife, Saray Mulk-khanam, as his chief wife (Marozzi, 2004, p. 44). She represented the link to the greatest warrior the world had seen up to that time: Genghis Khan. She was a princess of the line of Genghis Khan and daughter of the last descendant of Genghis Khan to reign in this region.

Why was this so important? Just 130 years before Timur came to power, Genghis Khan had roared into central Asia with his Mongol generals and Turkish warriors, totally vanquishing it. Timur's home town was razed without a trace. So many women were impregnated that even now one finds Mongol characteristics among the central Asian population. After Genghis Khan died, one of his sons and then a grandson (Chagatai) ruled this area, so for the young Timur, the Mongol Empire was the latest and greatest. If Timur is Karimov's model for power, Genghis Khan was Timur's; he called himself "son-in-law of the Great Khan."

Timur's Mongol wife, known in Uzbekistan as Bibi Khanoum, was evidently very beautiful. When we visited Samarkand, we saw the huge refurbished

The Bibi Khanoum Mosque in Samarkand.

mosque of Bibi Khanoum built with the riches of Timur's India campaign. We heard that there had been suspicions of trysts between her and the architect, but when accused, the architect jumped from the high tower of the mosque and flew away! Other legends report that Timur was so jealous that his wife had to wear a veil, and thus started the practice of veiling in Samarkand.

Timur died in 1405, but in the golden age of his empire, his grandson, Ulug Beg, became a world-renowned astronomer-mathematician. In Samarkand, Clint and I climbed up and peeked into his huge observatory by which he found unknown stars and corrected mistakes in the positioning of known stars. He invited Islamic scientists to meet in the ornate school (*madrassa*) that he built next to his grandfather's mosques, and there tourists can still see their bronze statues appearing to be deep in discussion.

The astronomer Ulug Beg met a horrible fate: beheading by his eldest son on his way to Mecca—the center of Islam. His bones ended up, however, beside his grandfather Timur's grave in a tiled mausoleum in Samarkand. Today the mausoleum overflows with visitors from school children in t-shirts to elderly people in flowing gowns, for it is considered a place of pilgrimage for the nation.

In this mausoleum dedicated to Amir Timur lies a fascinating story that attests to his continuing power even after death. In 1941, Russian anthropologists wanted to unearth Timur's body for scientific examination. The Uzbeks cautioned them not to because written on his gravestone lies a warning: "Whoever disturbs my tomb will be defeated by an enemy mightier than I." Indeed, as soon as the Russian anthropologists removed Timur's body, the Nazis invaded Russia. But it gets stranger. Right after the bodies were returned to their graves in 1942, the Germans surrendered in Stalingrad! Maybe Karimov's choice of Timur as the most powerful cultural hero for his nation was on the mark after all.

BENEFITS OF TIMUR AS A NATIONAL HERO

What is to be gained by having Timur a national hero? Judging by the statue of Amir Timur astride his horse in the Tashkent park, he was a tall man with a broad chest, but often rode a horse to hide his leg, lame from a battle wound. As I looked up at him, I reflected on what Karimov achieved in his choice of this man as cultural hero. Karimov credits Timur as the founder of a Turkic nation, with Uzbek, a Turkic tongue, as the main language—much like Uzbekistan today. Indeed, Timur comes from a Turkic tribe (Barlas) that may have been one of the many tribes generally known as Uzbek at the time. He undoubtedly spoke a Turkic language.

Karimov also finds in Timur a champion of Islam who gave thanks to Allah for his victories, but one who put Mongol arts of war and governing above religiosity, and indeed killed many a Muslim soul from Baghdad to Damascus. This combination suits Karimov, for while he is Islamic and supports Islam, because the free practice of Islam was one of the prizes of independence from the Soviets, he is wary of it as well. Islam can act as a center of power that could compete with his government. Karimov wants a secular, independent state without influence from Islamic forces from outside.

WAS TIMUR REALLY UZBEK?

The halo around Timur's head blinds Uzbek citizens to certain complexities of the history of this area. One, it hides questions about the origins of the Uzbek tribes and their kingdoms. As some argue, Timur may not have even been an Uzbek. History is murky on the origin and historical uses of the term Uzbek or Ozbek, but Timur in fact attacked and conquered the Uzbek kingdom that ruled one of the parts of the Mongol empire to the west (Sengupta, 2003, p. 20). That was not very Uzbek of him!

The first "Uzbekistan" or early state ruled by Uzbek Khans[1] really took form in 1428 after Timur died. It arose out of the area to the west in the Caucasus that Timur had conquered. These Uzbek warriors took back their territory and even the heart of Timur's empire in Samarkand and Bukhara barely fifty years after his death. A ruler named Shaybani—whom Karimov could also have chosen as cultural hero—brought all the main oasis cities that are now modern-day Uzbekistan under his rule and called it an Uzbek state (Sengupta, 2003, p. 27; Yalcin, 2002, p. 31). But he was actually more Islamic than Timur, and used sharia (Islamic) law along with customary law of this area. Karimov would not welcome the use of sharia law in Uzbekistan these days.

HARD TO IGNORE THE TAJIKS

The spotlight on Timur as the national hero—a Turkic leader of a Turkic nation[2]—also hides the fact that Uzbeks who are Turks came to this area much later than the Tajiks who are a Persian-speaking group that came from Iran (Sengupta, 2003, pp. 20–21). The Tajiks came to what is now Uzbekistan from eastern Iran in the middle of the first millennium BCE.[3] Turkic people emerged historically in China in the middle of the fifth century AD when as nomads, they moved westward towards central Asia in search of pastures (Foster, 1939, p. 13).

In the sixth century, there is mention of Turks trading with the Sogdians along the Silk Road (de la Vaissiere, 2004). This is a detail of history in a Chinese text, but is interesting here because the Sogdians are ancestors of the present-day Tajiks in Uzbekistan. The Sogdians were major traveling merchants on the Silk Road from the second century BCE to the tenth century AD (Wood, 2004, p. 65).

Thus, the Tajiks were city-dwelling people who actually met the nomadic Turks when they came to central Asia. The Persians believed in Zoroastrianism,[4] vestiges of which still can be found in Uzbek culture. The Turks took over from 552 to 745 AD with the Gokturk Empire and brought their own religion of shamanism. But Persian-speaking groups took over the area from them in 819 to 999 AD, establishing the Samanid Empire, spreading Persian culture and language as well as Islam, which the Arabs had recently brought to the area. The Turks gradually became Islamic. A man named Muhammad al-Bukhari who is famous in the Islamic world for bringing together all the sayings of the Prophet Mohammed in one book lived during this time. He is famous to the extent that Uzbeks visiting American mosques sometimes receive shouts of joy and embraces because they come from this important part of the Muslim world.

Many more Turks came in with the Mongols under Genghis Khan in the thirteenth century, and Timur's tribe was one of them. Genghis Khan's army murdered civilians and leaders, but eventually merged with the amalgam of Persian and Turkic cultures in the area as well as Islam. Timur himself with his superior military might and Turkic base started from a small, rural city and took over the Silk Road cities of Samarkand and Bukhara, where many Persian speakers lived. However, in his capital of Samarkand, Persian continued as the language of administration and literature.

Over time, Turkish-based languages like Uzbek became written literary languages, but the Persian language never disappeared and still is the tongue used in everyday life in Samarkand and Bukhara. Likewise, Turkish-style food of the nomadic conquerors remains in meat kebabs barbequed on a stick (*sashlik*) or Kazakh dishes with horse meat (*norin*), but the highest status food is the Persian rice dish of *palov*, which even Karimov eats to celebrate matters of state. In many ways, this history does not jibe well with Karimov's decision to make Uzbek the national ethnicity and language.

This snippet of a long history illustrates that Uzbekistan is an inextricable mixture of Turkic and Persian cultures and languages. It is difficult for Karimov to claim that Uzbekistan is mainly Uzbek when the Tajiks who still speak a dialect of Persian have lived here in one form or another for almost twice as long. Karimov's use of Timur as a Turkic cultural hero for an Uzbek-Turkic nation ignores the complexities of history in which Persian language and culture have also figured prominently. We will return to the consequences of this situation in the chapter on ethnicity in present-day Uzbekistan.

SILK ROAD DECLINES

Because the Silk Road that linked Europe and Asia went right through central Asia, this area remained dynamic for centuries. But these days we don't know much about this area. One of the reasons is that the Silk Road and its caravans became irrelevant. About a century after Timur's empire ended in the late 1400s, European explorers were trying to find a way to China by sea. Christopher Columbus did not find it as he hoped, but Vasco de Gama found a way around Africa, and from that time on the Portuguese developed trade with Asia by ship. This is one big reason why central Asia was left in the dust, so to speak, in the 1500s.

THREE KHANATE KINGDOMS: KOKAND, BUKHARA, AND KHIVA

In the 1500s, central Asia broke up into Khanates or kingdoms, Khan being the Turkish word for ruler. There were three by the 1700s: one centered in Bukhara and including Samarkand, the area we have been talking about; a second centered around Khiva in the far west near the Aral Sea; and a third, about which we will talk more, centered around Kokand, a city in the eastern Ferghana Valley.

The Khanate that included Bukhara and Samarkand is interesting because studies of it indicate the co-existence of Persian-speaking Tajiks and Turkish-speaking Uzbeks. City people were usually bilingual, and some groups intermarried. Life brought both groups together in commerce and religion. Later in the book, I discuss the Tajik-Uzbek relations in contemporary Uzbekistan, so it is important to note here a relevant proverb of the times: "There is no Persian except in the company of a Turk, just as there is no cap unless there is a head to put it on" (Sengupta, 2003, p. 67).

People identified themselves not as Persian speakers or Turkish speakers, but by their cities, as Bukharans or Samarkandis. If they were rural, they identified with their tribes or clans. Secondarily, they identified themselves as Muslims. The Uzbek pride that Karimov claims from history was not important during this time (Malikov, 2005).

The eastern Kokand Khanate oversaw the largest territory. This is the home city of Usman, the pizza lover from Chapter 1. When he showed us around his city, he took us to the palace of the Kokand khanate. He sat his six-foot frame down on a huge, ornate bench that he loved as a child, and marveled at how small things seemed now. He took us to the tombs of the Khans and their wives, and particularly pointed out the grave of the wife of a Khan named Nadira. Kokand is proud of her as a brave and wise poet—wise because she warned cruel rulers who succeeded her husband: "If a king cares not for the poor man's life, his grand rule and sublimity is all in vain" (MacLoed & Mathew, 1999, p. 120), and brave because when attacked by the Khan of Bukhara, her husband already dead, she adamantly refused to marry the enemy, opting to die instead.

The castle of Kokand Khanate as it has been refurbished with intricate tile work.

THE RUSSIANS COMETH

In the 1860s, the world was changing. There was the Civil War in the United States and the forced opening of Japan and Korea to American commercial interests. And in Uzbekistan, the Russian Tsarist government sent soldiers into the three Khanates. Playing the "Great Game" of colonization with Britain, Russia established administrative control in this area Russians called "Turkestan"—the land of the Turks (Yalcin, 2002, p. 35).

In all of Turkestan, Russians were hardest on Kokand, Usman's hometown. In 1876, they attacked the newly built palace and completely demolished most of it. Usman told us how the back half of the palace with the harem and gardens was completely destroyed. The Khan remained only as a puppet, and Kokand became part of Russian Turkestan. Later the Russians subdued the other two Khanates as well, but gave them slightly more independence.

Life shifted. The Uzbeks of these Khanates started thinking of themselves first as Muslims, in opposition to the Christian Russians. The effect was not only on the government, but also on women's lives. In Bukhara, aristocratic city women wore long, heavy horse-hair veils and were not usually seen on the streets, but in the countryside Uzbek women did not wear veils. In Tashkent and Kokand, women only infrequently wore veils. However, confronted with Russian soldiers and later Russian merchants on the streets, women started to cover their faces more often and to stay inside their courtyards in seclusion (Northrop, 2004). Veiling and seclusion are not mandated by Islamic scripture, but vary according to the custom of the place and time (Mernissi, 1985).

The Russians also affected agriculture and commerce for they were not only seeking territory, but also wealth. The wealth they created in central Asia was built on cotton. Curiously, this prosperity relates directly to the United States. The Civil War had cut into cotton production in the United States and created a niche in world trade for Russia. Russian merchants backed by military force developed cotton plantations and experimented with various kinds of cotton, ending up with the variety popular in the American south!

THE JADIDS

"Let me tell you about the Jadids!" a woman at the institute where I taught cornered me one morning. "Uzbeks were trying to modernize Islam before the Soviets came! They had schools for women," she said with pride. Her testimony alerted me to the Jadid movement, which sought to modernize Islamic beliefs and practices. This movement originated in the late 1800s in western Russia among Turkic-speaking Muslims known as Tatars. They brought their ideas to fellow Turkic-speaking Muslims in the Russian Empire in central Asia.

The Jadid movement's first priority was expansion of education to include subjects that represented the realities of the modern world and its local variants. Thus, Jadid schools offered Turkic language, math, and science as well as the Qur'an, the Islamic holy book, and Arabic. Second, Jadids demanded national pride for Turkic Muslims under Russian colonization; in Central Asia this translated into pride in Turkestan and desire for its autonomy. Third, Jadids pushed for women's emancipation, their rights to schooling and public participation. Jadid schools for girls developed in Kokand, for example, taught by women who had learned to read and write from women religious leaders (*otin*) (Kamp, 2006; Sengupta, 2003, p. 64).

Women teachers also came from western Russia, where the Jadid movement began. They were Tatars, who like Uzbeks were Turkish Muslims in the Russian Empire. Uzbek women felt amazed when they saw these women working in public, unveiled. Of course, they also saw unveiled Russian women who had moved into central Asia, but these women were Christians and thus not seen as models. The Tatar teachers started to raise questions in women's minds about veiling and seclusion (Kamp, 2006). Thus, the Jadid movement was a movement not just against Russian domination, but also made people question the feudalistic ways imposed by their own conservative rulers and priests.

The Jadids actually sided with the Bolsheviks, who were victorious in the Russian Revolution in 1917 and led the Communist Party of the Soviet Union, because Bolsheviks talked about nations, freedom from feudalism, and need for modernization. But the Jadids dreamed for a united, free Turkestan, and that was not to be. Later under Soviet repression, the Jadid movement disappeared. Soviets replaced Jadid ideas with the ideology of communist-type modernization. Ironically, however, the Soviet's harsh repression of Islam ended up making Uzbeks turn away from their own ideas of modernizing within the Islamic faith, and towards a widespread desire to simply return to Islam as it used to be.

FOILED ATTEMPT

One of the first places in Kokand that Usman showed us was the hall where Muslim representatives from all over Turkestan met to declare their own independent Turkestan against the Tsarist Russians. Many of these leaders followed the Jadid movement and they took the Russian Bolsheviks at their word that nations should be free. We looked at pictures of the men lined up for a picture on the same spot, dark eyes hopeful and grimly determined. They were in Kokand from 1917 to 1918 to set up a government, but the Red Army of the Bolsheviks soon arrived by train. Their ideas of freedom did not match; the Bolsheviks had meant national freedom only within the Soviet fold.

Bolshevik soldiers gunned down the men who had established an autonomous Turkestan, and went on to punish the citizens of Kokand. For three days in the cold of February of 1918, the Bolsheviks killed ten thousand or more townspeople. Kokand was burned to the ground so that it would not rise in resistance again. Usman's hometown of Kokand has never yet regained its former size or status. This remains a bitter pill for him to swallow, and now the Soviets themselves have admitted it was a mistake. The massacre caused ongoing resistance throughout the area in the 1920s.

THE FORMATION OF REPUBLICS: ETHNIC MIXES

Soviet leaders at first joined together all of central Asia in a Turkestan state because they thought it represented one ethnic group, but local people soon complained (Sengupta, 2003). If Soviet "nations" were supposed to represent mainly one ethnic group, as the Soviets[5] suggested, big differences existed among Kazaks, Uzbeks, Turkmen, and Kyrgyz. Later the Tajiks claimed the Soviets ignored them, too. The Soviets listened to local advice on how to divide the Republics, at least for a few years. They were not averse to breaking up Turkestan, because Soviets were wary that all the Turkish-speaking peoples and all the Muslims in the Soviet Union might unite and rebel. They also thought experience of nationality was a necessary step in evolution towards the ideal, modern communist society—as long as the nations ascribed to the ultimate Soviet nation.

The final result was the five 'stans': Kazakhstan, Kyrgystan, Tajikistan, Turkestan, and Uzbekistan. Although by names it appeared that the Soviets had divided up ethnic groups neatly among these nations, it was impossible. Uzbekistan ended up with a majority of Uzbeks, but the populations of old Silk Road cities like Bukhara and Samarkand were highly Tajik. At first, Tajikistan was part of Uzbekistan, but later it became its own small, mountainous republic. Sizable groups of Kazakhs and Kyrgyz found themselves in Uzbekistan as well. Uzbekistan's far western part is an autonomous zone added on later; it is inhabited by Karakalpaks who are a Turkic group different in language and customs from the Uzbeks.

Map of Uzbekistan. Note the complicated borders in the Ferghana Valley.

The birth of modern Uzbekistan occurred in 1924 as a republic of the USSR. Among central Asian republics in the USSR, Uzbekistan fared well for land, receiving an area a bit smaller than California. Uzbekistan includes all the territory from the Aral Sea to the Ferghana Valley and between two big rivers, the Syr Darya to the north and the Amu Darya to the south. The majority of the population has always lived in the more fertile eastern part of the country so the population near the Aral Sea is very sparse, whereas the Ferghana Valley population is especially dense.

The Soviets divided the Ferghana Valley among Tajikistan, Kyrgystan, and Uzbekistan, creating a jigsaw puzzle with crazily shaped pieces to foil the players. This valley has been and still is a center of political and religious ferment, and later in this book I will discuss the tensions in this area.

MODERNIZING CENTRAL ASIA: GET RID OF ISLAM

The Soviets viewed central Asians as backward and superstitious. A major goal of the Soviets was to free people of their traditions so that they could modernize and become equal citizens in the USSR. But how could they do that in central Asia? Much as in other parts of the Soviet Union, the first targets were rich people and religious clergy. The theory was to hand over the power of these elite groups to peasants and workers. Larger landowners, merchants, and Muslim clergy lost land, wealth, and titles. I interviewed a man who was 90 years old in 2005. As he was growing up in the 1920s, his parents and grandparents, landowners at the outskirts of Tashkent, lost their orchards, grapes, and wheat. His parents soon died, and his grandmother raised him.

He also described the attack on Islam by the Soviets. He said that by the 1930s, "People's faces would turn white if you suggested that they perform some Islamic ritual for you. They were afraid that they would be turned in and sent off to Siberia." Uzbek who were Communist Party members and officials would lose everything if they attended a Muslim funeral service, even if it was their own father who had died.

On the face of it, Islam disappeared, but in reality it went underground. Secretly, prayers, rituals, and even education in reading the Qur'an continued. Ironically, the women religious practitioners (*otin*), who had lower status than the male clergy, sometimes could carry on Islamic services in homes and get away with it.

The attack on Islam set up a conflict among Uzbeks that continues to this day. As we have seen, the Jadid movement already was working to reform Islam to become more modern. But when the Soviets came down so hard on everything Islamic, people simply wanted to get back what they had lost. Tradition—the way it had been before the Soviets—no matter how old-fashioned, came to represent the antithesis to the Soviets. As a result, a conflict between traditionalists and reformists arose and continues to cause dissension about the proper practice of Islam and the morality surrounding women (Tokhtakhodzhaeva, 1995).

MODERNIZING CENTRAL ASIA:
GET RID OF THE VEIL

What other strategies did the Soviets use to make Central Asians into modernized communists? Veiled women were not initially viewed as a problem. However, by the late 1920s, both Russian and Uzbek Communists had decided that the veil was a symbol of backwardness and if they got rid of the veil, modernization would follow. They started what was known as 'the attack' (*hujum*) against the veil, demanding that women de-veil—first dancers, then wives or daughters of Communist Party members, teachers in Soviet schools, and finally even women in villages. In the late 1920s, Communist Party demands to throw veils in fires in public squares spread throughout Uzbekistan.

For some women this was traumatic. If a woman had not gone out of her courtyard without a veil since she was 13 or 14 years of age, to suddenly strip her face in front of non-family males at the age of 40 or 60, seemed like exposing herself improperly. Even the Jadids, who wanted to improve women's status within the practice of Islam, had not advocated de-veiling. Instead, they said, the worse evil was keeping women secluded within their homes and courtyards without letting them come out in public or go to school. Let women be veiled if they can emerge and get educated, they argued. On the other hand, there were many educated women who welcomed the opportunity to go out in public unveiled (Kamp, 2006).

The catch was this: Uzbek men sometimes objected strongly to de-veiling. And thus, women were caught between two powerful forces: the state that wanted them to de-veil and some of their fathers, brothers, and community

An historical rendition of a man pleading with officials for his wife to remain veiled.

leaders who wanted them to stay veiled—to the extent that they murdered women who de-veiled. It was an impossible quandary. Sometimes village women de-veiled in the square and then went on wearing the veil in their everyday lives to protect themselves.

The state in other places such as Turkey had encouraged women to shed their veils, but the men there, though they were patriarchal, did not murder de-veiled women. In Uzbekistan, the history of the late 1920s shows examples of brothers stabbing their sisters after they de-veiled; Muslim clergy inciting fathers to kill their daughters after they de-veiled; and even communist village officials raping de-veiled women (Kamp 2006).

Marianne Kamp struggles to answer the question as to why such atrocities occurred in Uzbekistan. She concludes that it was not a show of resistance of Uzbek men against the Soviets. Rather, it was a show of Uzbek men's power over their women at a time when the Soviets were stripping village leaders, landowners, merchants, and clergy of their power. Male dominance was the last bastion of power when the Soviets were overthrowing all the traditional power bases. About 1000 women died in the de-veiling campaigns. By the 1930s it was over, and by the 1940s and 1950s younger women were accustomed to wearing nothing but a headscarf tied behind their necks, Russian style.

Did the Soviets completely modernize Uzbek gender relations by the de-veiling campaign? No, they did not. Taking off veils does not a gender revolution make, any more than taking off corsets. But women as Soviet citizens were able to come into the public work world in Uzbekistan. They did the double duty that women do in most parts of the world, coming home from work to cook and clean, although day care centers and cafeterias for families helped them. Women's positions did not change completely, but as a result, women in Uzbekistan have greater equality in education and work than in many parts of the Islamic world.

MODERNIZING CENTRAL ASIA: CREATE A COTTON PLANTATION

Agriculture was another beachhead in the struggle to change Uzbeks into modernized Communists. The Soviets expanded on the policy of the Tsarist Russians to make Uzbekistan a cotton plantation for the rest of the Soviet Union. Implementation required land and control over its uses. First a land reform took place in which the land of the rich was taken from bigger landowners and re-distributed to those with little or no land. Those who were willing to shift into the cash crop of cotton and expand their lands to grow cotton received favorable loans. Some rich landowners were sent to Siberia, but others were able to move away and participate in the next step of agricultural reform in other parts of Uzbekistan (Kamp and Zanca, 2008).

The second step was collectivization. In the late 1920s and early 1930s, the Soviets brought private farmers together to farm collectively. Agricultural collectives gathered land and labor together with one goal in mind: to produce cotton. Uzbekistan had factories to clean the cotton, but the Soviets extracted the most value for themselves, shipping the cleaned cotton to Russia for more sophisticated processing, and selling cotton clothes back to the Uzbeks. Likewise, they sold food to Uzbeks that Uzbek land itself could have grown if it were not growing cotton. Uzbekistan remained an undeveloped underbelly of the Soviet empire.

The land also suffered from the cotton regime. The Soviets pushed nomads off their land and reclaimed it for irrigated cotton farming. They increased irrigated land again in the 1920s, and again from the 1950s to the 1980s. The expansion of cotton would be nothing but an interesting historical fact if it weren't for its consequences: one of the great ecological disasters of the world. The Aral Sea in western Uzbekistan is disappearing. Since 1960, the Aral Sea has lost 75% of its volume, and its surface area has shrunk by 50% because irrigation draws huge amounts of water from the two big rivers that feed it. Moreover, the water distribution system is inefficient and applies more water than is necessary to the cotton (Yalcin 2002).

FOOD FOR THE PEOPLE

The USSR promised equality in food, but in fact did not guarantee food sovereignty (control over food) and food security at the national level for Uzbekistan. The effect on food in Uzbekistan was similar to the effect of the many places in Africa that have shifted from growing their own local food to cash crops for the world market: food insecurity and hunger. In Uzbekistan, the saving grace was the household plots—small parcels of land allotted to each family. However, families were supposed to grow vegetables for themselves and their two cows (if they had them) on plots that averaged less than one-quarter the size of a basketball court (0.1 hectares, which equals 1076 square feet). Good luck!

In 1933, the confusion caused by the reorganization of farmland into collectivized farms caused a famine. A woman 80 years old remembered her hunger as she held out her gnarled hands for proof of her hard work. "I can remember when I was small eating the greens from the edges of the fields that only the cows had eaten before. And we even dug up roots of a tree to get enough nourishment." Determined to never have that happen again, she still got out and dug in the earth in her courtyard garden.

Over time, people adjusted to collectivization, the food supply increased, and food habits began to change. Public Soviet food was substandard Russian food: cabbage soup, boiled potatoes, and buckwheat porridge, prescribed in a standardized manual (Mack and Surina, 2005). This food is what students ate at school, adults ate at work, and families ate at evening cafeterias. Plates and forks came into people's lives, partially replacing bowls and large platters from which everyone shared (Zanca, 2003). An elderly rural woman told me that she remembers her Russian neighbors introducing them to cabbage, potatoes, peppers, dill, and parsley, and teaching them how to can tomatoes and tomato juice in big jars. Indeed, when their stock from their own gardens ran dry, Russian fare is what the market had to offer, and potatoes, tomatoes, and dill became important to Uzbek food.

However, many Uzbeks claim that potatoes do not fit them (Zanca, 2003). The 90-year-old man stuck to the Uzbek tastes of his childhood. "I still don't like potatoes. My grandchildren eat tomatoes and potatoes and they think that is Uzbek food. But when I was a boy, we never ate them." His daughter-in-law beside him, wearing a black and red scarf, nodded her head with a pleasant but rueful grin. "When I use potatoes, I have to make something special for him."

WORLD WAR II

While we were in Uzbekistan, the fiftieth anniversary of the fall of Berlin occurred. Schoolchildren strew roses over names of dead soldiers carved into marble on World War II memorials across the country. About one million Uzbek soldiers died for the Soviet cause in World War II. A huge picture in a Tashkent museum shows a woman with her young children sadly watching a receding line of soldiers. In 2005, the men who survived stood proudly at the ceremonies in their old uniforms to receive praise from their government.

An elderly man who rarely emerged from the third-floor apartment below us strutted into the courtyard that morning with medals shining. He said, "I bet that in America they don't even remember the fall of Berlin." We had to admit that was true, but here, to have lived through the siege of Stalingrad and have marched to Berlin was to have faced hell and survived.

Even the 90-year-old man who harbored many bitter memories of the Soviets felt pride and gratitude at having fought and survived. He claimed that he survived because of his sixth sense. Separated from other soldiers, he took refuge with a Russian woman who let him sleep in her house. He had a strange feeling and could not sleep, so moved to a nearby barn. Later that night her house was bombed and she died.

A monument to World War II in Bukhara with children strewing flowers to remember the fallen.

World War II was a burden, but it was a time when Uzbeks could take their place as full Soviet citizens along with their Russian peers. Although they experienced prejudice from Russians, World War II was a watershed in making Uzbeks feel part of the Soviet Union and allowing many Uzbek men to learn more about the Russian/Soviet world.

Early in the war, the major cities of the western USSR were in German hands or under siege. Because Tashkent was far from the German front, the Soviet Union used it as a safe haven for important factories. Uzbekistan became the unlikely home to a modern airplane factory (which is still there) and various armament factories. During the Cold War, it was the repository for nuclear weapons and chemical weapons. When the Soviets pulled out in 1991, they took the nuclear weapons, but the chemicals remain.

Uzbekistan also had the dubious distinction of being the place of banishment. A Russian woman in Tashkent told us the story of her grandfather, a Russian Orthodox priest, who got caught in Vienna during World War II while his family was still in Moscow. When he managed to return to Moscow, Soviets accused him of being a spy and sentenced him to execution. Clever planner that he was, he had brought some silver candlesticks from the Viennese church, and offered them as a bribe to escape execution. Instead the Soviets sent him and his family to Uzbekistan, where he married the daughter of a Russian sent down to mine gold. His blonde, blue-eyed granddaughter told us the tale over a delicious Russian dinner.

POSTWAR UZBEKISTAN

After the war, Stalin died. He was the dictator who ruled the USSR from 1922 to 1953 and ordered the killing of millions of Soviet citizens. But he also fought with the Allies against the Nazis. Khrushchev came to power (1958–1964), debunking the name of Stalin who in the1930s had sent many Uzbek citizens to Siberian labor camps for being too nationalistic. The Cold War was raging between the United States and the USSR. While I was growing up in the United States, I participated in drills crouching under my desk in case the Soviets bombed us. However, Khrushchev tolerated increasing nationalistic sentiment in the USSR. Thus, the Uzbek Communist Party encouraged a nationalist writer to publish an Uzbek recipe book that paid homage to ibn Sina, an eleventh century Persian medical philosopher whom Uzbeks claim as their own. No matter that the book borrowed recipes from other central Asian republics, its main point was to sharpen the boundaries of Uzbekistan as a nation (Mack and Surina, 2005, p. 62).

My Russian teacher lived in what she called a Khrushchev apartment. The smallness of Krushchev apartments was a sign of equality. We always sat in the main room where the couch stood within an arm's length of her daughter's bed and the postage stamp kitchen. She also had a tiny bedroom. It was one among acres of apartments built in this style in 1966 after the Tashkent earthquake of 7.5 magnitude in which the mud and straw walls of older Uzbek houses crumbled, leaving 300,000 people homeless. From all over the USSR, workers came to make Tashkent into a city of parks and wide boulevards. Many of those workers stayed and Tashkent became the fourth largest city in the Soviet Union!

In the heyday of the USSR under Brezhnev (1964–1982) the advantages of being Soviet were clear, not only for the Russians but also for the Uzbeks. Looking back in 2005, Uzbeks could see the advantages of the Soviet years when the postal system worked, medical care was free, and public schools were well-run. A high school teacher talked of travelling to conferences and trainings in Eastern Europe. The smartest Uzbeks attended the prestigious University of Moscow. One woman's husband had worked for the railroads and she remembered the delicious cheeses, fat turkeys, and expensive vodka he brought home with him. Admittedly, that was not Uzbek cuisine—and Muslims were not supposed to drink alcohol—but life was enjoyable and meat was not so expensive.

By 1985, however, the USSR was in trouble from an enormous budget deficit—too much military spending and too much corruption. Meat was hard to find in Tashkent. Mikhail Gorbachev came to the helm hoping to solve things by allowing new openness (*glasnost*). Uzbeks were once more allowed to practice Islam, and many mosques re-opened. But the new freedoms got away from Moscow when East Germans started streaming through the Berlin wall in 1989. Even in Uzbekistan, people in Kokand rioted against a group of Meskhetian Turks, deported by Stalin from Georgia in 1944, whom they felt had received unfair advantages. The unruliness of the riots demonstrated that resistance was now a possibility.

INDEPENDENCE

The genie was out of the bottle—both the desire for freedom and the wish to get rid of Soviet power and corruption had become unstoppable forces. A new spate of Uzbek cookbooks emerged as a sign of nationalism. Uzbeks were freshly resentful because Soviet elite in Moscow had been skimming cotton profits off of the backs of Uzbek peasants, in collusion with Uzbek elites. Although they did not push as hard against the USSR as Eastern Europeans, Uzbeks were ready for a declaration of independence in 1991. Elected to the presidency was a man who had become the Communist Party's first Secretary of Uzbekistan in 1989: Islam Karimov. He stood up for Uzbek ways against the former Soviets, waving the Qur'an and declaring that his name was Islam.

Yet from the beginning of his rule, Karimov established a harsh style of fighting his political opponents and it lasts to this day. His government suppressed students demonstrating over poor living conditions at Tashkent University in 1992. The students carried signs supporting two opposition parties: the Birlik (Unity) and Erk (Freedom) parties, founded in 1988 and 1990 respectively. Both supported a secular, non-Islamic, democratic state. Birlik was the larger of the two and rejected Karimov's accusation that they were actually Muslim extremists. The same year, security forces beat up Birlik's leader and closed their offices. The legislature took away their party registration. Erk lasted until 1993, when it was also stripped of its registration. Opposition leaders frequently disappeared without explanation (Yalcin, 2002, p. 55).

Economics and politics worsened in the mid-nineties. By 1994, Uzbekistan's economic situation had deteriorated because it no longer received manufactured goods or raw materials from the Soviet Union. In 1996, the world price of cotton plunged, threatening cotton exports and government coffers, for cotton constituted over a third of Uzbekistan's exports. When the president stopped foreign companies from converting Uzbek currency into dollars, most of them left the country. He declared that their departure did not matter: "We have many tomatoes in Uzbekistan. We should be making our own tomato sauce" (Whitlock, 2002, p. 238).

For a moment in 1995, Karimov opened a dialogue with the Birlik party leaders in the United States in an attempt to assuage his authoritarian image, but it was short-lived. In 1996, Karimov gathered journalists and proclaimed a freer press, yet today, the state maintains complete control over television, radio, and newspapers, and journalists can take no chances (Yalcin, 2002).

In the late 1990s, Karimov returned to suppressing all political opposition. When there was any trouble, particularly in the eastern Ferghana Valley, he blamed Islamist groups and had police arrest young men quietly at night, going from house to house (Whitlock, 2002).

In 1999, government officials blamed Islamic militants when car bombs went off in downtown Tashkent, narrowly missing President Karimov himself. Cynical citizens claim quietly that Karimov himself planned the attack so that he could crack down on dissidents, while others think political opponents were targeting Karimov and his government. At any rate, Karimov took advantage of it, taking down the ubiquitous loudspeakers at mosques from which to call the faithful to prayer five times a day. Karimov made his stance painfully clear against political dissidents: "I am ready to rip off the heads of two hundred people … to save peace and calm in the Republic … If a child of mine chose such a path, I myself would rip off his head" (Whitlock, 2002, p. 244).

After the bombing, police arrested young men who prayed five times a day and belonged to conservative religious organizations, associating them with the radical Islamic Movement of Uzbekistan. Police also arrested the brothers of these young men on trumped-up drug charges, and made sure that their fathers lost their jobs. The government tortured suspects to extract confessions, held a trial that most citizens discredited, and executed six men. One of the men executed was the brightest grandson of an Islamic mystic (Sufi) from Bukhara who had spent time in Siberia. The mystic had taught his grandson Muslim prayers and Arabic language in secret, hoping that he would become his spiritual successor (Whitlock, 2002, p. 262).

The Birlik and Erk Parties have persisted in Uzbekistan despite persecution. However, in 1999 and 2001, security officials killed regional Birlik Party officials, and now leaders of both parties live in exile abroad. Karimov's agencies repeatedly refuse to allow these parties to register. Karimov will risk no real opponents, preferring to establish his own approved opposition parties! Elections continue, but Karimov controls the results.

KARIMOV'S DAUGHTER

Remember Karimov's colorful daughter and her black SUV mentioned in Chapter 1? Her father may try to extend his power by backing her candidacy in the future. Gulnara Karimova has continued to keep Uzbeks amused. She made a music video in Russia under the name Googoosha, her father's nickname for her, and has started a jewelry line in Switzerland where her children go to school. You can find her on the web.

But Gulnara is not to be taken lightly. On a blog, Uzbeks in the United States tease that none other than their own Dr. Googoosha—she has an MA from Harvard and a PhD from the University of World Economy and Diplomacy in Tashkent—is now Uzbek's Ambassador to Spain! No mean position as Spain now has the presidency of the European Union. She is also rich, head of a company in Uzbekistan that controls a mobile telephone network, and sponsor of her own Guli brand of clothes. In short, both economically and politically she is well-positioned to succeed her father.

CONCLUSION

In the first part of this chapter, I showed how Karimov transformed the history of Amir Timur into an Uzbek myth in order to bolster Uzbek ethnic nationalism and Karimov's own power. His exercise of power will come to an explosive climax in Chapter 7. Karimov's version of Uzbek history projects Uzbekistan far back in time and denies the rich ethnic mix of this area. I will focus on the ethnic diversity of Uzbekistan in Chapter 6.

The Soviet Union's attempts to communize and modernize Uzbekistan have left a legacy of conflict and contradiction for Uzbeks surrounding how and to what extent modernization will occur. The Soviets set up the expectation for less class difference and more equality in modern Uzbek society. In Chapters 3 and 4, we will meet the negative feelings emerging as inequalities between rich and poor in urban and rural areas increase. This chapter shows that women's traditional roles, associated with Islamic morality, were a special target of Soviet modernization, leading to particular problems for women in Uzbekistan, which I will take up in Chapter 5. Uzbek women represent, on the one hand, the chance to return to traditional morality in a newly independent Uzbekistan, and on the other hand, the hope to participate in the modern ideals of a global world.

ENDNOTES

1. Khans are rulers in both the Turkic and Mongolian languages.

2. Turkic here means that these are people that speak a Turkic or Altaic type of language and are descended from Turkish tribes originally from China.

3. "Tajik" originated from the Turko-Mongolian word for non-Turk, and historically came to designate Persians and speakers of Persian in Central Asia.

4. Zoroastrianism started in what is now Iran by Zarathustra and is historically recorded in the fifth century BCE. The religion believes in one god, creator of good. Fire is a medium of spirituality, and water is the source of wisdom. Some uses of fire in ritual in Uzbekistan, such as jumping over fire, carry echoes of Zoroastrian beliefs in the region.

5. I will refer to the leaders of the USSR as Soviets, a word that refers to the authoritative governing councils. Soviets began as democratically elected work councils, but after the Revolution became ruling bodies. Soviets existed at the central level in Moscow as well as at the level of republics like Uzbekistan. They were nominally elected and consisted of Communist Party members.

Chapter 3

Urban Class Differences and Food Security

This book is about the right to food. Food security means having enough food to survive, but real food security promises guaranteed access to food socially and economically, as well as the right to both nutrition and cultural preferences—that is, to be able to get what you ought to eat and what you like to eat, as influenced by your ethnicity or class.

Food security sounds simple, but it requires adequate income or land, knowledge, freedom to be who you are, and freedom of the market. I go to the refrigerator in the morning and number one, it isn't empty (right to survive). Number two, I choose orange juice instead of Coke (right to nutrition). Number three, I have oatmeal or a fried egg—not unlike my German and Scottish forbearers (right to cultural preferences). Number four, my husband drinks specialty coffee such as Ethiopian Mocha; I drink Irish Breakfast Tea. Although it is not in the definition, the right to keep up with the trends drawn from the global market is associated with higher class people like us who are very food secure.

EXPLORING FOOD SECURITY IN UZBEKISTAN

Food security in Uzbekistan varies greatly. This chapter focuses on Tashkent, the capital city. Overall, Tashkent city has higher food security than other parts of Uzbekistan with 9.2% food poverty and 2.9% extreme food poverty in 2003—about 13 times better food security than the rest of the country (WFP, 2008, p. 11). However, there is sharp inequality among households in Tashkent, some bargaining for every penny at the cheapest outdoor markets, and others paying high prices for packaged food at shiny grocery stores. Furthermore, in the rural areas almost all families have household plots to grow food, whereas in the city the size of land is small, and more than half is covered by buildings or houses (WFP, 2008, p. 4). City dwellers usually must buy food, and thus, urban differences in income impact access to food directly. For Uzbekistan as a whole, the highest 20% of the population controls 44% of the household income and the lowest 40% controls only 19% (2003-2008) (Unicef, 2010). I will illustrate differences in access to food in this chapter where we meet a poor family, a rich family, and an aspiring, middle-class family.

As for the knowledge aspect of food security, Uzbekistan is well-educated for its level of economic development—adults literate at 97%; youth literate at 99%; and 100% of children attending primary school (Unicef, 2010). Everyone learns about nutrition in school.

What about cultural preferences? Uzbekistan has its challenges. Variation in income makes a huge difference. In this chapter, I ask how people of different socioeconomic levels in Tashkent are able to fulfill their cultural preferences for *palov*, the national food that Karimov touts as the reward of Uzbek independence. This dish of mutton, rice, carrots, and onions is at the top of almost all interviewees' preferences. They thought they deserved this dish as part of a diet replete with meat and the good taste of fat, but some could not afford to have it often.

How did food security compare among people of vastly different socioeconomic levels in Tashkent?

LOW-INCOME HOUSEHOLDS IN TASHKENT

On a rainy day in early spring, I walked through the gates of an Uzbek neighborhood (*mahalla*) in Tashkent. Each neighborhood had its own local leaders, but they helped the national government keep people in line. I felt the first hints of warmth in the air as I passed along the narrow streets between white walls surrounding courtyards where I could see the tops of fruit trees beginning to bud. After several blocks, Shahnoza, my interpreter, and I found a house recommended to us by colleagues at the institute.

We entered a metal blue doorway and stared at a courtyard about twenty square feet with a small area of soil turned over, and the frame of a bed that would be used for lounging through the hot summer. The courtyard was surrounded by several teeny houses—two of one room and one of several rooms. Across the courtyard were cow stalls, though no cows were in sight.

Turning to our right, we went up onto a porch, through a worn blue door and into a little room where a small elderly woman sat on a blanket behind a low table. "*Assalamalykum*" (Peace be upon you). She motioned us to seats of honor on a blanket farthest from the door. An old wooden stove was plastered into one corner of the room, but it sat cold on this Saturday morning. Although Uzbekistan has high production of natural gas, poorer people did not necessarily receive it.

Dressed in a long brown velveteen dress and leggings, her hair covered with a tight brown under-scarf and a red, white, and blue wool scarf tied under her chin, Nagira had eyes clouded with cataracts, but talked alertly. She brought her hands together like a book and prayed as soon as we all sat down. I gave her tea that I had brought, and she prayed again, this time for me. "Take me to America," she half-joked after she had wiped her hands over her face. I laughed outwardly, while taking the statement inwardly as a vote of dissatisfaction about her life. Her face wrinkled in laughter, too, and showed one remaining tooth in her bottom front jaw.

"You have a nice garden," I ventured.

"I'm afraid this rain will knock the blossoms off the fruit trees," she said, speaking in Uzbek. Nagira pantomimed shoveling. "I can still dig in the garden, though it is harder since I hurt my back last year. But we can't grow much here anymore because we have no water to garden with. We used to be able to use the water from the street, but not anymore. We can grow some corn, parsley, and dill, but no potatoes or onions." Her teenage granddaughter brought in tea and poured it for us.

I asked Nagira what she had eaten yesterday, hoping to get an honest representation of a recent day. "Tea, sugar, and bread for breakfast. *Shipildok* for lunch made of small green lentils (*mosh*), onion, and cumin. For dinner, we had *atala*: milk, oil, and onions." No meat, I noted. I knew that at least the price of bread was kept low by the government, benefitting urban poor people in particular. Also, poor people got special hand-outs of food on national holidays. Nonetheless, people in the poorest fifth of the population consume about half the protein that they need and even lack adequate levels of fat intake (Musaev et al, 2010, p. 53, 56).

"Who cooks?"

"My daughter. She lives here with me and five grandchildren. She is divorced. Her husband was Tajik and lived over in Tajikistan, but when the war got bad over there, she came home. I also have a handicapped son. We all eat together right here out of the same pot."

"Do the children eat different foods sometimes?"

"No. I have to have soft foods and that is what they eat, too." Wow, that's respect for the elderly, I thought.

"What are your favorite foods?"

"Macaroni, fried spaghetti (*shavla*), but I don't get them all the time. When I am sick I might like soft fish or meat, but I can't ask my children for it." Not enough money for that, I finished her thought in my head.

It was clear that these people had a hard time and used a lot of pasta, potatoes, and onions to get by. She and her daughter stuffed long floor pillows and sold them, but that effort brought in little money. Even in Tashkent there were too many people for the available jobs because industries disappeared and declined after the Soviet Union withdrew. The service sector had not developed as it had in America and other societies in the West. However, Uzbekistan gave free health benefits and more welfare to the poor than other central Asian republics (Welfare, 2007).

"What foods don't you like?"

Her eyes got big. "I like them all." She then put her hand over her mouth, giggled, and quite unexpectedly said, "My daughter said that I shouldn't say anything about the president."

The interview dissolved into laughter. I could only imagine that her daughter had warned her not to criticize the president even though she disliked him. Any questions on 'dislike' brought him up!

I had been told that a characteristic of Uzbeks is that they buy large amounts of wheat, onions, and potatoes in the fall and store this food to save money, so I asked her if they buy food in the fall. I found that she lived hand to mouth. "No, we can't afford to buy much. If we had $5 we would buy ten kilos, but we can only buy a few kilos at a time. You don't know what will happen tomorrow. I am thankful for today." She was philosophical for she had faced famine when young, but at 80 had outlived most of her friends. The life expectancy in Uzbekistan is about 72 years of age—75 for women (CIA 2009).[1]

I asked her if she shared food with friends and neighbors, as many Uzbeks are proud of doing on ritual days. "Yes, before we did," she answered, remembering this neighborhood in better times. "But neighbors I knew have died. Before there was everything to eat and now there is nothing."

My question about eating in restaurants seemed irrelevant here, but she answered it with aplomb. "When we went outside we used to eat ice cream, but we don't eat outside anymore."

Later on, Nagira's niece, her sister's daughter, arrived. A hefty middle-aged woman, she was without a headscarf and wore a newer-looking beaded sweater vest over her dark dress, her fingers polished with red. The teenage granddaughter again came into the room with tea and echoed her grandmother's refrain to me: "Please take us to the United States."

I laughed, "Will you fit in my suitcase?"

She shyly shook her head and added, "Our neighbor won the green card lottery." She was referring to a lottery in which people applied to the American embassy for an immigrant visa. A hundred or so, depending on the year, would receive permanent residency in the United States—if they paid the fees, filled out paper work correctly, and passed the interview process.

Her quiet words shouted out that life was difficult here. My presence as an American conjured up idealistic dreams of America where all the streets are paved with gold, and where they could escape both poverty and the president they dare not mention for fear of reprisal.

Nagira's niece spoke for the young girl. "She is in high school, but it would be too expensive to get more schooling." Only 56% of ninth graders continue on in school to general, vocational or academic high schools (UNDP, 2005).

The niece brought with her samples of a dish that her brother had made for a family birthday party. "You make it by putting meat, water, and wheat into a pot. You cook it all night for five to six hours until the bones get very soft." The interpreter and I both sampled the pasty dish of mashed potatoes along with a few strings of meat. I said I liked it, but I was definitely neutral. If this was all the meat they ate, it was precious little.

Although she was clearly better off than her elder aunt, the niece had her own tale of sorrow. She and her daughter had been robbed and lost everything, including all the carpets and dishes she had saved for her daughter's marriage. They then came to live with her brother and his family. Now she helped her

Women selling vegetables in an unofficial market along the street in Tashkent.

sister-in-law to make dumplings, which the sister-in-law took to the market to sell—a sure sign that the family was having difficulty in making ends meet.

WHAT KIND OF FOOD SECURITY?

It was time to move on to other houses in the neighborhood. I wished the old woman long life. She bid us goodbye with a last prayer for health and happiness. As we went out the door and down the street to the next house, I talked with Shahnoza about what had happened.

"It seemed like the niece came so that they could save face and serve us something more than tea."

She agreed. "The woman didn't want to be ashamed. Uzbeks want to be hospitable with their food, and families help each other out. That's all people have to depend on now when times are bad."

Her remark made me think. Uzbeks often told me with pride: "Americans eat out, but Uzbeks like to eat at home," and "American families aren't so close, but Uzbek families are very close." My husband and I would always protest "—No, we do eat at home. No, our family is close!" But now the statements made more sense. They were more about them than us, and made virtues from necessity. A close family eating at home together was a good thing about the Uzbeks, but it also cast a rosy light on strategies for survival. How would this family ever have survived without each other? With low-paying jobs or no jobs, they had no choice but to stick together.

Like Nagira's silenced remark about the president that popped out when thinking about foods she didn't like, these statements carried truths that had to remain silent. Living without enough food was not the way independent Uzbekistan should be, but it was politically risky to criticize a food policy so strongly embraced by the president. People could not complain about not having enough food because it would be non-patriotic and possibly dangerous.

Nagira's family had enough food security to survive, but not necessarily food that gave them adequate nutrition. They were likely part of the 22.5% of urban Uzbeks who consume less than 2100 calories a day—the amount necessary to maintain their health (WFP, 2008, p. 28).[2] Although they were Uzbek citizens, the economy under President Karimov did not give them access to the culturally preferred foods that they felt they deserved. As Nagira showed, food was just barely a safe topic, only a hair's breadth away from dissatisfactions about hunger and poverty.

HIGH-INCOME HOUSEHOLDS IN TASHKENT

The sun peeked in and out of the clouds as we walked past various houses in the neighborhood, but nowhere did the sun shine brighter than when we knocked at a thick-walled gate answered by a security guard, skirted our way between an SUV Mercedes and a sedan Mercedes, and climbed marble steps into a big marble entry hall. A bright green and yellow parrot hung in a cage. This house was little more than a block from Nagira's place, but it was a completely different world. We sat on a rounded leather sofa in front of a table with flowers and chocolate. My gift of tea seemed paltry, merely symbolic, here, whereas in Nagira's home I felt it was actually appreciated.

Zahro had long-hair, and was petite and pretty in her pink track suit. Her 12-year-old daughter cuddled up next to her, still pudgy with baby fat. The conversation was in Russian, the language of the conquerors, but now the language of education and sophistication. For Zahro's husband, Russian was the language of business. As it turned out, the family's wealth came from a chain of stores that he owned in Russia. They were the "New Rich" that people spoke of—the few that profited from economic differences that emerged in Uzbekistan after the fall of communism.

Zahro's husband was there when we first came in, and he said, "Would you like tea, coffee, vodka, cognac, martini?" I staggered backwards in surprise and made it a joke, "I can't drink on the job," I quipped, but it was not lost on me that he was showing off his wealth and generosity with alcohol, and alcohol beyond the normal wine or vodka easy to get in Uzbekistan.

He left for work, but not long afterwards he kept calling on the cell phone. Zahro answered again and again patiently, and laughed as she held up the phone so that we could hear him shout the English words he knew through the phone. He evidently liked to keep his finger on home even from his office. According to Zahro, her husband decided what food to buy and cook, and the chauffeur bought it at the bazaar.

Between calls Zahro talked about food. "Yesterday I didn't eat any breakfast because I am worried about my weight." Actually I had thought she might be pregnant because she was thin except for her stomach, but luckily I hadn't said anything. It turned out that she had been ill, and simultaneously dealing with her mother's serious illness. Watching their weight was a worry that Nagira and her family, just a block away, would like to have, I thought.

Zahro talked about her lunch yesterday: three to four salads, borscht (Russian beet soup), and *kavardak*—fried vegetables and meat. "At 5:00 we have tea like in London, and then in evenings we have fruit, and my husband and daughter have sandwiches. My son is 22 and has been studying in England for five years. He wants to work there and get a green card. He even thinks in English now! When he talks in Uzbek, his word order is funny, like English."

"He's really immersed!" This family had attained the dream of a son or daughter studying abroad that came almost like a side dish in every conversation.

"Who cooks?" I asked.

"The cook is a woman, a Russian. We like her food. I taught her to cook things properly as my husband likes. He likes beautiful, delicious meals."

"Does he ever cook?"

"No, he just lifts up the lids and smells it and says whether it is good. But on special holidays, he makes *palov* out in front of the house and serves everyone in the neighborhood who comes. On *Hayit* we kill a ram and serve the neighborhood, too." Ah, so in spite of the alcohol, forbidden in Islam, he still performed service to the community like a good Muslim.

We changed to the topic of favorite foods. The contrast between this family and everyone with whom I had talked with so far was stunning. Like the majority of people, Zahro and her daughter remained loyal to Uzbekistan in saying that their absolutely favorite food was *palov*, the preeminent national food. But afterward Zahro quickly shifted to expressing preference for international food to which most Uzbeks had no access: "Japanese sushi. In London it was so good. In Malaysia, I loved the tiger shrimp and in Thailand the papaya."

Her daughter continued: "I love the french fries and chicken sandwiches at McDonald's." I knew there were no McDonald's restaurants in Uzbekistan, so I looked at her mother. "She gets this [food] when we are in London or Moscow."

After the interview, Zahro invited us to have lunch. We walked across a Western-type lawn behind the house to get to a small, well-built house with kitchen, dining room, a few soft chairs, and the cook's bedroom. The cook had everything ready—three salads and soft *shavlar osh*—*palov* recooked to be really soft. While Nagira's meals were mostly meatless except for holidays and celebrations, Zahro's daily meals had meat at their center. Her husband could demand and afford this symbol of wealth that was increasingly out of reach for common Uzbeks.

Zahro proudly described the special dish of *shipildok*—lentils and horse meat, boiled with onion and cumin. Nagira had mentioned eating the same thing yesterday, but at her house it had been lentils, onion, and cumin minus the horse meat.

Higher income young women at a festival in the park with Coca Cola umbrellas behind.

After lunch, the 12-year-old drew a picture of a pregnant woman and gave it to my interpreter who was pregnant at the time. The mother chuckled and told us that her daughter had wanted to go to the store and buy a younger sibling.

Zahro displayed a family picture with her handsome son, well over six feet tall. "Will he marry soon?" I asked, as I knew this was a concern of all Uzbek families. "When he finishes studying. He doesn't want to marry an English girl because they are too independent. I do what my husband says, and if he wants me home, I stay. But English girls don't." Trained as a pediatrician, Zahro had stayed home at her husband's request for ten years. Such an arrangement was also a sign of his high status.

FOOD AND CLASS DIFFERENCES

Asking about food revealed class differences that people might otherwise have avoided in our conversation. A study in France found that people's tastes for food, and even for body type, varied by class. Working class people preferred meat, potatoes, and full, stocky bodies. Wealthy people preferred shrimp, vegetables and taut, thin bodies (Bourdieu, 1984).

In the United States, people find class differences embarrassing because of the cultural ideal that we are all supposed to be equal. Students don't like to talk about this topic either. We try to wipe out visual evidence of class by all wearing jeans, Nike shoes, and eating pizza—or by blaming social friction on ethnic or racial differences instead of class. Food studies clearly show that class differences involving food and diet exist in the United States. For example, obesity is higher among low-income people (Berg, 2008). In Chapter 8, food interviews conducted in Oregon will show how low-income people have food tastes and limitations in access to food that relate strongly to class and help to explain the mystery of class-based obesity.

Uzbeks who well remember the communist ideal of equality do not like class differences either. Ordinary people talk of the New Rich with a derogatory bitterness, as they are all too aware that their own woefully low salaries do not always get paid. However, export industries such as cotton, natural gas, and oil products were thriving from the annual growth in GDP—around 3% in 2005, going up to 8% in 2009 (WFP, 2010, p. 13).

I was surprised that Zahro's and Nagira's homes were located in the same neighborhood. Meals without meat were consumed almost within sight of houses where meat was common fare. Inevitably negative feelings and resentments arose among citizens, though President Karimov forbids their public expression. Sharing within families and sharing with neighbors on feast days could not make up for basic inequalities in food security.

Wealth differences increased after the fall of communism in spite of President Karimov's ideology of a unified national identity built in part around the right to consume national food. Now a few individuals such as Zahro's husband can go to Russia, start businesses, and become a lot richer than their neighbors. They can afford to eat at French or Turkish restaurants in Tashkent. Although Karimov had promised bread at a stable price for everyone in the country, food in general had become more expensive for those who could least afford it. People in Nagira's family did not have access to water, land, or income to attain food security much above basic survival. For them eating out is only a dream.

Food lets us see ourselves for what we are able to give to our children or to guests. A material thing that goes into our bodies and is shared while sitting with others again and again, food communicates meanings that we feel in our guts even if we are not supposed to talk about them. In this case, food tells us that life under Karimov is getting worse for many people.

Objects become meaningful for us when they "resist our own gestures" (Heidegger in Keane, 2003, p. 417). That is to say, if food cannot give Uzbeks what they want, if it resists their gestures to be full-fledged citizens of Uzbekistan as expressed in the right to consume national foods, then food opens up mutual feelings and ideas that may instigate actions of resistance. Uzbeks rarely risk taking part in public protests, but in the city parks people had torn up many of the nationalistic posters glowing with steaming *palov*, mutton, and plump melons. These acts indicate that contradictions and resentments fester in people's minds.

TASHKENT MIDDLE CLASS: PLENTY OF FOOD AND UNFULFILLED DREAMS

On a weekday in April, we were gathered in a middle-class Tashkent apartment around a dining table that sat the eight of us comfortably. I was put at the most honorable end of the table far from the door and kitchen, facing Bahora, the hostess, at the other end. In between us sat our mutual friend Dikloram, an English teacher and tutor to Bahora's children for many years. To my left sat the women's daughters, giggling 10-year-old friends from school, and Bahora's

13-year-old daughter, who was jumping up and down to serve the food and saying little. To my right, most serious of all, sat Bahora's son, 19 years of age, next to Dikloram's daughter, 20 years of age.

The table was already covered with food when we sat down: two round loaves of bread; two plates of dough-wrapped dumplings (*manti*) made by the 13-year-old, one with mutton and potatoes and the other with rice and vegetables; a big bowl of fruit—bananas, pears, oranges, apples—in the middle; two plates each of hard candy, almonds, raisins, and walnuts broken for guests. Honey cake made by Bahora's sister also sat waiting. The table rejoiced with evidence of food security, family cooperation, and perhaps most of all, with the Uzbek virtue of generous hospitality (Zanca, 2003).

Bahora broke the bread and passed it around. Our blue, cotton-blossom teacups were filled, and Bahora urged us, "Please have some dumplings."

"This is a big, friendly family," said Dikloram, the neighbor who had brought me. "When we walk in the evenings, we go with them. The two youngest girls are in the same class at the Russian school, and they love to dance."

The little girls beamed. "Shall we show her?"

"Not yet," the mothers laughed.

The large hutch beside the table held lots of teacups—both European style with handles and Uzbek style without—and a picture of the parents when they were younger. Bahora's husband owned a furniture factory, and the eldest son, not present at this gathering, was in training to take over the business. The company had done well enough to afford this refurbished apartment in an older building, with good heat, a television-living room, a kitchen on the enclosed balcony, and three bedrooms for parents, sisters, and brothers. The front hall had walls of cross-weaved wood like bamboo, two inches thick.

Juxtaposed with the plethora of food and décor was another message of desire unfulfilled. Although the conversation was ostensibly about food, I ignored at my peril the conversation that they wove into it, a conversation that centered on questions about the futures of the 19-year-old son and 20-year-old daughter. These families were not only in between Shahnoza and Nagira's families as measured by food consumption, but also in their dreams for education abroad. Shahnoza's family could easily support their son studying abroad; Nagira's family did not have a hope beyond stowing away in my suitcase. Bahora's family had hope and vague plans, but political and economic barriers remained formidable.

Bahora's family and Dikloram's family, both considered middle class, were equal in goals and education, but their financial resources differed. This difference was reflected not only in the amount of food they served at each home—it had been mainly soup and bread at Dikloram's home—but also in the fortunes of the two college-age children. Dikloram was a single mother, widowed seven years ago, and struggling to support her three children through private English teaching.

Practicing his English, Bahora's son reported, "I study at Tashkent Economic University, with a major in economics. I like computers and like to communicate on the Internet."

"Do you have a computer?" I asked him.

"Yes, I have one at home."

"We can write e-mail."

"I don't have an e-mail address." I hesitated, realizing that Internet access was mainly through commercial Internet cafes where you paid by the hour.

His mother watched him intently as he said, "I will finish university, and then I will go to America and continue my studies." He needs access to the Internet, I thought.

Dikloram's daughter spoke much less, but used better English. She had already showed me the cards and exercises that she and her mother made for teaching English to children at a private kindergarten. "I go to a technical institute now, but I am studying to get into the World Language University."

"Were you two in the same class together?"

Her big dark eyes widened in shock. "No, I am 20 and he is only 19." We all laughed, except for the two young adults.

One year was an important difference at age 20, I conceded to myself. But now despite her seniority, Dikloram's daughter was getting left behind her neighbor's son because of a lack of money. His parents could afford to send him to university on the contract system where students paid tuition and could get in with slightly lower test scores. She needed higher test scores to make it in as a scholarship student because her mother could not afford to pay tuition. Even then she had to pay many other fees. The tuition system had started in 1996, and now 66% of university students paid tuition (UNDP, 2005).

Ezoza, the thirteen-year old, brought in crescent-shaped hot rolls that she herself had made. "She made them in the gas stove," bragged her mother. "We train our daughters to be good cooks so they can find a good husband." I noticed that Ezoza never spoke for herself, and along with her mother, like good hostesses, hardly ate at all.

Amidst the talk of foods they liked and didn't like, Ezoza soon appeared again with a dish that was new for almost everyone: fried cauliflower. Dikloram exclaimed "Ah, this is like cabbage with more calories—good for health in the spring."

One of the little girls piped up with her negative review: "It tastes like fish!"

I noted that they were showing me not only the Uzbek national dishes but also new dishes that showed them off as a middle-class, modern family. Their concern with education was another reflection of their status. We had a kind of reciprocity going: they fed me and told me about their food, and I told them about educational opportunities in the United States.

"Where do you want to study in the United States?" I asked Bahora's son.

"I don't know. I will study English language for a year and then I will take tests. I might have to study for a year to pass them. After this I will study. But I will try to do it on my own money. I don't know yet. Visa is the first problem—to get to the United States."

Dikloram backed up his dreams: "He wants to work in the United States as a good manager, God willing. His elder brother will work in the furniture business with his father here."

"Please stay here," the son said to me. "Teach me English."

His mother urged me to eat. "Look at the cauliflower!"

I felt their pride in Uzbek food and dreams of America bouncing off me like crosswinds.

Almost filled to the brim, I was amazed when Ezoza brought in more: *manpar*, soup with dill, meat and homemade noodle pieces set off with fried vegetables and tomatoes from one of the 100 jars of tomatoes Bahora had canned last summer. It all looked easy now, but this middle-class hospitality was the fruit of much female labor—a point we return to in Chapter 5. I continued to eat while Bahora's daughter Ezoza watched me intently from the other end of the table.

Dikloram's elder daughter was not saying much, although she showed her superior English by prompting Bahora's son with English words. Her mother spoke for her: "My daughter is like a son. She wants to go as a man and not get married. First she wants to study abroad. I will help you, I tell her. It is your choice, I say. We will pray that God will save us in New York City ... or Oregon."

Dikloram had told me earlier that her daughter had high demands for a husband, if she did marry. She preferred an English or American husband to an Uzbek. I marveled at how political power based on American industry, military, and education shifted into romantic appeal! Linking up with an English or American man was one more possible path to gain control over her life, or so it seemed.

Neither of them had many concrete ideas of how to go about getting to the United States or what to do when they got there. I knew that getting visas was very difficult and expensive. I had heard of people having to pay $100 just for an interview at the American embassy to see if they were eligible to apply. This amount compares to a typical wage for a fairly good job of $30 to $50 a month in 2005. They would need more money later for documents and proof of having a savings account, to say nothing of the cost of an international airplane ticket.

"Bahora is angry at you for not eating enough!"

A middle-class family eating out on a holiday.

I could do nothing but laugh as Ezoza served me cake. I was stuffed just as I should be by Uzbek standards!

The two 10-year-olds tapped my arm to show me their pet turtle and do their dance for me.

UZBEKS IN THE UNITED STATES

As Dikloram, her two daughters, and I left the apartment building for the bus stop, I felt compelled to express more than my gratitude.

"Dikloram, you know, life for people coming into the America from other countries isn't always easy. Getting the visa and having enough money to go is one thing, but, well, the other day I was talking to a girl who had spent a year in the United States when she was 19, and went to college on a scholarship from the American government. She was there the year of 9/11, and people said some mean things to her—like "Muslims go home. We don't want you here." and even "Murderer." Some people can be very nationalistic and closed—even though most are friendly and mean well. Some people don't even want to hear an accent—especially in the Midwest where she was living." Dikloram and her daughter were listening with pained expressions, but I followed my urge to warn them.

"And I was talking to a doctor the other day whose children are studying in Florida. He can't practice over there because he doesn't have a license, so he visits when he can. But he doesn't want his children to be there alone, so his wife lives over there and cooks Uzbek food for the children. He talked a lot about how children don't respect their parents in the United States and talk back to them, so I think he doesn't want his children to turn into Americans!"

"Maybe he is worried they will marry Americans and stay."

"Probably. He said they would marry Uzbeks for sure. It probably depends how Americanized they get."

"Well," said Dikloram, "Bahora and I don't want our children to stay in the United States forever and marry Americans. Home is best. They want to eat good Uzbek foods and be near family, but we want the opportunity to learn."

And then Dikloram said something that caught the flavor of the dream held by these families with middle-class ideals.

"Going to the United States to study is like a fairy tale, but sometimes we have to believe."

Her 20-year-old daughter—usually so silent—bent her head around towards me, her black hair falling to one side and replied with fervor: "I believe!"

And who could blame her, in a country where competition for jobs is high? The working age population (15 to 64) in Uzbekistan comprised 60% of the population in 2007, up from 50% in 1990. Moreover, the population will rise because 28% of women were of child-bearing age in 2007 (Ergashev & Akhmerova, 2010, p. 23). However, this young woman was focused on education, not child-bearing; she wanted to help her widowed mother support the family.

TURKISH RESTAURANT FOOD

Later that week, Clint and I met several of our student friends at their favorite Turkish restaurant. They were middle class enough to have a taste for restaurant food on special occasions such as now when they had finished their exams.

From afar we spotted Shahnoza, my interpreter who was a female university student, and Usman, a male university student whom we met in Chapter 1. They were standing among washing machines out on the sidewalk. Shops selling digital cameras, cell phones, and vacuum cleaners flanked the restaurant. The geography of the place had its own lesson to teach. Small stores that hugged the narrow sidewalk along the four-lane street were filled with goods that even middle-class Uzbeks could hardly afford because of the high tariffs. Most people swept or shook their carpets rather than using expensive vacuum cleaners. Rumor had it that Gulnara, Karimov's daughter, owned the huge furniture stores nearby as a way to monopolize valuable real estate.

Behind the stores ran a shallow valley that until recently had cradled many traditional Uzbek houses built close together, courtyard to courtyard on narrow streets. This was the old Uzbek section of Tashkent, parts of which still existed, although when we were about to leave the country, the government was in the process of tearing down more old houses to build a highway. Karimov tried to persuade people that razing old Uzbek houses would bring modernity and urban beautification. However, the crashing plaster echoed Karimov's fear of a rebellion in this part of town where many people were only getting poorer under his rule. Lining the area with stores selling goods far out of reach of the normal person seemed strange, but it created an aura of wealth as a matter of national pride.

We bundled into the restaurant, warm from the open meat barbeque. "I love this restaurant," Shahnoza exclaimed. "Something delicious comes bubbling on an iron platter … beef with lots of tomato sauce and bread with cheese inside." She smacked her lips. Soon Clint and I were looking across the iron trays at Usman and Shahnoza. "The interviews are really going well," I said, "but it's nice to relax and not have to ask questions or take notes, just eat!" Shahnoza nodded in agreement. Interpreting was exhausting.

The food was still too hot to eat. "As we do these interviews, I realize more and more how few people can enjoy coming to restaurants like these," I said. "And it's interesting how much people talk about the wish to get education."

"They all want to go to the United States," added Shahnoza. She and Usman had been exchange students in the United States and knew its advantages and disadvantages.

It didn't take Usman and Clint long to ignore the heat and dig in. "Education here is really disillusioning," Usman said between bites. "Since Independence, students and parents have started bribing the teachers, and now it's like an institution—you pay so much for a B, a little more for an A! I study for tests and pass them for real, and I tell the teachers I shouldn't have to pay bribes, but the teachers still demand them!"

"That's not fair," said Clint.

It wasn't only the food that was boiling now, and Shahnoza added fat to the fire. "I have still not finished university in my hometown, but I got offered this job working for an international group that has money to loan to businesses here. I have to judge the businesses to see if they are loan-worthy. I can learn more doing this job than going to school, but I still am taking classes at the university."

"How do you do that?" Clint asked. He stopped eating for a second to figure this out.

"I live here in Tashkent, but I'm enrolled there. I just pay for the grades. It isn't good, but in this case it is the best way." She plunged in her fork.

Clint and I looked at each other and raised our eyebrows in amazement. "You make more money this way." Clint acknowledged. "... and build your resume," I added.

Shahnoza didn't flinch; this was simply a way to strategize within an unfair system. "My family doesn't have much extra. When I told my mother that I was chosen to study in the United States, she was so worried about money. I told her my way was paid for a year, so she said okay. She went to a party with me to accept the award to study in the United States. There was a lot of food with meat there, and she kept telling me to go up and eat the food because we rarely had beef—usually only rice and potatoes and bread, some tomatoes. But I was too shy. So before we left, she went up and gathered a bunch of meat onto a paper plate and took it with me out the door. I was so embarrassed." She grimaced. Usman was chuckling at her chagrin and maybe her mother's brashness.

"My mother told me that I had to become more bold," Shahnoza was giggling now, too. "Well, I did become bolder in the United States. I had to. My family actually tried to Christianize me, but I told them that I was a Muslim and wanted to stay one. That was hard."

"Oh, that was not what a host family should do!" I said.

"Well, my teachers were good," Shahnoza said, saving face for us Americans.

Usman countered, diving back into the Uzbek situation. "The teachers here—some of them are good and really teach, but they don't get paid much at all. So they have to moonlight to make ends meet. So sometimes they don't try too hard or they might not even show up."

Clint had been lecturing now and then at a university. "Ever since the coup next door in Kyrgystan, last month, they check me every time I come in the university gate. And another teacher said there was a quite a fat file on Clint Morrison in the office!"

Shahnoza said, "Yeah, they think that American non-profit organizations helped to bankroll and supply equipment for the Kyrgyz coup leaders.[3] I don't know if it is true or not, but the 'manager' is really worried that something will happen here, so he's keeping track of Americans."

Clint and I looked at each other, puzzled. The manager? Then we both realized at once that she was referring to the president. "Ah, he who shall not be named! I've started calling him Voldemort," I said. Both of them had heard of Harry Potter and laughingly agreed it was a good code name for him.[4]

"The inspections have really picked up at my university," said Usman. "Ever since the 1999 bombings, teachers have to take attendance carefully, and the staff come in and look at who is in the class. If they never see you, they start to wonder. But now after the trouble in Kyrgystan, government officials are coming in and demanding to find out where people are if they aren't present. I had to go home for medical treatment for a week and I was worried. But I got an excuse from the doctor so it was okay. They are afraid that the students are going to start something."

"Yes, government people have been checking people's research projects more closely at the institute, too," I said. "A master's student there said she doesn't get much done anyway with all the meetings. But now that they have to write reports on their research for the government, it's worse."

Hot, sweet tea in little glasses had come, and we were sipping our way back to face everyday life.

"This was so good!" Usman said. "It's such a break from cheap students' food—macaroni and more macaroni!"

Usman and Shahnoza were among the few Uzbeks their age in university. Only 6.4% were attending university in 2001—down from 14% in 1992—and this decline had hit women in particular because poorer families put scarce resources into boys and married girls off early (Ismalov, 2004).

Although Usman ate on a shoestring budget, and Shahnoza was only starting to save money, they were only temporarily poor, or at least they hoped so. Between their educations and their English speaking, they would probably be able to find employment in the sector with the highest salaries—international non-profits, companies, and agencies. Their promise of upward class mobility stood in contrast with the downward class mobility faced by most people, except the ones at the very top in business and government.

Questions about food security brought answers that nuanced the landscape of Tashkent life in lights and darks of class difference. The rich had a fashionable, global level of food security; the middle class had the food security of citizens fully participating in the food of the nation, although working hard to maintain that position; and the poor lacked all but the bare minimum of food security. Varying degrees of access to education also predicted their futures. Poverty and lower levels of education went hand in hand in Uzbekistan (Musaev et al, 2010, p. 49).

ENDNOTES

1. People over 65 years of age make up only 4.9% of the population in Uzbekistan, quite low compared with the United States at 12.6% in 2009 (U.S. Census Bureau, 2009).

2. Urban food poverty had actually gone down in the four years before this research (32% decline from 2000 to 2004), but it would decrease little in the years to come (6% decline in 2004 to 2007) (WFP, 2008, p.18).

3.   In April 2005, while we were in Uzbekistan a largely bloodless coup occurred in Kyrgystan, the neighboring country, in protest of election irregularities. The new leader named Bakiyev who took over with the help of the military, was ousted in another bloodless coup in April, 2010. In June 2010, widespread violence broke out involving Kyrgyze against Uzbeks living in southern Kyrgystan. Some suspect that Bakiyev or his son instigated the conflict.

4.   Voldemort is the villain in the series of books about Harry Potter by JK Rowling. In the novel people avoided saying Voldemort's name out loud because of political risk. Mentioning Karimov's name is also deemed dangerous.

Chapter 4

Rural Differences and Food Sovereignty

In this chapter the spotlight moves from food security in Tashkent to questions of food security and food sovereignty in rural Uzbekistan. Rural people—65% of the population—had a much higher poverty rate than urban people. According to a United Nations study, rural poverty was 30% during the year I was there, and urban poverty was 18% (Ergashev & Alchmerova 2010, p. 18). Since then, poverty has declined a bit, but more for urban people than for rural people. I wanted a closer look because the nature of food security or insecurity would be quite different in rural areas, especially where people live in the midst of arable land.

Food security was only one question that I brought with me on the bus as we left Tashkent, and I sat gazing at rows and rows of greenhouses for vegetables and fields newly planted with small green shoots. We passed orchards of apple trees just starting to bloom and fields of grape vines. These lands produced many of the fruits and vegetables that filled the Chorsu Market and other bazaars in Tashkent.

We headed south several hours where huge fields reached out in all directions, some green like the bottom stripe on the Uzbek flag, and some dark brown. Clint and I were travelling with Umid, a student friend who had invited us to his parents' home as a way station into the countryside. Umid told us that the fields with taller green grain were wheat. The cotton fields were just getting readied for planting around April 15, and for now stretched like black clouds to the horizon.

Wheat was for bread to feed Uzbek citizens, and cotton was to sell on the world market for government revenue: this was Karimov's basic plan for the wide, irrigable stretches of land in Uzbekistan. And this raised the second question that I brought with me to rural Uzbekistan. What is the nature of food sovereignty in Uzbekistan?

FOOD SOVEREIGNTY

Via Campesina, a group of farmer organizations from Latin America and Europe, formulated the original principles for food sovereignty in 1996 (Family Farm Defenders, 2005). They called for reform that would give ownership and control of the land to landless and farming people, especially women, indigenous peoples, and other disadvantaged groups. Their reasoning was that if many small farmers had secure rights to their land, they would care for the soil and water with less use of agrochemicals, because they would pass the land on to future generations. The goal was to make crops a source of nutrition for the people of the locale and the nation, rather than an item of world trade. Both sustainability and equality would increase.

The problems along the road to food sovereignty take different shapes in different parts of the world. In Latin America, peasants fight against land ownership by a few rich families and global corporations, often owned by American concerns and headquartered in the United States.

What were the challenges for food sovereignty in Uzbekistan where there were few corporations and tight borders? Food sovereignty started with the use of the land, and I found no better place than a farming village to investigate it.

UMID'S FATHER'S HOUSEHOLD GARDEN

Umid was overjoyed to reach his parents' home in a small city from which we would drive into the country the next day. A graduate student married to a graduate student, he and his wife lived in Tashkent, but their 2-year-old daughter lived with his parents under grandmother's watchful eye. Nigora nestled in her father's arms and when tired of that, jumped into her grandfather's lap or toddled over to her grandmother in the kitchen. "She was sick when she was a baby, so we thought she would grow better out here," Umid told us, hugging her as if his arms were hungry.

Nigora was growing up with a well-tended household garden within the walls of Umid's father's house, located at the edge of an industrial city where most industry had closed. Her grandparents had both just retired, the grandmother from a factory accountancy job and the grandfather from a government agency. If Nigora got up early enough, she could watch her grandfather milk several cows they kept at the back of the courtyard and go with her grandmother to collect eggs from the turkeys that gobbled their way around the yard. Both animals provided valuable fertilizer. In the garden they grew corn for the cows and some vegetables for Nigora, her grandparents, and her parents in the city.

In the morning, we feasted on creamy yogurt (*katik*) that his mother made from the cows' milk. As we set out for his relatives' village, Nigora left tearfully behind, Umid elaborated on his situation, revealing both his respect for and obedience to his father. "My father is a strong and good man. I am the eldest son and this is his first grandchild, so he wants her near him. He has been a great

Household plot located at the edge of a regional city with house at one end, outhouses in the middle and barn at the far end.

influence on me. He wanted me to be a government administrator, but I wanted to study history. So I have promised that after I finish my graduate work, I will work in university administration." His serious brow met his wide smile to show his path to compromise.

QUESTIONS ABOUT FOOD SOVEREIGNTY

We sailed over paved roads and jostled over dirt ruts, driving to his uncle's house in an old Russian Zhiguli, a car that they had repaired again and again over the years.[1] Umid said that going through relatives was the only way our rural visiting was going to work easily, because approaching strangers would require permission from the local government. That could get messy for all of us. Yet he reminded us with pride how things had changed in Uzbekistan.

"You know, we had the old collective farms under the Soviets. They were nothing but cotton. After Independence, Karimov shifted about 40% the land into wheat production so Uzbeks could be self-sufficient in wheat."

I noted that—Karimov gave his people food sovereignty in wheat.

"So do people have their own farms now?" I asked.

"Well, kind of yes and kind of no. The government still technically owns the land, and farmers get the right to use it for a number of years. My cousin runs a small farm, so let's ask him."

"And what about the collective farms?," I asked.

"They became *shirkat*—cooperative farms. They contract their production out to small family-based farms who are members, and then the cooperative farm fulfills its quota to the government for cotton and wheat. But I'm not sure what's happening with them. Maybe we can talk to a village official and he can answer your questions better than I can."

I could see that assessing food sovereignty was going to be interesting. Food sovereignty usually stands against corporations buying up land from peasants or contracting with farmers for cash crops. In Uzbekistan, the government takes the place of corporations: they just took over the collective farms of the Soviet Union and shifted them. The Uzbek government basically controls the land except for small household plots and keeps 40% of the arable land in cotton, mainly for export, and almost 40% in wheat for domestic consumption (WFP, 2008, p. 2). The goal of self-sufficiency in wheat fits very well with food sovereignty, but the control of the land does not.

A RURAL HOUSEHOLD

We were met at the courtyard gate by Umid's aunt, a tall woman in her sixties with a purple scarf tied at the nape of her neck, and his uncle, a tall man with gray hair topped by the typical Uzbek hat (*doppi*), black with paisley-like white embroidered patterns worn by middle-aged Muslim men. They were a distinguished looking pair, whose lined faces showed that they had worked hard in their lives. They had no telephone, but they had received word from a neighbor that we were coming.

Umid's uncle motioned to the stone foundation of a house to the left of the gate. "This was our old house. We tore it down, and we will rebuild it. Now we are living in our older house." He motioned to trees on the far side of the garden. "Those are the kind of trees we can use for building. We've already cut some to use." That's self-sufficiency, I thought, growing your own wood. I knew that rebuilding a house was done over time as people could afford it—first the foundation, then the structure, and later the inside. The whole process could take several years.

Umid's aunt ushered us past a bunch of white cotton lying on the sagging wooden porch floor beside a half-stuffed futon-type mattress and into the small house. The front room looks colorful in the photos we took: red, blue, and green traditionally patterned rugs on walls and floors, good for keeping out the cold. On one side was a low table with mats to sit on and pillows to rest on against the walls. On the wall by the door hung two posters of desserts and wine, perhaps hung more for color than anything, but the wine implied that they were not extremely serious Muslims.

Umid's aunt introduced us to an older woman sitting on a cot that took up much of the small room. "This is my husband's sister. She is very sick," she said. The older woman was lying on her side watching a small television on a stool across from her bed. She sat up as we came in and we greeted each other, but then she started talking non-stop as she swayed back and forth. As she talked, she cried as if she were powerless to stop. "Maybe she's had a stroke," I muttered to Clint. I thought of my own mother who had had a stroke and had little control over her emotions after that.

My mother had gone into a nursing home and received professional care with steady visits from relatives, but in rural Uzbekistan, relatives had to do the primary caring, both by virtue and necessity. Such care was difficult because many rural houses such as this did not have dependable access to Uzbekistan's ample natural gas reserves for warmth and lacked access to indoor plumbing (Ergashev & Akhmerova, 2010, p. 29). Umid's aunt watched her without apology, and said to us: "You must be tired from the journey. Relax awhile before I show you my garden."

Soon the daughter-in-law (*kelin*) brought in a teapot and cups made of the typical cotton-flower patterns in blue and white so popular throughout Uzbekistan. The aunt and uncle lived with their middle son, his wife, and two children. The daughter-in-law always served the food, and on this occasion she placed a bowl of unwrapped white candy and a loaf of bread on the table—not sumptuous hospitality, but this was early spring, the spare time for farmers whose stored food from last summer and fall was running out.

The bread was smaller, thicker, browner, and more irregular than city bread. "Do you make it here?" I asked.

The aunt answered proudly, "We bake it for half an hour in the *tandoor* oven." We saw the oven later behind the house; it resembled a three-foot high adobe beehive. "We prepare 15 loaves together at one time—30 every week. Many relatives come here so we can always give them bread. We use cotton sticks for heat and it is so good." She broke the bread and gave us each a piece.

"Nancy, Clint, please eat!" Umid urged us. "I remember the taste of this bread from when I was little. It's always the same, even though the daughter-in-law makes it now."

"I taught her how," said the aunt proudly.

My teeth sank into the bread, coarser than town bread, made with local wheat, lower in quality than imported wheat. "This is local food sovereignty," I thought to myself, but Umid's aunt soon interrupted my intellectualizing with a joke.

"I told my granddaughter that I would be going to another world someday. 'Where?' she asked. 'Paradise,' I answered. 'Can I go along?' my granddaughter asked me." She held Umid's arm and rocked with laughter as we all joined in.

THE HOUSEHOLD PLOT

We did not stay long enough at the table to finish the bread—its symbolic value for hospitality being the point—but went out for a tour of the garden located in a space approximately 60 by 100 feet behind the house. Umid's aunt led me along low beds in the front covered with plastic stretched over low hoops. "I plant tomatoes and radishes here and then transplant them. Here are some greens that come up in the early spring. We use them to make delicious *somsa* (stuffed dough-wrapped, oven-baked dumplings)." A few radishes were already developing in another bed, and she pulled a few tiny red bulbs for us to taste. She watched with enjoyment as we crunched on the crisp taste of early spring from her garden.

Umid's aunt picks us some radishes to eat from her household plot in early spring.

"We live by this garden. We plant lots of potatoes and onions, enough to get us through the year." She looked out of the corner of her eye at me. "We hope!" she added. "If there is no meat, we eat potatoes a lot. Right now we still have onions from last year, but not potatoes. We have to buy them at the bazaar now."

"Do you get potato bugs?" I still remembered my grandfather complaining about them. "No, we burn cotton stalks, and the smoke goes over the potatoes and keeps the bugs away."

"What about chemical fertilizers? Do you use them?"

"No, we can't afford them. The cows are our fertilizer."

"Ah, good way." There was a faint smell of manure in the air, I realized, but this was the trade-off for a cycle of natural resources right here on this farm. I saw the cycle with idealistic eyes, but Umid's aunt had no choice in the matter. It was economic necessity.

"And who plants all this?"

"I do." She pointed to herself with a winsome smile, still pretty as a grandmother. "But the family helps. The men help with the heavy work." This must be a huge job, I thought, and her family of seven depended on her garden produce for adequate nutrition. She seemed undaunted at the moment.

"These are peppers," she said, pointing to sprouts in a bucket. "We'll plant carrots, cabbage, eggplants, parsley, and dill, too."

As her smaller, four-year-old granddaughter was prancing around the garden at her heels, the older woman caught her in the folds of her long dress. "When I came as a bride, we didn't grow cabbage or potatoes. Our neighbors were Russians, and they showed us how to cook cabbage dishes. Now we all like them. This little girl thinks they are Uzbek foods!"

The little girl giggled as she tried to escape and ran back to the house where her sister was helping her mother stuff cotton into pillows. As she stared back at us, I was happy that her height looked normal for her age. I had read that almost a quarter of Uzbek children under five years of age were short or 'stunted' because of under-nutrition, especially in rural areas (WFP, 2008, p. 49). The wind blew the grandmother's purple scarf against the blue sky.

"After Independence, the government allotted us twice the size of plot we had before under the Soviets." Her sudden seriousness underlined the importance of this improvement on her life.

"Are you able to sell any of the food for extra money now?" I asked.

"We can sell vegetables, but we don't have enough to sell. We sell fruits if it's a good year—especially apricots. People just come and buy. Last year we sold a lot of apricots, and we had enough pomegranates to sell and eat for the winter. Please come back and eat some!"

Umid had been talking with his uncle, but he heard us as we approached. "Uzbekistan has wonderful fruit. You have to taste it. It's the best! We weren't allowed to grow so much during the Soviet times because everything was cotton. But now we grow a lot."

I looked at the hay covering the back part of the garden, and Umid's aunt followed my gaze. "Back there we plant corn for the animals. We can't plant enough, but we can get through part of the year. We get butter and yogurt from the cows, and some meat. We have four chickens and … sometimes we get eggs," the aunt laughed. "So really we only buy macaroni, rice, and some meat at the market. Oh, and candy!" The little granddaughter had come close again, and with big eyes, patted her stomach and licked her lips. Her grandmother hugged her to her legs. "That has come into the market in recent years. If we have a little extra money, we buy it for them."

THE KEY TO FOOD SECURITY

I had found out one thing. The key to food security in rural areas is the household plot. The government allotted each household a plot—both under the Soviets and after independence. The average plot is now 0.17 hectares in Uzbekistan, including garden and buildings (WFP, 2008, p. 4). This is about one-sixth of the area inside of a 400-meter track.[2]

Families can grow what they want, and they can sell the extra in the market (if they have any). These household plots "provide more than a quarter of the food consumption of rural households, and 7% of the food consumption of urban households" (WFP, 2008, p. 4). With only 11% of the land, they produce 60% of agricultural output. Their productivity is high because people are highly motivated to produce a lot—to feed themselves and sell privately in the markets.

However, I reasoned from Umid's aunt's story that this system required a lot of work, experience, knowledge and fortitude. Given that they were now running out of food, this was food security by the skin of their teeth and the sweat of their brow.

At a household level, Umid's aunt and uncle had fairly secure food sovereignty. Nevertheless, the government had given this land to them, and could take it away. They also had sovereignty in terms of ecological sustainability. They had their own small sustainable cycle of cow dung for the soil which

A household plot located in a rural village with grape arbors in front and cow barn to the right.

grew the corn which fed the cows. However, their non-use of agrochemicals was a matter of necessity. They had no money for fertilizer, and subsidized fertilizer went to cotton and wheat. Finally, they had few children, which helped them escape from being among the poorest households in Uzbekistan: rural households with many children have high levels of poverty (Musaev et al, 2010).

MONEY

I still wondered how they found money to buy other necessities under this system, because in rural areas on average people had to purchase three-quarters of the food they consumed (WFP, 2008, p. 39), but I was soon to find out. The men in our group, Umid's uncle, his cousin (the uncle's son), Umid, and Clint, sat at a picnic table in the front of the courtyard, and we joined them there. The daughter-in-law kept working, but the granddaughters came over to join us.

The grandfather had a twinkle in his eye as he said. "You have banks, but our cows are our banks!" Clint chuckled. "What do you mean?"

"We can have as many cows as we want now since Independence. We only have two cows now and one little one. But last year we bought a house for our son for marrying, so we sold a cow then. And we sold 19 cows for buying a car last year, a used Damas."

The thought twisted my brain a bit because it was a whole new way of figuring things: how many cows for a car?

Clint nodded, his lips pursed. "I'm not sure I'd put my money in the banks here either. I might have to pay to get it back!"

The grandfather didn't respond yes or no. He just rolled his eyes upwards. The younger granddaughter clambered up onto her grandfather's lap and he helped her up.

Umid said, "My uncle has a job where he supplies everything to everyone for wedding ceremonies—the big pots for making *palov,* the camera, the tables, everything. They are really busy in the summer. He was a schoolteacher but he is retired now."

"Schoolteachers don't get paid much. I can make more this way because Uzbeks pay a lot for their weddings. And even though I get a small pension, you never can be sure when it will be paid."

Umid chimed in. "They say that Uzbeks don't have air conditioners. They have to save all their money for weddings!"

It made me realize that when we talk about food security for Uzbek households in the context of their local communities, we had to talk about more than everyday food in the household. Culturally appropriate food security must also include access to food for a community of friends, neighbors, and extended family at rituals such as weddings, funerals, and feast days when meats (that you could cut corners on everyday) were necessary.

Later Umid told us that the central government sets limits on spending for rituals, including weddings and funerals, through the power of neighborhood organizations in cities and village committees in the countryside. The government wanted economics to be less devoted to the "wasteful" social realm of connections and status by inviting fewer guests or having fewer ceremonies around a wedding. But people's status depended on this so-called wasteful spending, so it was hard to control completely.

Umid's uncle was interested in what things were like in the United States. "How much do schoolteachers in your country get paid?" he asked me. I was hesitant to say, because it would sound ludicrously luxuriant, the standard of living and expenses faced by families being wildly different. "About 1,000,000 *sum* per month" (about $1000 per month), I said, knowing that in fact it was a lot more. Even at that the uncle's mouth dropped open. "We would sleep in the school for that kind of money!" he exclaimed.

The aunt was sitting beside me. She reached out her index finger and with the tip of it touched the opal ring I always wear. "I like your ring."

I smiled and told her it had belonged to my mother. I admired her earrings in turn—big pink stones in gold settings.

"That's what we buy when we have some extra money. We convert our cows into gold and gems." She glanced over at her husband with a flirtatious smile and said to me: "About a month ago we were in a bazaar in Tashkent looking for building materials, and I wanted to buy a necklace that cost 150,000 *sum* ($150) for my daughter. But my husband decided not. 'Why this?' he said. 'We will buy a horse for my daughter to give to her son when they do an initiation ceremony for him.'"[3] He nodded, agreeing that he had asserted his male power and his wisdom for carrying out social and familial customs.

I had found the answer to my question about money. They did not have a lot of money, but they patched enough together to exist with dignity in the community through their cows, the grandfather's informal work, his unsteady pension, the sale of fruits, and, as we would see, from the farm of Umid's cousin. They then invested their money in jewelry, houses, and animals to protect it from the government.

FOOD SOVEREIGNTY FOR A FARMER

Umid's cousin had a sharp-featured ruddy face that shone against his dark hair. In his mid-to-late thirties, he did not wear an Uzbek hat like his father, only a worn cotton green jacket, the callused hands of a farmer sticking out from the sleeves.

Umid acted as master of ceremonies. "My cousin has been an agricultural worker up to now. But just recently he got land from the government. He submitted his name to the local government, and a commission judged the people who applied and gave the land to the best person. He won. He felt that after years as a worker he could do it now." His cousin nodded with a shy smile.

"Do you own the land now?" I asked, knowing it wasn't that simple.

"Well, not exactly. But I have the right to use it for 10 years. The government is increasing that to 50 years, so I hope to leave it to my sons. To be a farmer is good. It is one good job."

"I hope you can leave it to your sons," I said, knowing how important it was in a patrilineal system where girls married out and sons stayed with the family, but then I clapped my hand over my mouth. He didn't have any sons. Umid saved me, "He hopes for sons. His wife is pregnant now."

Umid's aunt and I exchanged smiles. Dressed in her muumuu-like dress with leggings, the daughter-in-law hid any signs of pregnancy. This child would put them a bit over the average fertility rate of 2.3 for Uzbekistan (Unicef, 2010). As in many patrilineal systems, parents desired a boy to inherit the land and care for the parents, but the population ratio between sexes is not skewed here as it is in India or China.

Attention on the farm, I reminded myself. This was a chance to find out about how much control or sovereignty a relatively small farmer had over his land and its crops.

"How much land do you have?"

"I have 14.9 hectares (37 acres) in cotton and wheat. I'd like to increase that to 50 hectares (123 acres), God willing. This year I will plant it in cotton. It is useful for growing and also good for economic conditions. Last year I sowed half of my land in wheat, and that helps the soil, so now I can do cotton." These small "private" farms must grow a certain percentage of cotton and wheat or rice which they must sell to the state (WFP, 2008, p. 4).

"Is there more profit from cotton or wheat?"

"Cotton, because the price is higher than wheat. And also you get oil from the cotton and soap, and useful things to feed animals like cotton cake (*kunjara*) that is left after you make the oil."

His four-year-old daughter was tugging at his arms. He turned to the side and swung her around a bit to keep her happy. Perhaps he was sparing his wife just now, I thought.

"How do you sell your crops?"

"I have a contract with the state for wheat and cotton. The government buys it. So if I plant 115%—15% above the contract—then I can have that 15% to sell."

"How do you decide how much is 100%?"

"The state decides. The state knows my condition. So they—along with the village officials—figure how much cotton and wheat I should make—how many tons per hectare I should produce. I discuss with the local government people what percentage of land will be in cotton and wheat. By that we decide how many tons I need to sell to the government."

"Okay, so then if you produce more, you sell it yourself on the market?"

"Well, wheat, yes. I can sell the extra wheat if I sell it within Uzbekistan. I can get about twice what the government gives me."

"So in a way you can get more profit from growing wheat," concluded Clint.

"Well, yes…" he seemed to be feeling out if it was safe to be candid with us. The government demanded cotton because that was what they could export and one should not seem reluctant to grow it. Perhaps he decided to trust us because we were with his cousin.

"Yes," he repeated, and after bouncing his daughter on his foot continued. "Another good thing about wheat is that the growing season is November to July, so after July the workers and I can plant other crops, like tomatoes or carrots and we can sell them for money in the wholesale market or the bazaar."

He clarified the situation for us: "I'm allowed to plant up to 30% of my land in wheat. But mainly I must plant cotton."

I was trying to think quickly about how much control he had over his land. He had to grow either wheat or cotton. He could sell part of his wheat—a third to a half, depending on the abundance at harvest—on the market for a higher-than-government price. I was unclear if he could sell any of the cotton at a higher price on the market.

"And what about selling the cotton?"

"It's a crime for a private person to sell cotton to any other person in the Republic of Uzbekistan."

"Ah." That was clear. I wrote it down.

Umid reminded us. "Cotton is the main export of Uzbekistan. The farmers are helping the country." The government gets the money—needs the money—from the international trade of cotton, so they must control it completely. Individual farmers get no dibs on cotton. In 2004, the government made about $350 per hectare for the cotton and wheat farmed on about 80% of the cultivated land in Uzbekistan (WFP, 2008, p. 11).

"So how much do you get paid for the cotton?"

"There are five levels of quality." I should have known this would not be a simple answer. "The first harvest gives the highest quality. There are three harvests and with each one the quality gets lower."

He was evasive about the price, a dicey topic. I had read that the government only paid about half of the world rate for cotton. When it came to the growing and selling of cotton, Uzbek farmers had precious little sovereignty.

"Has it been difficult for you starting out with your own farm?" I asked.

"In the first season it was really difficult to meet the cotton plan [set by the government]. But now I have my own tractor which I got with a government loan so it is easier."

"You said you want to grow to 50 hectares and be a medium-size farmer. Will you be satisfied when you get to that level?"

"Yes, if you are a big farmer, you have big problems. If you are medium, you have medium problems" He gave his first big smile. "They are easy to solve. And sometimes medium farmers make more money than big farmers. I actually have an income of about 70,000 *sum* ($70) per month."

"That's good compared to a lot of people," his cousin Umid inserted with a hint of admiration.

I asked the next question carefully. "Do you have any problems that don't allow you to develop as you want?"

He hesitated, but said, "Sometimes the state doesn't pay our money on time." He ran his fingers through his hair.

The conversation was getting precarious. For all his excitement about farming, Umid's cousin also experienced the sovereignty of the national coffers that took precedence over his personal control of his land—how to farm it, what to grow, and how to sell it.

Umid switched us towards other topics, and a neighbor who was a worker on someone else's farm came by. His story will answer questions raised by our visit to the village office, so we will hear his story later.

Soon Umid moved us along. "Let's talk to the official in the village agricultural office." I gripped the arms of Umid's aunt, saying goodbye at the gate. I had grown to like her humor and strength.

THE GOVERNMENT'S POINT OF VIEW: NATIONAL FOOD SOVEREIGNTY

Although we came unannounced, when Umid identified his father who had mostly grown up in this village and brought his bride here—even had his first son Umid here—the village's economist extended his hand and clapped chests with Umid the way Uzbek men are accustomed to do.

He ushered Clint and me into his office in the old wooden government building. He sat at his small, wooden desk, dressed in a Western style suit, his head properly covered with a traditional hat and his traditional thick robe (*chapon*) hanging on a hook behind him in case he needed to attend a funeral or wedding. A patterned decoration was stenciled in blue around the walls of composite board with no source of heat in sight. I shivered to think how cold it would be in winter, because it wasn't warm even now. The beads on a big abacus sat idle on one

Office of a village official.

side of his desk as he figured percentages on his calculator of the various sizes of farms in the village area.

He read out his results. "Big farmers make up 20% percent of farmers with 11% of the land. Medium farmers make up 40% of farmers with 84% of the land. And small farmers make up 40% of farmers with the rest of the land." That would leave about 5% of the land for them, I thought.

"Around here big farmers have at least 100 hectares—some even 200 hectares. There are many big farmers around here. Medium size farmers have about 40 hectares each. The system is changing a bit now. The government is giving the land to the farmers who can plant and achieve their government quota of cotton and wheat."

I thought of Umid's cousin who still had only 14 hectares and had trouble making his quota. What did this change in the system mean for him? I tried to put my concern into a general question that would let me know the fate of a smaller farmer.

"So how will things change?"

His big fingers reached over to flick a few of the wooden beads upwards on the abacus, and he leaned back in his chair, seeming to enjoy the chance to educate us.

"After independence we had the *shirkat* farms—unions of small family farmers made by the government."

We nodded. Umid had told us about these farms.

"The *shirkat* agrees on a quota for cotton and wheat with the government, and then they contract out to small farmers who have quite small farms—about .16 hectares on average. The small farmers have the right of possession to their bit of land as long as they plant and achieve their quota. But it turns out that the farmers have not satisfied government production quotas, and a lot of the *shirkat* are in debt."

He rearranged his hat and sat up straighter as if this were the crux of the matter.

"Now the government is taking the land away from the *shirkat* and giving it to medium and large farmers to grow the cotton and wheat. So in the future, there will be no small farmers, and the big farmers will increase. For example, in one village I know, last year big farmers farmed only 40% of the land, and this year they will farm 70% of the land. In two years, there will be no more little farmers. It won't happen quite that fast here, but…"

We both registered surprise. What would this mean for Umid's cousin if he could not manage to get more land? That led to Clint asking about the criteria for becoming a medium or large farmer. "How do they decide who will get the land?"

"It's a competition. They decide who has the life conditions to do it, and who has the ability. The big farmers are men who have technology—machines and fertilizer. They are good for the state, not just for people, because they produce a lot. We can't have farmers who say they will grow 50 tons of cotton and then grow only 30 tons!" I noticed Umid nodded in agreement. It made sense from a national point of view, but I wondered about the household level.

"What will become of the small farmers?"

"If small farmers have good techniques, they can become big farmers. If not, they can work for big farmers. They will be paid money. They also get food from working on the land. Like wheat after the harvest and cottonseed oil and soap after the cotton picking. And they can grow their own potatoes and carrots in their household plots. These plots are enough for people's own eating. They can also have as many cows as they want. An ordinary family has 10 to 15 cows now! Under the Soviet Union, everyone was limited to two personal cows. It is okay," he added as if to wipe the worried expression from my face. The village economist leaned his bulk forward in his wooden chair and thumped the desk with his thumb, trying to persuade me of the goodness of the government's plan.

"The big farmers take care of the canals. You know, irrigation canals had become full of silt in the Soviet days. Now big farmers clean the canals. They improve the land. They pay the workers on time. Life will become more modern because of the big farmers. They use fertilizer and oil. They work in the interest of the state. And they become rich. Come! Let's go meet one and you will see!"

His stately figure led us out of the government building, and we all piled into Umid's car to go meet a big farmer. On the way over, the economist told us proudly from the front seat: "I myself have 20 hectares of land now! I grow cotton and wheat. I employ six male workers. It wasn't bad during the Soviet times. I was never hungry. But it is better now"

"Do you have animals?" Clint asked, wondering perhaps about his "bank."

"Yes, I have 30 cows, 150 sheep and 20 horses. And chickens too. My family cares for them."

"Wow," Clint exclaimed. "And does your family have a household plot?"

"Oh yes, of course. I have five sons and six daughters. We have 0.5 hectares where we raise vegetables. Now we grow tomatoes, potatoes, melons, watermelons—all the things we missed during the Soviet days."

I winked at Clint in the back seat. It paid to be a government administrator! In rural areas, the ability of a household to produce food was a huge advantage because the largest share of rural income derived from household production and richer households can provide almost a third of their food for themselves (WFP, 2008, p. 39).

BIG FARMERS: THE ANSWER TO NATIONAL FOOD SOVEREIGNTY?

We found the big farmer at the edge of one of his broad cotton fields with several workers. They were standing beside a big American-size tractor that had just finished plowing the field for the cotton planting.

We stepped out of the car and talked by the side of the road. "This farmer has 150 hectares (370 acres)," the village economist said by way of introduction. The farmer, dressed in jeans and a dark denim shirt, smiled broadly. If success in Uzbekistan could be measured by the girth of his well-fed stomach, then this farmer was successful.

We listened closely as he told his occupational history, both of us wondering what experience or connections enabled him to climb to the rank of big farmer.

"I became a farmer in 1998. I used to work for the collective farm as a truck driver. Then after Independence, I was a trader for awhile and then came back to work in the government administration. When they had a competition for large farmers, I got chosen. I got advice from older men to learn how to do it. The government gave me 16 million *sum* of credit ($16,000) to help me buy tractors like this. I can use the land for 50 years if I am successful."

I looked over at the big red machine outlined against the blue sky and pulled up beside the small trees at the end of the field. It sounded like the right connections, more than experience, had procured this land for him. If so, Umid's cousin would have to work on his government relationships. I remember that he too had received a government loan for a tractor. Maybe that bode well for him.

"What are your biggest expenses?" I asked, curious whether it was true that big farmers had big problems as Umid's cousin had said.

Tractor and workers in a field that is being prepared for cotton for a big farmer.

"The wheat doesn't require a lot of expenses, and if we have extra wheat, we can sell it on the market. I sold about three tons of wheat on the market this year because it was a good harvest. I had three tons left after giving some to the workers as part of their pay. But the cotton is expensive—for machines, oil, chemical fertilizers, and pesticides. And cotton takes a lot of labor. I pay for all of this."

He glanced at the village economist sitting on the dirt beside us, perhaps realizing that the government's ears were present. He was only powerful as long as he kept the government happy, so he should not be too enthusiastic about wheat. Without missing a beat, he continued. "I grow about 60% cotton. But the government buys the cotton and pays 80% of the bill seven days after the harvest. That is good. If you produce more than your quota, the government pays you 25% more for that. I could sell it to other people and they might pay me more, but it is more comfortable for me to sell cotton to the state."

I noticed that he spoke as if he could sell his cotton privately, but I knew that the food sovereignty of even the big farmer did not go that far. He would remain a big farmer only as long as he supplied the state with as much cotton as the land could bear.

I watched the male workers taking a smoke over by the tractor, checking the tires, and looking at the engine as they talked idly among themselves. I was concerned about the fate of the workers, especially since it looked like their numbers would be increasing with fewer small farms. "What about the workers?" I asked him.

"I am the oldest at 58. The workers range in age from 22 to 40. There are 40 altogether—19 women. The regular male workers get 40,000 *sum* a month ($40) and 50 kilos of oil after the cotton harvest." That was a decent salary in Uzbekistan, I reminded myself.

"The male workers also get one ton of wheat per year, 800 kilograms of rice per year, and 500 kilograms of green lentils per year. If a worker has a wedding or funeral in his family, I give big money to them. I pay for half the party."

He made it sound like a good life, although I was sure that these jobs were the cream of the crop when it came to agricultural jobs around here. But he had only told half the tale.

"What do the women workers get?"

The farmer ran his hand over his balding head. "They only work for short periods and there are several systems. Each woman gets 200 kilograms of wheat after the harvest. If women take 2 hectares of cotton land as her responsibility at harvest, then we pay her 5000 *sum* per hectare ($5) and she gets 15 kilos of cottonseed oil. But we also have the system of hiring many women at a time and paying them per kilo picked. Last year I hired 150 women to pick the cotton in two days to get the highest quality cotton."

"How did you gather so many women so fast?"

"I said something to several village women that tomorrow we will start to pick the cotton, and the news spread from mouth to mouth. They were waiting."

"What do they get paid?"

"They get from 39 to 40 *sum* per kilo. It depends on the woman how much they pick per day. Some do 70. The very best do 160, but that is rare. I pay them once every five days."

I did some quick figuring. If a woman picked 100 kilos, she would get 400 *sum* a day—$4.00. That would be great if it were everyday, but for only two days, it's not much to go on. Obviously a woman without a husband or a male relative to depend on in the countryside would have a very hard time getting much reward beyond the products of her household plot.

It was hot sitting in the sun, and the government economist did not look comfortable squatting there with his stocky frame. He stood as he spoke admiringly of the big farmer. "He is a good Muslim. Sometimes there are women without families or invalids who need help. He practices charity (*zakat*). He comes to me and says, 'Give me a list of the needy people. I can help.' Every month he comes."

Both women's amount of work and their pay implied that their agricultural labor was simply supplemental to men's work. Women living alone in this system have a hard time. They receive traditional forms of community help, according to the men. Yet sometimes the men running neighborhoods or villages did not give so generously to divorced women of whom they did not approve (Human Rights Watch, 2003).

Such moral-based giving is precarious. If Islamic morality grows stronger in the community, men making judgments about allocation of resources under local religious standards might ostracize certain women. On the other hand, if Islamic morality weakens, and Karimov increasingly appeals to big farmers' secular wishes to get rich, the wealthy farmers might ignore disadvantaged people in the community. Either way, increased mechanization will decrease the work that women now do at the busy times of planting and harvest, and reduce their income. Households headed by women are few in rural Uzbekistan because it is very hard for them to make it economically or socially (Muraev et al, 2010).

BACK TO GRASSROOTS FOOD SOVEREIGNTY

From various points of view, food sovereignty was not looking so good in Uzbekistan. With the goal of self-sufficiency emphasizing wheat production and the target of high exports supporting cotton production, and with the government buying both at cheap prices, Uzbekistan has a "hidden taxation of agriculture and the rural population" (Musaev et al, 2010, p. 56). If big farmers increase and mechanize, and the cooperative farms disappear, then there will be less employment for agricultural laborers. Fewer workers will have formal contracts and get paid on time, and the unemployed and underemployed will increase (WFP, 2008, p. 37). The government wanted fewer small farmers and more industrial agriculture in order to attain economy of scale—greater output per unit of land by means of larger farms, and more intense methods using larger machines and more agricultural chemicals. This might yield more cotton and more export dollars, but at what cost?

If we refer to the principles of food sovereignty composed by Via Campesina (Family Farm Defenders 2005), one calls for "sustainable care and use of natural resources." One of the costs of this shift to larger farmers in Uzbekistan would be the opposite—use of more irrigation and more chemicals on the land. Via Campesina also calls for "smallholder farmers [making] direct input into agricultural policies." Another cost to the shift in Uzbek agriculture is that small farmers will become agricultural laborers rather than landholders, and their voices will go unheard in policy making. Finally, Via Campesina principles require that "rural women...must be granted active decision making on food and rural issues." In Uzbekistan women already have been blocked from equal agricultural employment, and with fewer jobs overall, they will have even less chance to become involved.

Interviews in rural Uzbekistan show that food sovereignty has many different angles to consider. The realization that more and more rural Uzbeks would become agricultural laborers rather than small landholders has huge implications for access to land, control of how farming happens, and the ability to have enough food, or money to buy food. As the government official assured me, "They have their household plot...they can have as many cows as they want," but I had already seen that a comparatively big household plot with four adult workers did not feed a three-generational family year around. And cows do not drop from heaven; if they are the bank, someone still has to deposit the money, or in this case, buy the cows.

I wanted to gather more information, particularly on how agricultural workers were faring.

AN AGRICULTURAL WORKER

Male workers seemed to do rather well if they had a formal job on a medium or large farm where the farmer had long-term responsibility for the land. I recalled the neighbor who came into Umid's uncle's courtyard.

The clomping of cow hooves on the packed dirt road and the clanging of cowbells wafted over the wall. Umid's cousin went to the gate, evidently knowing that this meant that his neighbor, an agricultural worker on a local rice farm, was passing by. Clint and I joined him to see a boy of about 12 years of age grasping a rope tied around the horns of a big cow, with several more following behind. I counted six in all. The boy flashed Umid's cousin a smile. His father sauntered behind. The uncle went over and asked if he would be willing to talk with these Americans.

The boy's father was glad to help out his long-time neighbors because it was April, still the off-season for farmers. He settled into the picnic table among the men. A farmer in his early forties, he had dark stubble on his face and I could see around his neck three somewhat tattered sweaters that he was wearing to keep warm. He talked with a bit of a smile on his long face.

"Nice cows," said Clint.

"My son is taking them to the rice field that I farm. They can pasture there in the winter and then eat around the edges in the summer."

"Your son's already a bank manager, I see," said Clint with dry humor. The man got it. A son and six cows: his face shone with satisfaction. These cows meant money for the future, as well as meat and milk.

"I have always lived in this village. I grow rice just like I did under the Soviet Union. We begin work in the spring and go to the autumn, but the farmer pays me a salary all year. I get 32,000 *sum* per month ($32) for taking care of four hectares of rice. I get 8000 *sum* for every hectare. There are two workers because the farmer owns eight hectares of rice. There were four, but the farmer cut them down to two, so now we will get more per worker."

It sounded like the farmer was rationalizing to increase profits, and this worker was one of the four original workers who had hung onto his job; two others were out looking for work. The wind blew the hair on his cowlick as he talked.

Clint offered, "We lived in Japan so we know that rice takes a lot of work." He looked Clint in the eye and gave an emphatic nod.

"I plant, fertilize, weed, and regulate the water in the field. The harvest is easy because a combine comes to do the harvest—an American combine." He laughed, making the connection between the machine and us. "The workers are free during the harvest." This was a good example of mechanization making work easier, but cutting into workers' chances to earn money.

"Do you get rice as well as money?" I asked.

"Yes, last year the farmer distributed three tons of rice between two workers. I can sell my part on the market. I get 135 *sum* per kilo during the period of the harvest. But if I hang on to it and sell it like now, I would get 270 *sum* per kilo."

"Big difference! Do you have any now, in April?"

"No, only to eat now." He wrinkled his brow.

"Do you get enough rice to eat for the whole year for your family?"

"Yes. I have four children who are younger now, and there is enough for us. But if we do a wedding it is not enough."

This man was not doing badly as a permanent agricultural worker, but not as well as Umid's cousin who farmed his own land. I wanted to get a sense of his family's self-sufficiency.

"Do you have a household plot?"

"Yes, it is 0.2 hectares."

Umid's cousin and uncle exclaimed, "He has one of the biggest plots in the village! It's bigger than ours."

The worker protested: "It isn't so big! Even if I grew corn for my cows on the whole piece of land, I wouldn't have enough to feed my cows for a year. Now my wife grows vegetables on about a quarter of it, and the rest is in corn."

I later read that with so much of the land in cotton and grain, land for fodder had shrunk since Independence. It was hard to grow enough fodder on the household plots along with enough food for a family to eat and sell. Fodder areas have declined by two-thirds between 1991 and 2004, and consequently cows give less milk and have fewer calves (WFP, 2008, p. 9, 11). I thought back to the village economist's plot of 0.5 hectares and 30 cows, and understood the intimate relationship between access to household plots, food sufficiency, and cows—the mark of wealth and status in the village.

"Well, it looks like agricultural workers can make a fair living," I ventured to the group at the picnic table, hoping to draw out their responses.

Umid's cousin nodded his head in affirmation. "Of course it depends on the season. I had six workers last year for the wheat. I paid them 30,000 per month ($30) during the work season and then 15,000 monthly ($15) during the winter." The average agricultural wage was only 23% of the average industrial wage in 2002, yet there were 2.2 million agricultural workers (WFP, 2008, p. 21).

FOOD SOVEREIGNTY: A SUMMARY

To sum up, food sovereignty in Uzbekistan has twists and turns that differ from the United States, where our main worry is global agricultural industries and policies that support them. In Uzbekistan, the government is sovereign over the vast majority of the land, its use, and its products.

Yet if we look deeper, both systems relate to the world market. The Uzbek government uses the land to gain government revenue, but like American corporations, it competes on the world market. Uzbekistan was the world's third largest exporter of cotton in 2007, but the total amount comes to only 8% of world exports, whereas the American share is 55% (Workman, 2007). Furthermore, American cotton farmers receive rather high government subsidies, thus allowing them to export at prices below their production costs. Luckily, China needs cotton imports and has a trade pact with Uzbekistan, so Uzbekistan can sell to China.

The use of land in Uzbekistan for cotton decreases citizens' food sovereignty in several ways. Most obviously, they cannot use the land to grow food. Second, most of the cotton profits go directly into government coffers. Third, the land is indirectly under the control of the global market. If competing with American cotton means prices for Uzbek cotton must be lower, then the Uzbek government pays the farmers less. Alternatively, they put more land under cotton cultivation, putting a strain on the land, and further reducing farmers' opportunity to make money from planting wheat, rice, or vegetables.

At present, pressures from the world market for lower prices push the Uzbek government towards a policy mandating larger, more efficient industrialized farms at the expense of the more democratic dispersal of the land that Uzbekistan leaned towards after Independence. Increased focus on intense production also threatens food sovereignty, because such farming emphasizes high production with high irrigation, high fertilizer use, and rapid rotation of wheat and cotton, rather than sustainable use of the land for generations to come. Eighty percent of the irrigated land goes to cotton and wheat fed by inefficient irrigation systems soaking up 90% of all water (Ergashev & Akhmerova, 2010, p. 24). The only hope is that the government might lighten the pressure for intense cotton production as the exports of natural gas are superseding exports of cotton by the end of the 2000s (Ergashev & Akhmerova, 2010, p. 10).

The loss of small farms in turn affects food sovereignty in terms of the supply of food for domestic markets. Luckily, household plots will remain. Household plots and small farms are amazingly productive, making 95% of the milk; 94% of the cattle and poultry; 90% of the potatoes; 71% of the vegetables; 63% of the fruits; and 54% of the eggs in Uzbekistan in 2003 (Suleimenov et al, 2006, p. 287).

In recent years productivity on household plots has grown. Rural Uzbeks are more fortunate than people from other countries because they can do intense cultivation in their own gardens, but with only 11% of the cultivated land, growth is limited both at the household and national level. Analysts figure that although Uzbeks have enough vegetables like tomatoes, onions, and cucumbers for domestic consumption, they lack enough potatoes, fruits (which they export), oil, and particularly meat and dairy products. Even rice, the mainstay of the popular dish *palov*, has risen in price because its production has almost halved from 1994 to 2004 (Spoor, 2006, p. 196).

As a result, food security suffers in both quality and quantity for the whole nation. Between 1992 and 2003, the available daily energy supply in calories per person per day has decreased from 2700 to 2312. The decrease has come in protein-rich foods like meat, milk, eggs, and nuts, although animal fats and sugars have also decreased. Some foods have increased, but they are starchy roots, oil crops, and alcoholic beverages (WFP, 2008, p. 14,15).

Even though 2312 calories are available per person per day, inequality means that many people do not consume that much. In 2003, seven million people in Uzbekistan, almost a third of the population, consumed less than 2100 calories per person per day. More than a third of these food-insecure people (11% of the whole population) consume less than 1500 calories per person per day (WFP, 2008, p. 23).

Ironically, rural people who grow the food receive much less nutrition in proteins and fats than urban people (Musaev et al, 2010, p. 53). About half of rural workers are farmers or agricultural workers. Despite their industriousness, they have the highest incidence of food poverty in Uzbekistan! (WFP, 2008, p. 37).

Yet this new agricultural policy turns more rural people into potential agricultural laborers. This flies in the face of the Via Campesina principle of food sovereignty that demands "ownership and control of the land farming people work" (Family Farm Defenders 2005). Because of mechanization, medium and big farmers will hire fewer permanent male workers, and male unemployment will rise. Inequality between men and women agricultural laborers is already well-established, and this new policy will likely only narrow women's access to opportunities.

Lower employment for agricultural laborers is particularly problematic because the rural population is growing more rapidly than the urban population in Uzbekistan, and the population is young. While the urban population has increased 13.5% between 1991 and 2005, the rural population has increased 35%, and villages are undergoing a process of 'densification' (Ergashev & Akhmarova, 2010, p. 24). Furthermore, 34% of the overall population is under the age of 14—as compared to 20% of the United States population. (CIA World Factbook 2009; US Census Bureau, 2009).

Food sovereignty implies social, economic, and political control over land and resources so that true food security is attained. At the national level, Uzbekistan has one version of food sovereignty in the sense that the country does not have to depend on wheat from other countries like Russia or the United States to survive. The national coffers have money from cotton, and some of that has been going into rural improvements. But this version of food sovereignty is not sustainable because it offers neither adequate nutrition to its people nor sufficient nurture to its land.

ENDNOTES

1. Uzbekistan has a low-level of car ownership. People use busses and both officially approved and informal taxis. For example, there are no traffic jams in Tashkent, a city of 3.5 million people (Nuttal, 2009).

2. A hectare is 100 square meters or 107,639 square feet and 0.17 hectares is about 18,300 square feet.

3. The male initiation ceremony takes place at the age of 3, 5, 7, or 9. The boy, accompanied by his male relatives, is circumcised by a medical practitioner at home as a religious practitioner reads from the Qur'an. Afterwards, money and sweets are thrown on the boy. Several weeks later, the boy's maternal grandparents ideally give him a horse, and he rides it, now likened to an adult soldier. In modern times, a horse may be borrowed and furniture given instead of a horse. A morning feast of *palov* for men, and a feast with a sacrificed sheep where men and women usually sit separately, celebrate the occasion.

Chapter 5

Women, Relationships, and Food

It was spring and love was in the air. Eager young male hands reached for ice cream cones, vanilla or chocolate, at the corner kiosk outside of our apartment complex and handed them to their waiting girlfriends. Evenings softened into warm strolls down Navoi Street under the greening sycamore trees. Several couples with enough money ventured into the movies to watch *Devona*, a story about overcoming the barriers to love in a small Uzbek village. Clint and I, also having toasted our much longer troth with ice cream, followed them inside.

The movie answered the mood of the evening: food, the language of love. *Devona* dripped with grapes—huge clumps hanging ripe in the heroine's courtyard, setting off the beauty of her long dark hair and her furtive glances at the muscled hero who worked for her father. Despite her father's opposition to this union of mutual attraction, the grapes, turned locally into wine, saved the day. Wine warmed up the relationship between her father and the hero's uncle and, after various misunderstandings, sealed the agreement that the two could marry. The movie ended with the hero and heroine in the orchard, finally alone. He hands her an apple as the symbol of their love and promised union.

We exited into the dark night, and Clint wondered whether the green radishes ripe around that time would do for me as a sign of love. "No way," I informed him. "How about a pomegranate?" We both remembered the bas-relief hanging on the walls of a Tashkent metro station. It was named after the national poet, Alisher Navoi. Two young lovers, immortalized in Navoi's poetry, sit facing each other in traditional central Asian dress. The young man is offering a pomegranate to his lover. The pomegranate full of many seeds, and red juice flowing is an obvious symbol of sexuality and fertility.

Young couple strolls arm-in-arm past apartment buildings on a holiday morning.

LINKAGE AND CONFLICT

This chapter will illustrate how food constructs relationships in courtship, marriage, post-marriage and marriage phases of life, mainly from the point of view of the women I interviewed. In its ideal form, food links people to each other and mediates their relationships. It brings lovers together as well as elders whose approval they need in order to marry. Food reaches out and secures suitable mates in contemporary Tashkent, where many parents feel responsible to find a good spouse for their children.

Linkage is just one of the themes of this chapter: the other is conflict. As we will see, food does not always succeed in its goal to bring potential marriage partners together. Even if it does succeed up to the point of marriage, food almost inevitably sets the stage for conflict after marriage. Household conflicts occur both within and across genders: between mother-in-law (*kainona*) and daughter-in-law (*kelin*) and between husband and wife. Food gives material shape to lines of authority and simmering resentments.

In this chapter I ask several questions. How do food and the flow of food construct differences and power dynamics between men and women as well as between women of different generations in the household? How do these power dynamics translate into food sovereignty on a personal level for women in their husbands' households? Furthermore, how does food help to shape the socially ideal woman, increasingly seen as the revitalization of a modest Muslim, Uzbek woman? Yet how do women use food to negotiate for their own ideas and feelings, drawing on both Muslim ideals and models of the modern woman striving for equality with men?

FOOD, COURTSHIP, AND STATUS

One day three young university women whom we had met at the celebration for the new bride in Chapter 1 visited our apartment. When I brought in cookies and tea, they teased me that I was like a newly married woman (*kelin*) who always serves the tea and food. They sat next to each other on the couch and at first talked seriously of how being Uzbek means serving a lot of food to guests.

The smaller, thinner Siervara said, "You can't meet guests without food. You show your respect by giving them food and by what you cook."

Her friend Mukadas, taller and more abrupt in her speech added, "If you don't serve food when guests come, even for five minutes, you are not a good person. Food connotes connection."

The third, named Samila, was plump with longer hair and a quick smile. She added, "People bringing guests must put all they have in the house on the table. It is our tradition. We have a big square plate that we fill with everything—nuts, apricots, pomegranates. It is especially for guests." Samila blushed slightly and started to giggle, glancing at her friends.

"And when you have a daughter and she gets older, they put it on the table ..." The others motioned with their hands for Samila to go on, while teasing smiles lit up their faces.

"A woman comes to your home and asks for the heart and hand of your daughter. You really put out good stuff and lots of stuff," Samila finished.

Mukadas added a bit cynically, "You put out things like expensive chocolate. Expensive is the main word here."

"You want to show that you are rich and you can afford to make a wedding. Like maybe for 300 guests. Expensive means high quality," said Samila. "And high quality shows respect for the boy's family," added Siervara.

Samila took up the story again. She was going through this courtship process right now as various mothers of prospective husbands came to visit her mother. "My mother wants me to get married soon. I am late because I am almost finished with university. Parents want us to marry by 19, but we like to wait a few years longer. There is a food called *ozru havas*. It means 'the parents' dream' maybe a dream that this food will make us seem rich enough to satisfy the boy's mother and catch a really good man!"

"They want to have the best wedding, the most modern, the most fashionable. Of course not all can afford it. It is a dream," added Mukadas.

"The mother of the boy usually comes to talk and check out the girl's home and family—and the food—and of course the daughter," said Samila.

"I think every Uzbek woman is a go-between. After she marries, she tries to set up marriages for her friends. It is the main thing that women talk about!" said Mukadas with a cynical twist to her lips. She herself wanted to work for a while before marrying. Neither were young men so eager to marry early because they then had to shoulder financial responsibilities for a family. Men could put off marriage to as late as 30 years of age, but the pressure was on them, too.

Samila's eyes were shining. She enjoyed talking about her current courtship adventure. A shadow passed over her face, however. "It is very difficult to do things right for girls here. Everyone is watching us, looking at us, following us."

"What do you mean?"

"If you go on the street with a boy, they say it is terrible. They say that he is your boyfriend. And then they tell the parents and don't interpret it in the right way. And then the parents…well, it starts problems." Samila's lips pouted.

Her friends nodded knowingly, but comforted Samila: "Your mother will find you a good man. She is a good cook."

FOOD TO THINK WITH

Food and gender: the relationship can seem like a many-splendored thing when a boy offers ice cream, apple, or pomegranate to a girl. But it has more than a single meaning. Look deeper and the relationship between food and gender is a many-fractured thing, spelling out as many differences as links between the couple.

Anthropologists try to examine meanings from multiple angles. The famous anthropologist, Claude Levi-Strauss (1963), said that people choose food not just because it is good to eat, but also because it is good to think with. He meant that foods serve as concrete metaphors for similarities and differences between groups. People in one clan are alike because they honor beaver and different from another clan because they honor duck. Living in Oregon and understanding the clan identities of its two largest universities, I thought I knew what he was talking about.

In many cultures, the differences between men and women represent the groundwork of how people understand the world (Bourdieu, 2001). For example, gender differences often underlie how we differentiate between social spaces and networks. This differs by cultural group, but in the United States the kitchen might be identified with the woman and the workshop with the man, or the stove with the woman and the barbeque with the man.

Gender differences are never set in stone. They are cultural and as such people construct them in different ways throughout history. They can and do change as people act them out with bodies and emotions in real time; people do not always behave "correctly" (Butler, 1999). Women are aware of their own feelings yet they are cognizant of the need to appear virtuous, so they strategize to live life the way they prefer, sometimes conforming, sometimes challenging norms and finding arenas of life where they can act as they wish (Rosenberger, 2001). But gender differences often change with great difficulty because they constitute the way we think about the world (Bourdieu, 2001).

FOOD DIFFERENCES AND GENDER DIFFERENCES

Gender differences often designate different sets of responsibilities. In Uzbekistan, women cook, raise children, and bless food with prayers to the household ancestors, whereas men entertain important guests, take care of community politics, and chant formal prayers in the mosque.

In almost every interview I conducted, I heard that men prefer heavy meat dishes, and that women prefer lighter soups and salads. On the surface people were making a statement about food, but on a deeper, cultural level they were saying that men and women are different and aim for different kinds of bodies. Symbolically associating men and women with different foods "naturalizes" their difference. In other words, their association with different foods makes male-female differences seem as if they are based in nature—the way it has always been (Yanagisako, and Delaney 1995). Associating gender with food also naturalizes the idea that there are only two genders and that they complement each other in heterosexual marriage—a fundamental and powerful assumption of Uzbek culture that can marginalize people who do not subscribe to this viewpoint.

POWER DIFFERENCES

Food differences also naturalize differences of power between men and women. A good example is when women I interviewed talked of serving their husbands heavy meat dishes for dinner, even though they themselves did not like them. "Why serve the soup I like in the evenings?" said one housewife. "My husband wouldn't eat it anyway." Thus, food tells a tale of power: males are dominant in the household. As we will see, women have various strategies to circumvent their husbands, but food underscores the cultural value that in the household men deserve respect and women should obey.

Food also helps to etch into reality another cultural difference between men and women: men represent the household to the outside world, whereas women's proper sphere is the inside of the household. The consequence is that men hold political and economic dominance in society. Although women's roles in public and private life were and still are a subject of debate in modern Uzbekistan, political independence from the Soviets has reinstated what is touted as Uzbek tradition. Present expectations are reinforced by conservative Islamic ideas: that women are best suited to remain in the household while men operate in the public arena.

Thus, I was puzzled when I heard repeatedly that men are the best *palov* makers. How did this finding fit into my interviews with women who reported making *palov* for dinner? Yet even these women said that their husbands or brothers make the best *palov*. Further interviews solved the puzzle.

When I asked farmers in Usman's village about why men are the best *palov* makers, they chuckled and answered honestly, "I suppose it's because we always make it for guests, so we don't hold back. We use the best meat and lots of it. Women are always being careful with the household budget [for everyday meals]." Men make *palov* for special feasts—religious holidays, marriages, funerals, and birthday parties when the family steps out of its everyday routine and publically displays its hospitality by sharing food with friends, neighbors, and extended family. So men's skill at cooking *palov* turned out to make cultural sense; men's control over meat on these occasions demotes women's daily cooking work and promotes the men as proper hosts with wealth and status as they represent the household to outsiders.

Meat laden *palov* also contrasts with *sumalak*, a sweetened porridge made by women from wheat sprouts in the early spring. Men enjoy making and eating *palov* at all-male parties typically staged beside a river or in a teahouse, whereas women enjoy *sumalak* parties at home or in the neighborhood in the early spring around the Persian New Year (*Navruz*). *Palov* marks men's virility around the year, whereas *sumalak* links women's fertility with the seasonal fertility of the land. All-women groups of relatives (mothers and sisters or in-laws) and close neighbors get together for all-night parties, bringing the wheat they have sprouted in their homes for three days, grinding it, and mixing it with oil, flour and sugar. Taking turns, they stir it for hours in a big vat as they talk, sing, and dance. One woman thought it appropriate to pray as she stirred, but others recommended wishing for what you want the most—a husband, a baby, a wife for your son. The first taste of *sumalak* often goes to women without children.

One warm night I attended a *sumalak* party held at a picnic pavilion in our apartment complex. Women from one building in the complex stirred the *sumalak* all night, older women in the lead. The next morning, a man came to make *palov* to add to the feast, and local women chopped the ingredients for him. Later, men, women, and children—including the local police and the foreigners—ate together, while teenage girls and children of both genders did the serving.

Thus, *sumalak* and *palov* naturalize gender differences and define appropriate spheres for male and female control. As we will see below, age and generational

Nieghborhood women stand around the vat in which they have stirred *sumalak* through the night.

The male *palov* maker serves *palov* to the women for the community feast.

differences also contribute to defining power differences and overlap with gender differences, in this case, to make older women more powerful.

GENDER AND FOOD SOVEREIGNTY

How do the ideals of food sovereignty relate to these gendered power differences that food helps to construct in Uzbekistan? "Food sovereignty implies new social relations free of oppression and inequality between men and women ..." states the *Declaration of the Forum on Food Sovereignty* (Declaration 2007). On the face of it this statement is transparent. If a single mother with no male relatives in a village cannot get adequate land or a job to feed herself and her children, she is oppressed. If a sister gets less food than a brother, or a young wife gets the dredges of the family's meal, the inherent inequality is a form of oppression.

However, in daily life the relationship of gender to food sovereignty is far from transparent because much of it occurs within the cultural morality of the household and the family—the values associated with relations of kinship. Gender differences are a key building block for kinship relations. Girls flowing in marriage to boys' families or boys to girls' families map kinship relations and give them substance and meaning. Uzbeks believe that their patrilineal system that traces kinship through a man's natal family is the essence of their culture. It underlies meaning, love, a sense of traditional morality—and relations of power.

Food sovereignty clearly requires equal access to food at all levels of society, but when it comes to questions of gender, food sovereignty is ambiguous. A household taken as a whole may have food sovereignty, and women and girl children in that household may have enough to eat. However, women's everyday lives in the context of a patrilineal family may make them less than equal when it comes to control over food. How do differences between food sovereignty at the household level and food sovereignty for women unfold in everyday life?

Nargiza was a woman in her late thirties who worked at the institute where I taught in Uzbekistan. She had married at age 19 into a multi-generational household in a typical Uzbek neighborhood where she had to live up to the social norms for a good housewife, or else risk both her and the family's reputation. She took on the cleaning and cooking for the family. Everyday she would ask her mother-in-law what she would like to eat that day. In return, her mother-in-law paid for her university education and helped with raising her first child. Then she had two more children that she herself raised as she worked part-time in teaching and continued her education. Her husband was a businessman, bringing in a good income for the family. He usually came home late to eat or ate out, but helped the family by shopping for food at the bazaar on weekends.

Later Nargiza began studying for a PhD and doing research part time. By this time her daughter was old enough to help cook the meals and take over the daily task of asking the grandmother to specify what food the family would eat. Nargiza's daughter also helped to carry food from the kitchen across the courtyard to the dining room located in another small house where everyone ate together. First they carried the main dishes and then the tea, regardless of the weather—sun, rain, or snow.

In this household everyone had enough to eat, indicating that they had food sovereignty at the household level. At a personal level, however, people of different genders and ages interacted with food in different and unequal ways. Nargiza had to give much more time and energy to food and its preparation than did her husband. Her control over cooking was limited by the ingredients her husband brought home and what her in-laws wanted. She had to train her daughter to help and thus was passing on similar skills and responsibilities to the next generation of women. Her husband had an entirely different responsibility—to earn an income and provide the food. In attending to her household responsibilities, Nargiza also gave up time needed for her education and career. Thus, according to the 2007 Declaration mentioned above, Nargiza lacked a certain amount of food sovereignty at a personal level. Although her situation is not a clear example of oppression, we cannot describe it simply as "social relations free of oppression and inequality between men and women."

But things look different from the point of view of the local cultural morality in a patrilineal kinship system. Neighbors considered Nargiza's parents-in-law and husband to be generous in allowing her the freedom to pursue higher education and a career. Uzbek men I talked with claimed that different roles did not mean inequality. Equality did not have to mean sameness, but simply that responsibilities differed. Didn't her husband provide enough money for food and do the shopping at the market?

Nargiza's participation in food preparation also enhanced her social position. Women gain emotional influence in their family and a reputation in their community through the food they cook and serve. They experience feelings of warmth and affection associated with their cooking that reinforces shared identity and unifies family members. In the community, women and their families acquire a reputation of virtue because of women's cooking. Nargiza's role as cook was especially important to her at this point in history, when the trend in society was to praise the traits of the so-called traditional Uzbek woman and assert a strong and independent Uzbek identity. It also aligned her with Islamic morality in demonstrating her modesty and sacrifice for others—characteristics that require self-cultivation (Mahmood, 2001). Conservative Islamic beliefs have a popular foothold in the neighborhoods of Tashkent, and women gain social status for themselves and their families by dressing and acting modestly.

In short, women's gender requires them to act certain ways in order to be acceptable in society and families. While this benefits them in their homes and neighborhoods, it penalizes their progress in education and careers. Nargiza is extremely fortunate in the support she receives, yet her position in the food life of the family affects her ability to perform equally with men in her profession. Although her household has both food security and food sovereignty, she experiences food security, but lacks food sovereignty in the sense of equal relations in regards to food. She has struck the "patriarchal bargain" in which compromise with the kinship system allows a woman increasing freedom as she ages, and in this case, freedom to further her career, at least part time (Kandyoti, 1988).

DEBATE ABOUT WOMEN

In post-independence Uzbekistan, a debate has raged about women and their roles in families and society (Tokhtakhodzhaeva, 2008). The Soviets attempted to force Uzbek women into modernity through de-veiling, getting an education, working outside the home, and being free to marry a man of her own choice in her later rather than early teens. Many Uzbeks still agree with the Soviet agenda and seek parity for Uzbek women with women in other parts of the world.

As Nargiza's story shows, the value placed on women's education under the Soviets, remains a strong point of pride in Uzbek society, especially among the urban middle class, though the number of women in higher educational institutions has decreased since independence in favor of early marriage (Human Rights Watch, 2001, p. 10). Careers have suffered even more. Nargiza had a career, but she had to compromise her commitment with the needs of her household and worked with the permission of her in-laws and husband. In general, Uzbek women work in lower-paid fields of education and health, while men work in higher-paid fields of transportation, communication, and construction (Welfare, 2007, p. 9).

Class intervened with gender to alter the situation for a younger woman in a poor household in Tashkent. I interviewed a daughter-in-law who had a low level bank job, and her mother-in-law, who worried about having enough money to purchase meat for her family. Her mother-in-law respected her right to work and gave her more leeway because she brought in needed income for the household. The daughter-in-law lived next door and used a kitchen separate from her mother-in-law. She cooked for her husband and children every day, but only cooked and served her in-laws on the weekends.

Conservative Uzbeks advocate for what they perceive as Uzbek traditions, intertwined with the Uzbek version of Islamic morality. They reclaim old ways as representative of an independent Uzbekistan no longer bowing to the forced social changes under the Soviet Union. Virtuous wives should marry in their late teens, work at home under the direction of their mothers-in-law, obey their husbands, cook for their in-laws, and raise children.

Nargiza's life is a testimony to trying to walk in two worlds, as symbolized by the scoop-neck red dress she wears to work and the loose leggings and longer dress she wears in her neighborhood. While she makes Uzbek food at home for her in-laws, she eats French food at restaurants with her colleagues. As I attended weddings and visited women in their homes in Tashkent, this double-ness of modest subservience and individualized independence characterized many women's experiences and their attempts to strategize for both security and opportunities in contemporary Uzbekistan.

WEDDINGS: THE PREPARATION

Weddings feature flows of people, food, and gifts that are rich with cultural significance, but also rife with power and status dynamics between men and women and between their families (Zununova, 2008). We already know that Uzbeks will sacrifice air conditioning or all of their cows for fancy weddings for their children, but I was interested in finding out what weddings have to say about gender relations in light of the current societal debates. Weddings tend to feature gender ideals, but in a society like Uzbekistan with its debate over traditional and modern ways for women, I suspected that weddings with their many ceremonies and exchanges of goods would show women off in a variety of ideal poses.

In the movie *Devona*, food and drink flowed from the boy's side to the girl's side to persuade Devona's unwilling father to give her to the boy's family in marriage. In this patrilineal kinship system, where inheritance flows through male heirs, the girl will leave her natal family and join the boy's family. The boy and his family must give up resources in order to secure the bride. By doing so, the boy's family exerts the greater power because the acceptance of their gifts means that the children produced by the marriage will belong to them. Yet the girl's family also must offer resources in a competitive marriage market to procure a bridegroom with a family that has education and assets that are equal to or above those of the bride's family. The bride's family gives lavish gifts to the newlyweds and the husband's family to secure good treatment for their daughter following the marriage, when the daughter will to some extent be at the mercy of her mother-in-law's authority. As in the relations between men and women, the girl's family (the wife-givers, as anthropologists say) is in a weaker position of power than the boy's family (the wife-takers).

As we saw above, the exchange of food and gifts starts from the first visit of the boy's mother to the girl's mother. So strong is the power of food to bind people together and make them feel responsible to each other that in some families in Tashkent, the boy's mother makes the first visit to meet the girl and her mother without food being served. When the girl's mother makes a sumptuous table for the boy's mother, the negotiations have begun in earnest. Already the girl's mother is showing her respect upwards to the boy's mother, and the boy's mother is evaluating the girl's mother's cooking prowess and the family's wealth and status. As Samila above indicated, wealth may be more important than the girl herself. As negotiations progress, if the girl's mother wishes to talk as an equal with the boy's mother about who will pay for the further education of her daughter, for example, she meets her in a neutral café where she is not proffering food.

In Tashkent, the boy's family pays a bride price (*qalin*) to the bride at the engagement party. It amounts to anywhere from $200 to $1000, depending on the family's income. Younger women often command a higher bride price than women over the age of twenty, even with a university degree (Human Rights Watch, 2001, p. 10). Critics say the goods, food, and money passing from his family to hers is buying a bride, and for this reason the Soviets did not like this custom. Supporters, even among contemporary young people, defend bride price: "It is like paying for the family having raised the girl." "It helps to pay for the things the bride's family must buy." The bride price confirms that the groom's family has now taken on responsibility for her, and will have control over her and the children she produces. Food figures in here as well; if the bride's parents are satisfied with the payment for the bride, they smear their lips with flour.

Usman talked about his brother's marriage in the Ferghana Valley of eastern Uzbekistan where the bride price features food.

"Several days before the wedding, we got a truck from my uncle. The groom rode in front, and the food was in the back. There was a sheep, a leg of bull, 30 kilos of oil, 50 kilos of rice, 50 kilos of flour, and some salt and tea. We took it to the bride's house and while the groom sat and drank tea, the men from her family unloaded the food."

Usman's family was also responsible for providing a place to live, either a new apartment or a room in the family house. The latter was the choice for Usman's brother and his wife. Even though he would immigrate to Russia for work, social norms required Usman's new sister-in-law to stay at her husband's house with her new mother-in-law. Otherwise, it would appear that there was conflict.

However, the bride's family also has vital responsibilities that mimic the subservience that the new bride should show to her husband's family. In Tashkent, the bride's family uses money provided by the groom's family to purchase and cook the food for the engagement party. They should humble themselves to the groom's family by helping with the hardest parts of the wedding. They must completely furnish the rooms or apartment of the new couple with new furniture, television, and carpets, and if the husband's family's status is particularly high, they might throw in a car!

The negotiations between the groom's mother and the bride's mother are particularly important. The groom's mother (the bride's new mother-in-law) often demands more gifts during the first year after the wedding, such as a vacuum cleaner, washing machine, or refrigerator. If the bride's mother skimps on meeting these requests, her daughter may be subjected to criticism and harassment by the mother-in-law. If the bride is still in school, the bride's mother must negotiate with the groom's mother about who is responsible for paying school expenses. They sometimes split these expenses, but the mother-in-law may agree to pay. In the latter case, the daughter-in-law may be put into a difficult situation.

A 23-year-old female university student explained, "My aunt and uncle say I'm getting old and should marry because family life is easier when you are young. But their son got married early, and his wife doesn't have rights. I don't want to be like her. If a baby would be born, it would get harder to work and study. It depends on the mother-in-law. My aunt is paying for her daughter-in-law's education. Then she says, 'I am paying so you have to follow my orders.'"

Sitting on the sofa in her parents' small home, she raised her eyebrows at me. "I think it is better to eat dry bread and be free!"

THE DAY OF THE WEDDING

In Tashkent I participated in the wedding of a friend named Rano. Rano had fallen in love five years earlier, but even though she and her boyfriend Muzaffar had their parents' agreement to marry, they had to wait for her older sister to marry first. Age differences are important to observe, but their day had come at last.

At 5:00 AM on the morning of their wedding, hundreds of male friends and family gathered for *palov*, paid for by the groom's family. I remember one woman complaining that she wished she had been born a male so that she could eat *palov* on wedding days! Women are not invited. *Palov* represents men's virility, generosity, and strength in the public social sphere. Many of the men in attendance at this event had received invitations, but supposedly any man from the community is welcome.

Blaring four-foot long trumpets later led the parade of the groom and his friends to the bride's house where he tasted *palov* and left some for his bride and her womenfolk to eat. *Palov* has magic energy that produces happiness in family life (Zununova, 2008). After eating they held a quiet religious ceremony (*nikoh*) led by an Islamic priest (*imam*) that emphasized the modest, even invisible, role of the bride vis-à-vis her new husband-to-be. The imam read the Qur'an while sitting beside the groom at a small, low table. The bride in traditional Uzbek dress stationed herself discretely behind a partly open door right next to the table. In this case, Rano and Muzaffar had dated for a long time, but here she took the pose of bridal modesty in front of her bridegroom, who in pre-Soviet times would not yet have seen her.

With a change into a white wedding dress of the latest global fashion, however, Rano shifted into a symbol of modern womanhood in Uzbekistan. She and Muzaffar were off to have their wedding pictures taken in front of the famous statue of the Tashkent earthquake victims. He, however, was dressed in a velvet wedding robe embroidered with gold threads (*chapon*)—a symbol of the traditional Uzbek gentleman.

THE WEDDING RECEPTION

That night the wedding hall was full of family and friends, eating and dancing to the constant jiving of a rock band. The huge trumpets announced the couple's arrival into the wedding hall,[1] accompanied by a best man and bridesmaid. Rano and Muzaffar signed the state registry by which they would be legally married, and the four of them floated up to the front table set on a stage at the front of the hall. Rano wore her white wedding gown and Muzaffar still wore his traditional robe with a wedding turban on his head. The rest of us, numbering 250 altogether, sat at long tables laden with food. Only 60 of the guests were from the girl's family, because the boy's family was paying for the wedding.

Customs of Soviet-style modernity featuring more Western food and women's equality, and historical traditions featuring Uzbek food and women's subordination interacted with each other in this wedding. At various times, the bride bowed in humility to the crowd, holding her veil out in front of her face. Yet later she danced, shoulders bared. Men and women sat at tables together, but the fare was traditional Uzbek food: *somsa* bursting with more meat than usual; special wedding soup; big dough dumplings (*manti*), two a piece; and horse meat with noodles (*norin*). We also ate European style salads and white wedding cake. Big bottles of Coke and Sprite bedecked the bride and groom's table, and we could have soda if we wanted it instead of tea. The men drank vodka, a Russian custom not acceptable in conservative Islam. If the wedding had been more conservative, no vodka would be served, and men and women would sit separately.

The band was in full swing, and young men gyrated their bodies more and more freely as they became intoxicated—arms outstretched and hips wiggling in a mixture of Uzbek dance emphasizing shoulder and arm movements, and Western disco dance targeting the hips. Women and young girls joined in, usually dancing together in loosely cut western style dresses, moving mainly their arms and shoulders in Uzbek style. I joined the revelry with the bride's aunt, Dikloram from Chapter 3, but Clint demurred. A few young women writhed freely in tight, low-cut dresses. I whispered to Clint, "Wow, that's over the top!" These young women were obviously secular Muslims.

"We should have gotten married in Uzbekistan!" Clint commented, as he nodded towards the money that people were placing between the fingers of the important people in the wedding as they danced. As the grandmothers of the bride and groom joined in a stately dance, and later the fathers danced together more boisterously, guests and relatives rushed up to stick the *sum* bills,

A bride bowing to her guests at the wedding.

small in value, between their fingers. Part of the money donated to relatives would go to the band and part to the bride and groom.

The crowd was going crazy now as they watched Muzaffar, who had shed his traditional coat to reveal white shirt and trousers underneath, descend for a dance with Rano. Twisting and turning, Muzaffar faced his bride, who swayed elegantly, arms outstretched, hardly moving except for the slightest roll of her bare shoulder above her ruffled dress. They won the money competition, their fingers overflowing with cash. Relatives had to hover around with baskets to catch the bills so that their fingers were free to accept more.

After the festivities, Rano and Muzaffar went to his home where the womenfolk of his family greeted her. They held out bowls of flour, oil, and rice—the basics of cooking. She placed her finger into the flour, thus making clear the acceptance of her womanly duties. Rano was now a true Uzbek housewife!

The next morning Rano's family hosted a separate ritual, the bride's wedding (*chalar*). Karimov's government had directed local leaders to discourage this extra ceremony so that people would save money, but it has persisted in its cultural importance. The bride's wedding celebrates the bride's virginity, proven

As the bride dances, she receives many small bills from guests in admiration and support.

during the first night. More of the bride's friends come to this wedding and presents pour in. The bride must have great strength to make it through the ceremony, for she must greet everyone individually saying *Assalamalykum* (Peace be with you) and bow continuously while extending her arms forward as she holds out her lacy veil to hide her face. She is once more the picture of modest subservience.

Rano's wedding represents middle-class Tashkent customs and serves to illustrate an important point in Uzbek society and its attitude towards gender and women. This wedding exudes compromise in the current debate about women, treading the line between customs considered as traditional Uzbek and resurrected for contemporary times, and ways considered as modern that put women on a more equal footing with men. Weddings are a constant negotiation of power between families whose exchange of food and gifts reinforces an unequal relationship between wife-givers and wife-takers, yet aims towards an ongoing reciprocity over time. These days, both families expect to share in the life of the couple and their mutual grandchildren.

In the following sections, we turn to relations between women, particularly mothers-in-law and daughters-in-law. Although they are both women, in these roles they define the differences between the man's family represented by the older woman and the woman's family, represented by the younger daughter-in-law.

BRIDE AND MOTHER-IN-LAW FACE OFF

In Uzbekistan, custom dictates that the bride and groom should spend the first forty days with his family, the bride cooking under the tutelage of her mother-in-law (*kainona*). "The groom can go out with his friends, but the bride must stay inside," my graduate student told me. She must act the part of the perfect house-wife, sweeping the courtyard in front of the house early every morning just as in the park posters extolling Uzbek nationhood. This task is visible so that the neighbors can see what a good daughter-in-law the family has received. Most important is her duty of cooking for the groom's family, proving her integration into his family by learning the food styles and preferences of the household.

Rano was a college-educated career woman, and her patience was tested, but she persevered, cooking for three younger siblings and his parents, with whom in time they would live. No honeymoon. Cook, serve, and eat last. "I had a really hard time," she told me later. "The mother-in-law is very strict. Like one day I made borscht (a Russian beet soup) and my mother-in-law came by and was looking over my shoulder. 'You're doing that wrong!' she barked. 'That isn't the way we do it in this household.' I didn't say anything, even though I didn't think it was a good idea to make it that way. I made it just as she said." Rano grimaced and laughed, her hand over her mouth. "It tasted terrible." At the table that night the mother-in-law motioned to the place beside her where she wanted Rano to sit, but Rano resisted. "I went and sat beside my husband."

In a compromise between the equally strong imperatives of modern and Uzbek ways, Rano found a subtle way to express her individual feelings, of which she was quite conscious despite her obedience to her mother-in-law's cooking directions. She let her performance of the obedient daughter-in-law slip just enough to get her point across (Butler, 1999). Older and more educated than the average bride, she maintained her own point of view in private and would soon return to her own career. However, in the larger household, if food sovereignty means control over your own food and its preparation, it was the older woman ensconced in her husband's family, rather than the younger one newly arrived, who held it.

SUPER MOTHER-IN-LAW

Food in the household is highly symbolic of the relationship between women across the generations. In patrilineal systems, males and their families hold the reigns of power, but women eventually ascend to power through the male family as mothers-in-law and wield power over the menu and the daughter-in-law (Kandyoti, 1988). Never mind that the mother-in-law herself suffered as a young bride! In conservative households, the earnings of the daughter-in-law are under the control of the mother-in-law as well, but in this case Rano intended to keep what she earned.

The power of the mother-in-law does not go unchecked. Because she is a woman in a male-dominant system, her power is attenuated, and modern ideas of individualism and free choice among the younger generation also work against her. In an Uzbek play called *Super Mother-in-Law* the mother-in-law ends up looking ridiculous and making the audience howl. She calls in an Islamic priest to divorce her son from his first wife who was a perfect cook and caretaker, because the mother-in-law is jealous and competing for her son's affection. This is a quick, but not legally accepted way to get a divorce in modern Uzbek society. Then she has the priest remarry her son--first to a woman with dyed hair who frequents nightclubs, and later to a muscle-woman who beats up the mother-in-law! Neither of these wives could cook well and always left the mother-in-law hungry. In the end the mother-in-law takes back the first wife— still legally married to her son under Uzbek law.

My sides ached from laughing with the audience at the farce wrought from Islamic law by which a man can divorce and remarry quite easily. In a sense it was funny because it was only partially realistic in today's Uzbekistan. By Uzbek law, men can have only one wife; divorce requires a legal process, and women can also divorce just as men do. However, some wealthy men sidestep the law and marry additional wives through Muslim weddings. By Islamic law, additional wives require the permission of the first wife, but wealthy men ignore that restriction.

The comedy criticizes the mother-in-law for exercising unfair power over her son and his first wife, and ridicules the religious practice of taking the easy path to divorce and remarriage. It also reinforces the virtue of a quiet daughter-in-law who stays at home and respects her mother-in-law. Thus, the mother-in-law is not beyond reproach, but it seems that she is nonetheless regaining power in contemporary Uzbek society over sons and would-be daughters-in-law.

CAUGHT BETWEEN EDUCATION AND MARRIAGE

The mother-in-law's power to enforce more conservative norms was clear in the story of 26-year-old Feruza who did not even have a chance to prove her ability to cook, so determined was her boyfriend's mother to foil her hopes of marriage. Dressed in a pink blouse and black slacks, Feruza had light brown eyes accented with eyeliner and green eye shadow. She sat in the apartment of Shahnoza, a young woman who sometimes acted as my interpreter. Feruza's bracelets illustrated her dilemma: one arm sported a gold chain bracelet much like the ones I had seen on the arms of single women in Japan, and on the other she wore a bracelet with two strands of eyes set among numerous green stones to keep away the evil eye. An ancient superstition still popular throughout central Asia and the Middle East, the evil eye comes from others' dislike or envy and causes bad luck. Feruza's bracelet protected her.

"I don't really believe in the evil eye but just in case ..." Feruza was trying to walk the tightrope between being Uzbek and modern. She had a master's degree, worked for a foreign company, and ate European foods at lunch with her friends, yet she lived with her aunt and went home every weekend, about an hour outside of Tashkent, to eat her mother's cooking. "It is our national tradition that women cook. My mother makes delicious *palov* and soup. And I talk with my mother about my problems."

Soon we turned to Feruza's love story that her friend Shahnoza wanted me to hear. Feruza started, "Before people appreciated a girl with work and education, and it was easy to get married. But now people want young girls. It is strange if they are over 20…."

Shahnoza chimed in. "The culture has gotten more conservative, more religious. Girls who wear pants and work outside are bad. People think they are showing off."

Feruza continued. "It isn't fair. I had a bad situation. I wanted to marry a man who worked at my company, but his parents were against it. It is stupid if two people who like each other can't be together. We were the same age. That was the mother's main reason against it. She wanted him to marry a girl six or seven years younger than he is. When I met with his mother, she asked me, 'Why didn't you get married before you were 25?' I said, 'I was getting education. I chose education.' She thought that I met one guy one day and another guy another day. I didn't meet with another before him."

Feruza's eyes filled with tears, but she held them back and went on.

"My mother was not against the idea of the marriage. His mother was. His mother came to our house, my mother bought a lot of good food and made delicious things, and they talked. But his mother said awful things. She was not respectful of my family. My parents were angry. First, it was my age, and then that I was not from Tashkent. She thought that he is a city boy, and I am a country girl who knows nothing."

Shahnoza added dryly, "She just thought that a younger girl would give her more power and cook all the food her husband wants."

"So the girl he married is six years younger than him, and she has no education or work. She just sits at home. She is her mother-in-law's slave. I think he will divorce. I don't speak with him, but he looks bad. I try not to meet with him."

Feruza bowed her head for a moment. "My mother wants me to get married to some other man. She made a wonderful table, and his mother came around. But how can I marry a man I feel nothing for? I am just relaxing now, breathing. I hope I will find my second love."

"I hope so. How long did you know each other?" I asked.

"About a year. At first we were just friends. How are you? How is work? We talked. Then he would go with me as I went home from work and we became closer. We would stop and eat at a café sometimes. I respect him, I told my parents, and I feel something for him. They told me not to act like this."

We were silent for a moment, sipping tea.

"The main reason was that his mother was worried about his money. He is the main money earner. She thought that I would take him away and live separately. I don't want to be like that. I would have learned her cooking. But she was jealous."

PROBLEMS OF 'OLDER' EDUCATED WOMEN

Feruza was typical of the educated young women I met who wanted to find a compromise between their individual feelings and the expectations of conservative, Uzbek society. Like many, she respected Uzbek culture and would have cooked for her lover's mother, but she also respects who she has become as an individual and receives comparable respect from others in her international workplace.

I came home that night and gave Clint an anthropological lecture over the meatball soup that we had paid the next-door neighbor to make for us. He grimaced, but bore up. "It's not like modernization theory we used to learn, you know, that everyone would become individuals in nuclear families—like us. Feruza is a good example. She is thoroughly modern, but she is also committed to being Uzbek—if only the mother of someone she loves will trust her at the ripe old age of 26."

Sitting at the little table on our verandah that had been shoddily closed in, we shivered a bit as we dug into cabbage slaw. Our neighbor was of Ukranian descent, and her food reflected that tradition. It was warm and delicious, and she greatly appreciated the ability to earn some extra money.

"Hard to find a boy when you aren't even supposed to be seen with them," Clint pointed out. "But actually we see couples all the time walking around!"

I brought up another case. "One girl I interviewed is in a bind because she had sex with her boyfriend who then won the green-card lottery and went off to New York City where he is driving a taxi. He says he will send for her, but so far has not. Now she refuses to marry and have sex with someone she doesn't love, but her parents are unaware that she lost her virginity, and they keep trying to match her up. She needs to tell them. The guy would have to understand! In the most conservative villages, they are starting to revive the morning-after-the wedding display of the bloody sheet—proof of virginity thing."

Clint said nothing at first and then referred to a girl in her late twenties whom I had interviewed at the apartment just the other day.

"I thought that girl had the ticket. She made a bunch of money in her job, and then she took up with that younger guy from her home city and is going to set him up in the ice cream business. That'll keep his mother and father happy."

"Yeah, and she said that she would never spend forty days cooking for his mother after the wedding. She would argue she had to work." I stared out the window at the dining room all lit up in the apartment across the courtyard. "She said they met when he was just calling random cell phone numbers and dialed hers. Do you believe that?"

"Not a chance. He knew."

We laughed and Clint added, "He's her boy now, but she will have to put him up on a husband pedestal after they marry."

I agreed. Young women had to step carefully in order to satisfy both sides of this debate that now permeated Uzbek society. Young women constantly had to weigh the consequences of their acts. To what extent could they act as individuals with rights—the assumption underlying the definition of food sovereignty, and to what extent did they need to or want to enact the roles of the idealized Uzbek woman?

A YOUNG WIFE, HUSBAND, AND FOOD

I emerged from a metro stop with a graduate student who was taking me to meet a friend from her university days. "That's her building right there." She pointed to the high-rise right beside the subway.

"Wow. That's convenient!"

"Her husband's family has some money." The concrete entrance was not fancy, but the steps were clean and the elevator worked.

"Sit down! Over there on the couch!" Takhmina waved us in. "That's where my in-laws sit when they visit on Sundays!" We scooted between the couch and the huge dining room table it faced. "Here, you sit there," she said to her small son, sitting him on a dining room chair facing us. "My parents gave us this Italian furniture when we married." She nodded towards the matching hutch that held a big television from which beamed a Brazilian soap opera.

Takhmina, 25 years old and married with a two-year-old child, lived with her husband; his parents lived apart for now. She was part of the puzzle I needed to solve about gender and food in Tashkent. I knew that mothers-in-law wielded their power over daughters-in-law through food, but what about husbands, and especially well-educated, urban ones? How did young husbands and wives parlay the societal debate between more conservative Uzbek ways that favored women at home and more liberal reformist ways that encouraged women to venture out into society?

Through interviews with housewives, I found that husbands and wives fought a quiet but steady battle around the food table. The question of food sovereignty for women, in terms of the right to buy, cook, and eat what they want when they want centered around questions of love, money, respect for the husband, and status for his larger family. At stake for the wife was her ability to endure, but also to tread two paths simultaneously and to strategize over time.

As I leaned back in the sofa, I could not keep my eyes from glancing at the show on television. I watched it between bites of bread broken and passed around by Takhmina, homemade Uzbek *somsa* (meat and onion-stuffed pastry) already on the table, and *mastava,* a soup of carrots, potatoes, tomatoes, and rice that Takhmina brought in. A man and woman kissed, his wife watching from around the corner, and soon the woman undressed into bra and pantaloons to perform a private belly dance for her lover. I felt like I was in a roller coaster whizzing through the paradoxes of twenty-first century globalization.

Takhmina was petite, but she was obviously up for the ride. Not only was she an accomplished Uzbek cook like her mother, but also she served garlic-dill toast, a French salad with boiled eggs and sausage, and a ten-layer Napoleon cake her sister had learned to make from a French cooking class. She described how to make fish Israeli style—a recipe she had picked up from television. "My mother-in-law is a shuttle trader who goes between here and Korea, so she teaches me some Korean foods, too," she added with a smile.

Takhmina wanted to be modern, and her food said so, yet she simultaneously respected and compromised with reconstructed Uzbek traditions "I made this to show you." It was *halvatar,* the same brown pudding that I had seen at the death day ritual in Chapter 1. "I make it every Thursday night (the day before Friday which is the Sabbath in Islam) and say a little prayer for the ancestors."

Her friend was startled. "Really? I never do. Maybe I should!" She too was trying to find her balance between tradition and modernity as a young married woman.

Takhmina's light-skinned face, framed with dark hair, nodded in agreement when her friend blurted out, "Takhmina didn't like her husband when she married him. It's a secret, but it is true."

"I didn't like him," she admitted. "My parents just gave him to me. He likes me very much, but I don't like him." She showed me a wedding picture.

"He's tall and handsome," I observed.

"Yes, but he is fat." She giggled and covered her mouth, laughing along with her friend who said with lascivious eyes, "At first I was worried about Takhmina because he was so big, and she so tiny."

"Did you have various choices of men?" I asked.

"Yes, but my parents chose this one. Sometimes I think of the others and wonder what it would be like. But I wanted modern parents-in-law, and I got them. They don't mind if I work later on." She turned to her son who was clambering for the bottle of soda on the table. She opened it and gave him a drink.

Her dissatisfaction with her husband emerged around food. "I only cook once per day and eat some of it at lunch, and then I serve it to my husband at dinner. I like European foods, but I have to prepare Uzbek foods for my husband because he likes them. He likes *palov* or dishes with noodles and meat because they fill him up. The dishes my husband likes are my least favorite!" She wrinkled her forehead and screwed up half her mouth.

"Even though he is fat, he can't be without tasty food. I exercise and he helps me, gives me advice." She laughed ironically. "I gained 20 kilos (44 pounds) when I was pregnant so I really want to lose weight." I didn't think she looked fat at all now.

"So if I am on a diet for that day, I might eat only once per day at lunch. Sometimes I just drink or eat fruit and vegetables. It used to be okay to be fat after you had a child, but now it is not okay."

Her friend agreed. "My husband is always warning me not to get too fat." I glanced at the super-thin women on Brazilian television once again and made a note that a global ideal of thinness had arrived in Uzbekistan. I had often heard people remark, "Uzbek food is delicious, but very greasy. Uzbeks like food that makes you fat." The ideal body image for women was changing, and young men shared in the trend, but for women more than for themselves! Uzbek women got caught in the middle of the shift, dieting, yet making fatty Uzbek food for their men. Among women in their forties, about half are overweight or obese, especially in Tashkent. However, for younger women the biggest problem across the country is undernourishment and anemia (WFP, 2008, pp. 54–55). I hoped Takhmina would be careful.

When I asked Takhmina where she bought her food, curious to know if she preferred modern supermarkets offering global food, the opposition between her and her husband emerged again. "My husband always goes to the bazaar. He always buys the food. He gets fruits and vegetables and the heavy things like onions and potatoes. He chooses the meat."

She glanced at her friend and then launched into an explanation. "See, I wanted to buy the food and did at first. I'd shop at the bazaar or one of the new supermarkets. But he said that I spend a lot of money and buy nothing. He says he spends a little money and buys a lot of good things." Takhmina looked at her friend in a resigned way.

It was clear from my interviews with married women that bazaar shopping was the husband's work. Women regard carrying heavy bags of onions and potatoes as man's work and a service they can provide. The husband's monopoly on food shopping is also a way for the man to control what the family eats, as well as the food budget.

Takhmina's heart seemed to soften towards her husband when I asked if he did any cooking. "Sometimes he cooks on the weekends. He makes fried, breaded meat, and pancakes (*blintzky*) for breakfast."

Her friend was surprised. "That's usually a woman's dish."

A little smile came to Takhmina's face. "He cooks well. It's nice on weekends. Maybe I am beginning to like him a little." She helped her son get down from his chair and we watched him climb into a little plastic scooter in the corner of the room.

She went over to the television to put on a video of their wedding. It showed her in her white wedding dress after the wedding reception sitting with her husband on their new bed. Women and children from his family sat in a circle at their feet, offering a prayer for the newlyweds. Takhmina did not look happy. We watched and talked for awhile.

"Will you live with your parents-in-law when you are older?"

"Probably, but for now we don't want to live with them—even though they want to live with us. Food is really important in my husband's family. Even if they didn't have anything else, they would have food and eat it together. My parents don't pay so much attention to food. But his parents always have to have national dishes."

Her friend echoed, "It is our happiness if we don't live together."

When the young, educated, urban voices of Uzbek women speak in the private of their dining rooms, their determination to minimize collective family life is clear, but their actions show that they only can go so far. As Takhmina skipped through the video to find other wedding scenes, she said something that revealed her strategizing behind the scenes, much as her ideas about food had indicated. "My husband didn't really want me to do this interview, but I did it anyway." She smiled with a hint of uncertainty in her eyes. "So if you ever meet him, don't tell him."

IDEAL UZBEK HOUSEWIVES

I heard echoes of Takhmina's story in the tales of other middle-class Tashkent wives. They accepted gender differences and submitted to their husbands' wills in food decisions as well as in decisions to work. Yet they used subversive strategies as well. A friend in her late twenties introduced me to several of the women whose young children she tutored. She thought I should meet "real Uzbek housewives." Her standards? "They are wonderful cooks. They make delicious Uzbek food for their children and husbands."

I watched in awe as a housewife named Camila spent her morning making noodles from wheat flour and eggs, rolling out the dough, and cutting it into small squares to wrap ground lamb and onions in little packages called *chuchuwara*. "My children like *chuchuwara*, and I try to make it the traditional way two or three times a week. They are nutritious because I put in eggs." Camila instructed me on how to shape them. "Just bring the two corners together and push to make a little hole in the middle with little ears sticking up on each end." I tried but could not approach her adeptness. In 30 minutes she had made 100 of them. Her elementary-age son soon came home to eat lunch with us. She claimed not to be good at saying prayers, so her son intoned a blessing in his high piping voice.

After lunch we all sat back with bellies full, basking in the sun shining through the balcony windows. Her son watched television in the next room.

Was Camila satisfied? In many ways the answer was yes. She was obviously fond of her three children and husband. She said that she had enjoyed learning to make bread and sausage from her mother-in-law with whom she had lived for ten years. She did not complain about her husband doing all the shopping or his preference for eating meat dishes in the evenings. These were simply the facts of her life.

"Do you like being a housewife?" I asked.

"Sometimes, yes. Sometimes I am tired of everything! I say to my husband, that I just want to go to America! My mother is there now because she won the green card lottery and she works as a nanny in New York City. He says, 'Okay, but what about the children?' I say, 'I will get a babysitter and go!'" She threw back her head and laughed at the preposterousness of the suggestion. "My husband can only fry eggs. He doesn't even make *palov* on holidays like other men."

"Do you want to work in the future?"

"Yes," she answered quickly and definitively. "But my husband doesn't want me to. He thinks it is my duty to raise the children."

"What would you like to do?"

"I want to start a small marriage agency to introduce people. Everyone around here would use it. I myself have a 12-year-old daughter to find a husband for someday."

"At what age would you like her to marry?"

"18. I am saving for her trousseau (*sep*)."

Working put women out in public and gave them money to live more independent lives, but husbands and parents-in-law saw it as a necessary evil. Laziza, a middle-class Tashkent woman I interviewed, hid her job from friends

The *chuchuwara* stuffed dumplings made by the ideal Uzbek housewife.

and extended family to protect the pride of her husband who had lost a lucrative job and now made much less as a security guard at night. Laziza worked as a cook at a foreign embassy, extending her cooking skills outside the household. On the side, she managed an informal cake business for friends and neighbors who needed fancy cakes for birthdays, which were well-celebrated occasions in Uzbekistan. For her, food was both a means of pleasing her husband and two children with good food, and a means of strategizing to support the family and continue to seem modest and subservient as a wife.

Laziza's husband did not let her visit her friends, even limiting her contact with her next-door neighbor. From her sidelong glances, I feared that domestic violence might be part of his power, but I had no proof. I knew, however, that domestic violence is widespread in Uzbekistan and poses a threat that can make women limit themselves. Women seek divorce because of abuse, usually going home to their parents, but the court, neighborhood elders, and even their parents often encourage them to try harder for awhile, implying that it is the woman's fault. The reputation of both families is at stake (Human Rights Watch 2001). One Tashkent woman I talked with was beaten while pregnant through two marriages, but her economic independence as an international worker allowed her to divorce twice and raise her daughters while living with her mother.

Work could even be a way for a wife to shame her husband. In another example, Gulzoda was burdened with an idle husband who was trying to decide whether to return to do white-collar work in Russia. She found a way to earn money by going out early in the morning to buy strawberries at the wholesale market and then sell them on the sidewalk near the market. This work was not fit for a middle-class wife with fancy furniture bought from her husband's earnings. Her mother had worked selling vegetables in a rural market, so she was not embarrassed by it, but if she had sold fancy clothes from Korea at the market, it would have been more honorable.

"I make 3000 to 4000 *sum* per day ($3 to 4) selling strawberries."

"It isn't good money. Only $60 a month or so," said her husband.

"As a (sewing) teacher I got only $15, then later $25 per month," retorted Gulzoda. Her husband, his elbows on his knees, chuckled quietly and waited for her to make lunch. He had told us before she came home that he was a picky eater, and that her food alone satisfied him. This conflict around her work as a food seller and her role as a food-maker was indicative of a larger conflict about where he would work. Gulzoda had not liked living in Russia when she tried it, but he wanted her and the children to accompany him.

As in all patriarchal cultures, women have strategies that subvert masculine power or simply evade it. Strawberry selling was one strategy, as was the cake-baking above. Camilla had another source of income apart from what her husband provided, a strategy that many women mentioned in interviews.

"Some neighbor women and I get together for a kind of club (*gyap*) once a month." She smiled happily at the memory. "It's a group of six of us who meet at each other's apartments. The hostess makes something delicious, and everyone brings a dish. It's really fun, but it's also a way to get a lot of money at one time. Everyone brings a certain amount of money, and it all goes into a kitty. The hostess gets it!"

"How much money?" I asked.

"We try to do $20 a month each. My father eats here every night, and he gives me a little on the side. My husband doesn't notice."

"So you get $120 every six months—that's good. What do you do with it?"

"I buy something for my daughter's trousseau like a carpet or dishes. Or else I save to visit my mother in the United States!"

These informal credit associations or savings clubs are common in Uzbekistan. Both women and men use them as a way to collect a fairly large amount of money without using the bank. They also cement friendships because people have to trust each other not to take the money and quit, but to share the proceeds evenly over time. For women these clubs are particularly important as a strategy to sidestep husbands' or in-laws' control of money and make little bits of money grow into larger sums that they can spend freely. Richer women gather at restaurants, and less rich women at each others' homes. The poorest cannot afford to participate.

CONCLUSION

This chapter illustrates several points about gender and food. Food is good to think with. It silently and effectively spells out differences between men and women. But it goes further. Food differences make gender differences seem natural, thus reproducing power differences between men and women over time. Food creates ties across gender lines between men and women, between the boy's family and the girl's family in marriage, and between mother-in-law and daughter-in-law. Yet sometimes it sows conflict across these same lines.

Food and gender are at the center of the debate about the version of modernity now evolving in Uzbek society. Women's roles have taken on strong, symbolic meaning in this debate, and their relationship to food is a large part of it.

The choice to strive for modernity is not without consequences for a country like Uzbekistan. It was basically a colony of the Soviet Union and now is one of the many "less-developed countries" in a global economic and political system in which powerful "developed countries" such as the United States and Russia continue to maintain and increase their advantage. Choosing the ways of modernity, including the equality of women, is tantamount to choosing the way of life of those who exploit Uzbekistan in various ways. Modernity seems to require giving up a sense of pride in one's own traditions and a stable sense of morality.

Traditions are selected and shaped for modern times. This process is easier for men to endure than for women because Uzbek 'tradition' gives more economic and political power to men at the household and community levels. The women I interviewed live at the intersection of reform continuing in the direction of modern equality for women started by the Soviet Union and encouraged by Western countries, and of contemporary impulses to recapture a traditional Uzbek identity linked with Islam and women's humility and modesty in ways that echo the past. Women's sympathies go both ways as they try to walk in both worlds.

This study of food and gender shows that women use food to make ties with their families and their men, who like themselves are oppressed by a government which does not favor a sense of political or economic rights, nor provide food security for all. Women respect the differences between genders that buying, cooking, and serving food denote. Yet women also understand food as a way for husbands and mothers-in-law to lord dominance over them at the household level and restrain their participation in society. Women make choices within these limitations as they strategize to act for themselves within a social and cultural environment fraught with tensions.

I return finally to the question of how food sovereignty plays out in the realm of gender. Food sovereignty means "new social relations free of oppression and inequality between men and women." From this study, it appears that even in middle-class urban, educated families of Tashkent, food sovereignty is difficult to claim for women. Women are as food-secure as their families, but the different roles demanded of men and women in relation to food, and the power of mothers-in-law and husbands over food in the household makes it a place of inequality for women. If we add this to the lessons of Chapter 4 on rural Uzbekistan, where women's labor is central to maintaining the household garden plot, but women's ability to hold agricultural land and earn money through agricultural labor is very limited, food sovereignty for women in Uzbekistan is certainly not free of oppression.

While global forces with the message of independence for women have become stronger in the world at large, contemporary Uzbekistan is not going in the direction of greater equality for women. Opportunities for women exist, but are limited by Uzbek morality pressuring women to be good housewives.

ENDNOTE

1. Most urban weddings today are held in commercial wedding halls that furnish large rooms with tables, chairs, and stages for the wedding party and band, as well as a kitchen.

Chapter 6

Ethnicity, Food, and Nationalism

Uzbekistan contains several different ethnic groups. According to official demographic statistics in 2000, 76% of the population is Uzbek, 8% Tajik, 5% Kazak, 3.4% Russian, and 1% Korean.[1] In this chapter I focus on two of these groups: Koreans and Tajiks.

Koreans look different and eat different foods than Uzbeks. Stalin forced most of them to migrate to Uzbekistan. The majority of Koreans now speak Russian, and the young have lost the ability to speak Korean. In contrast, Tajiks are natives, the settled city people of this area for centuries. Later, nomadic Uzbeks and other peoples moved into their territory. Tajiks speak Persian, an entirely different language than Uzbek, a Turkic language. However, over the years, Tajik and Uzbek food and customs have mixed through communal and marital intercourse.

The linguistic, cultural and historical differences between Koreans and Tajiks pose a puzzle. How does Karimov manipulate or control these very different ethnic minorities in order to construct "ethnic nationalism" centered on Uzbek food, language, and history?

BUILDING A NATION

After independence, Karimov struggled with the problem of how to build a modern nation with a strong sense of national unity. Put yourself in his shoes. How do you do it? Your territory, like any nation, is full of diversity by regions, ethnicities, and classes. The voices of difference will never stop whispering (Bhabha, 1994). The challenge is how to build a nation with a sense of unity against the pull of all this diversity. Nations are socially and culturally constructed, and must be constantly maintained as unities in citizens' minds (Anderson, 1991). How does Karimov do this in the face of ethnic differences?

Karimov knows how republics of the USSR were made. The Soviets faithfully researched the various ethnic groups located in their empire, and divided central Asia ostensibly on the basis of ethnic group boundaries—Uzbeks, Tajiks, Kyrgyz, and Kazakhs. However, Russian leaders controlled people in part by stigmatizing them as non-Russian ethnicities. Each was allowed to be different, but in all cases Soviet identity was superior and stood firmly at the center. Through education and politics Russian became the lingua franca, and through public cafeterias Russian food spread everywhere.

Now without that unifying factor, Karimov faces the same task of building a nation on the shoulders of many different ethnic groups. In this chapter I examine how Karimov molds national unity—first in the case of Koreans who are very different from Uzbeks, and second in the case of Tajiks who share similarities with Uzbeks. Finally, I show how Koreans and Tajiks respond to Karimov's policies and continue to survive.

PRIMORDIAL ETHNICITY

Karimov's strategy in dealing with ethnic diversity starts from his definition of ethnicity. He ascribes to "primordialism," an idea that derives from German and Soviet scholars. The primordial notion of ethnicity maintains that ethnicity is a non-changing entity, with a permanent cultural identity for its members that reaches back into history (Fenton, 2003).

Karimov creates a primordial story of ethnicity for Uzbeks by encouraging Uzbek scholars to reconstruct Uzbek history, and Uzbek cooks to confer Uzbek identities on foods that have actually come from other ethnic groups or from central Asia in general.

As it applies to Koreans, Karimov's philosophy of primordialism seems to work well. Korean phenotypic characteristics reach back into the distant past as primordial markers of their ethnicity. Under Karimov's direction, Uzbek scholars study Koreans focusing on diaspora as their history. The implication is that since they did not originate geographically in the Uzbek homeland, they constitute a separate ethnic group. However, this primordial philosophy succeeds only as long as people ignore the facts that Koreans now speak Russian and intermarry with other ethnic groups in Uzbekistan.

Karimov does not extend his philosophy of primordialism to Tajiks, as he does not think they are a separate group. He encourages them instead to give up their sense of having a unique ethnicity. It was a conundrum to me: how does Karimov manage to adhere to his philosophy of unchanging ethnicity and deny Tajiks their ethnic identity?

SITUATIONAL ETHNICITY

My training as an anthropologist in the West gave me a different concept of ethnicity: situationalist or constructivist. Accordingly, ethnic groups, their borders, and their identities change over time as situations change. Relationships between groups shift. Politics, economics, and people themselves construct and re-construct ethnic identity (Fenton, 2003). A situational view of ethnicity examines historical processes that have brought Uzbeks, Tajiks, or Koreans to this point and the ethnic ideology manufactured for political aims that keeps them where they are now.

When I was in Uzbekistan, I gave lectures about situational ethnicity in the United States. On one occasion as we sat around the table discussing my lecture, scholars were either quiet or refuted my ideas. After all, many of these same scholars had worked to write Karimov's Uzbek history and even to establish museums intended to prove the historical character of "Uzbekness", as I described in Chapter 2.

Later while we drank vodka, younger scholars began to express interest in looking at ethnicity as a changing phenomenon. They acknowledged the historical myths built up around Amir Timur, and admitted that the authenticity of national foods was suspect. "They take the foods they like the best, change the preparation a bit, and call it Uzbek."

If anything, Uzbek national food tells a story of many ethnic groups that have merged into and out of each other over time. But if these younger scholars wanted to tell this side of the story, they would have to be careful. Scholarship in Uzbekistan is a political game under the surveillance of security officials. When expressing their views for the public record, these scholars, young and old, still pay tribute to the primordial Uzbek identity.

ETHNICITY AND FOOD RIGHTS

Definitions of food sovereignty and food security emphasize the rights of various ethnic groups to what they claim as foods linked to their ethnic identity. Via Campesina's first principle on food sovereignty calls for "access to ... culturally appropriate food in sufficient quantity and quality to sustain a healthy life with full human dignity" (Family Farm Defenders, 2005). The definition of food security quoted in Chapter 1 includes access to "preferences."

The key phrases here are: preferences, culturally appropriate, and human dignity. People who identify as a unique cultural community first have the right to human dignity rather than inferiority and marginality in a world defined by another dominant ethnic group. The dignity accorded to a group is important both at their own tables and as they appear to others. They deserve to eat the food that satisfies them because of their history and upbringing—i.e., their food preferences. They deserve to eat the food that is meaningful for them in social interaction and cultural rituals, that is, culturally appropriate food. Their food preferences may change over time, but the nation and the people within it should honor them.

Returning to the statement of the 2007 Mali Forum, food sovereignty "implies social relations free of oppression and inequality between ... peoples, racial groups ..." (Declaration, 2007). As with gender, however, equality is hard to achieve. Sometimes ethnic minorities, such as Tajiks, change their food practices in order to survive in certain political situations. Other ethnic minorities, such as Koreans, emphasize their difference from the dominant ethnic group for the same reason. Inequality in exercising food preferences is unfair under any circumstances, but ethnic minorities have to weigh the achievement of food sovereignty against maintaining their own continuity in time and place.

UZBEKISTAN UNITED:
THE NEW YEAR CELEBRATION

A vignette from the celebration of Navruz, the traditional New Year in Uzbekistan, shows how the government would like citizens to understand various ethnicities within a united Uzbekistan.

Navruz originated from the Persian New Year welcoming the beginning of spring. Tajiks brought this holiday with them centuries ago when they migrated from Persia, and later it spread into Uzbek culture. Uzbeks and Tajiks celebrated the holiday in private during Soviet times, but now Karimov has made it part of the national calendar so that it can aid in creating nationalistic sentiments (Anderson, 1991).

On the morning of Navruz, official Uzbek television featured women stirring *sumalak*, and men cooking *palov* in courtyards and mountainsides. High school students competed in cooking contests between their homerooms, interspersed with pictures of Uzbekistan's natural beauty melting into the nation's three-colored flag—blue sky on top, white light in the middle, and fertile green on the bottom. On television Karimov delivered spring greetings to his nation.

We met with Usman and his friend, joining the crowds headed to a big city park where Karimov had arranged a concert of pop singers. Everyone was invited!

On our way to the big event, we cut through a sun-drenched park where a multi-ethnic celebration was in progress. Tables offered food from Kyrgystan and Turkey, while loud music blared from a pavilion. Stopping to stand on the edge of the crowd, one ethnic dance troupe after another appeared: Karakalpak dancers in bright silks from the far-western autonomous zone of Karakalpakstan; Korean women in long red and green *hanbok* dresses flowing down from big chest bows; Russian boys in red and yellow costumes kicking their legs out as they squatted; Germans in green and red vests with white shirts; and Uzbek dancers, all dressed in orange. Like good tourists, we swung our cameras into action to record this dazzling display of ethnic diversity!

The show ended with a parade of all the dancers in their ethnic costumes sweeping across the stage, each group waving white banners with the gold crest of Uzbekistan. They joined in a song that chanted: Uzbekistan! Uzbekistan! Uzbekistan!

We cheered with everyone and left to catch the other concert of pop singers, which it turned out could not accommodate all the people who wanted in, including us. As ubiquitous policemen strong-armed people out of the area, we

A Korean citizen of Uzbekistan dressed up and waiting to dance in the multi-ethnic performance during the holiday of Navruz—as she texts.

heard someone repeat the political joke that the actual national costume of the Uzbeks is a police uniform.

As we strolled, we talked about the ethnic spectacle we had just seen. Clint and Usman liked it. I was a bit more cynical. To me, this was a heart-warming performance, but one that was securely cradled in the message of Uzbek nationalism. It was ethnic expression limited to dance, music, and costumes. This demonstration spelled out the terms on which ethnic differences could exist in Uzbekistan—as spectacles of food and dance on national holidays ultimately contributing to the image of a united Uzbek nation that graciously tolerated ethnic difference. I also noticed that the show did not include any Tajik dances or dancers, as Tajiks officially have no status as a separate ethnic group.

KOREANS IN UZBEKISTAN

About 200,000 Koreans lived in Uzbekistan in 1997 (Yalcin, 2002, p. 119). Cattle cars brought most of the Korean immigrants. They were banished by Stalin from north of the Korean border in 1937, because he feared that Japanese spies existed among them. At first Stalin forced the Koreans to live in the countryside of Uzbekistan without any hope of higher education, and he killed the majority of Korean intellectuals. It was not until 1954 that they could move into the city or have access to higher education (Yalcin, 2002, p. 122). Now about one-third of Koreans in Uzbekistan work in agriculture, one-third in business, and one-third in intellectual professions (Yalcin, 2002, p. 119).

One Korean village west of Tashkent exuded prosperity, as I gazed upon its substantial houses and public buildings. For lunch, village leaders served up *kimchi,* a spicy, pickled cabbage loved by Koreans, along with spicy chicken and rice. They pointed proudly to their church spire, for they had brought Christianity with them from Korea where it had become more popular than in other Asian countries. Most Koreans in Uzbekistan are non-religious, but about 20% are Christian, a religion that was compatible with Russian Orthodox Catholicism (Yalcin, 1999).

Koreans survived in the Soviet era by assimilating more to Russian culture than to Uzbek culture. Once in Uzbekistan, Korean parents downplayed Korean language and encouraged their children to learn Russian because it was the language they would need to pursue an education. In contemporary Uzbekistan, Koreans still speak Russian in their homes, although many of them speak Uzbek reasonably well, and younger Koreans consider Uzbekistan to be their motherland (Yalcin, 1999). This assimilation belies their official designation as a separately marked 'primordial' ethnicity.

However, Koreans still have a strong feeling of being Korean (Kahn, 1998), and they have maintained their food traditions. Does this mean that they have

Three thoroughly modern schoolboys of Korean and Russian origins on a school trip. I asked to take their picture at a historical site.

food sovereignty? I remembered back to our early days in Tashkent when a friend took me to the Chorsu Market. Among the wooden platforms with vendors, we saw a whole line of Korean women selling their distinctive vegetable salads. Our Uzbek friend said with enthusiasm, "These Korean salads are so delicious! I like their flavor, and they don't make me fat!"

"Should I buy some?" I asked.

"Well, if you do, you should buy from that Uzbek woman over there." She pointed to a woman standing off to the side behind a table with bowls of salad that looked just like those of the Korean women.

"Why?" I asked.

"Because," she whispered in my ear, "the Koreans make their food in their bathtubs right next to the, you know, toilet. Uzbeks make them in the kitchens." Not wanting to offend Uzbek or Korean, I skipped buying any Korean salads that day.

On another occasion, an Uzbek college student remarked in an interview how much he enjoyed going to Korean restaurants in Tashkent. "They are quite popular now."

"What do you like?" I asked him.

He laughed. "Everyone wants to try dog meat! It's supposed to be good for you. But you have to be careful. People say if you eat it too much, your eyes will turn up at the corners like a Korean's."

"Oh." I was surprised again. Here were acts and language that implied tolerance for Koreans juxtaposed with underlying attitudes of prejudice.

My question about food sovereignty would be difficult to answer. Koreans could consume and even sell their traditionally preferred foods. Karimov allowed their restaurants to continue operating within a controlled economic world where he often shut down businesses he did not like by imposing exorbitant taxes and fees. What does this mean in terms of the human dignity and marginalization of the Koreans? What were the benefits and limitations of their ethnic right to eat and sell their food to Uzbeks?

KOREANS IN UZBEKISTAN: A YOUNG ADULT

Later in my stay, I had a chance to visit another Korean village about 30 minutes from Tashkent to explore these questions in more depth. This village had dirt streets and old houses, much like most rural villages in Uzbekistan. Yet it also had a Russian language school, a large Christian church, and two Korean restaurants.

Muneera, a Russian, had grown up in this village because her father worked there for the government. First she took me to the small, wooden house where we met Nadya, her best friend. I wondered what life was like for a young Korean adult in today's Uzbekistan and was pleasantly surprised.

We talked in Nadya's living room as her ten-year-old brother kept piping in with his comments. When I asked Muneera to name her favorite food, the boy beat her to the punch. "I like *kuksi* the best." *Kuksi* is noodles eaten cold with soy sauce and vinegar. She rolled her eyes and laughed, "I could eat my mother's *chimchi* three times a day. It is *kimchi* with rice and fried potatoes. The Korean table is rich. In Uzbek families they always eat the same foods. Korean food cuisine is so diverse!" she bragged. "Well, sometimes we eat Russian borscht and on New Year we even make *palov,* but ..."

"I hate borscht," Nadya's brother yelled.

Nadya was currently a math student at the university, but she made it clear that she had chosen math only to please her parents. What was her real goal? "I want to become a clothes designer." She showed us a long, flowing gown with sequins that she had designed and made for her graduation ceremony. After graduation, she would sell it at the bazaar. Clearly, she did not feel that her career was limited by her education. Economically things were not easy. "My father doesn't earn much money, but he cares about us children." She had two older brothers who helped out—one worked with computers and another worked in Russia and sent money home.

After she convinced her little brother to go outside to play, Nadya talked about the increasing pressure from her grandmother to marry. She was after all, 23 years old. She wanted someone strong, intelligent and caring, and could not find anyone that fit her criteria in her own community. Ethnicity did not matter, she claimed, but she did mention one ethnic barrier. For her the line was drawn to exclude Uzbeks, whose language and customs seemed too different, and whose men seemed too domineering. "I don't care about the amount of money my future husband brings in. I can give up a high salary to have a peaceful life."

Nadya and Muneera told me about a friend married to a South Korean man who had come to the village looking for a wife to take back to his country. "She's having a hard time," sighed Nadya. Because of a slight shortage of women in South Korea and preference for girls who are supposedly more submissive than modern Korean women, South Korean men seek Korean girls from Uzbekistan. In a search of more money for themselves and their families, some girls accept. Nadya continued. "Her husband is a lot older, and it's hard for her to learn Korean. When her mother gave two sweaters to the son-in-law, he was only interested in the expensive one." Another village girl who had married a Korean returned to Uzbekistan divorced, but an Uzbek singer who had married a rich South Korean man was still there. Nadya and Muneera would wait to see how their friend fared in a global marriage market that played richer countries against poorer ones.

The wind was blowing up a rainstorm as we left Nadya's house, and the clouds opened up as we reached picnic tables in front of a Korean restaurant. We lurched for the door and tumbled in.

KOREANS IN UZBEKISTAN:

A KOREAN RESTAURANT

We were met by the owner, a woman named Yana, who recognized Muneera and welcomed our business on an afternoon with few customers. She scurried off to bring us food and called her husband Vitalik to join us. He was happy to give us a lecture.

"Ours is historical Korean food from the nineteenth century. Even the dog meat is made differently here. Ours is less hot and we cook it for a long time. South Korean food is less pure now. It has been influenced by the Japanese and the Americans. It's sweeter. South Korean food now is absolutely different. If I could open a restaurant in Miami, I would have success. This is the most authentic Korean food in the world!"

Food was the foundation of Vitalik's pride in being a Korean in Uzbekistan. I felt surprise that food marked his ethnicity not only in relation to the Uzbeks, but also in relation to Koreans in the homeland, perhaps because South Koreans saw Soviet Koreans as inferior (Khan, 1999). He twisted the isolation and lagging modernity of Koreans in Uzbekistan into an ethnic benefit that had market value.

"Our food is pure. In our soy sauce and fermented soybean paste (*miso*), we use only soybeans that we grow right here. We don't add chemicals like in South Korea. It is very nutritious."

Yana soon came back with food from a kitchen located in an outer building. Rain was still pelting down. She shivered a bit as she and a waiter served us rice, marinated garlic, fresh vegetables from their greenhouse to dip into hot red sauce … and dog meat.

"Have you ever eaten dog meat?" Vitalik asked with a daring smile on his face.

"No," I admitted.

"You will love it," he proclaimed loudly. "Uzbeks like it for its medicinal benefits."

I had never eaten dog meat, and as an anthropologist, I knew all about cultural food taboos. They were just that—cultural, not physical in nature. Yet here I was struggling with one of my own taboos that I could not ignore. Should I eat the dog meat? Everything in my anthropological training said 'yes': eat the food of the people you are studying. I took a deep breath, willed myself not to think of my black lab, and bit in.

Watching me eat, the Korean owners laughed and cheered me on: "All different nationalities come here for dog." I smiled and told them it tasted good. In fact, it did.

"It improves your immune system so you don't get flu. Korean food is based on medicines to cure the body. Dog meat is like narcotics. Once a person eats it, he gets addicted and it is hard to live without it. It's good for sore throats and especially for virility. Everyone respects Korean cuisine."

I remembered an Uzbek friend whose mother had bought dog fat for him to smear on his chest to cure a cold. He had screwed up his face with distaste, but he thought it would help.

"Are most of the people who come here Koreans?" I asked as I sipped the *miso* soup.

"No, definitely not. Italians, Germans, Americans, and locals like Russians, Armenians … and Uzbeks come, too. This café is oriented to Tashkent people."

Muneera assured me that this was true. "People go out of their way to come here."

Yana sat down. "There is Korean food at the bazaar, but this is better. The old women here prepare the *miso* and soy sauce with their souls."

Vitalik dominated the conversation.

"We don't eat sheep. We eat pork and beef … well, usually beef because Uzbeks don't eat pork. But if we know they eat pork, we give it to them. You wouldn't believe it. Many Uzbeks come from the old city [the old Uzbek part of Tashkent] and ask for it, even though they don't eat it in the old city. Even from Samarkand, Uzbeks come to eat pig legs and pig feet."

According to him, the Korean food was so strong that it not only marked Koreans as different but also tempted Uzbeks to transgress their own cultural norms. I wondered about Vitalik's transgressions across cultural lines and asked him if he ate *palov*.

The tact of a person long used to living as a minority emerged in his answer. "We are used to Korean food, but sometimes when we get tired of it, we want to eat Uzbek food."

The lights suddenly went out and we could hardly see in the stormy gray. A waiter brought candles and placed them on our wooden table, as Vitalik rushed off.

The duskiness of the room brought out memories. Yana said, "My family came here early—three to four generations ago, but my husband's family came here under Stalin. In Soviet times, when we had collective farms, the Koreans did well. We are good farmers and made almost twice as much as the government quota required. So we convinced the head of the collective farm to sign a paper saying that the part of production above the quota had been raised on private household plots, and then we could sell it in the market here and even in Russia. Koreans seemed rich back then. We bought cars that others couldn't afford! Now the Uzbeks are also selling a lot, so we aren't so well off."

"How long have you run this restaurant?" I asked her.

"About ten years. I was a primary school teacher, but I got sick so I had to find a way to support my family. First we set up only an outside dining area with an outside kitchen and gradually we built everything. We got everything by hard work. My husband and children help, so we call it 'My Family.'" The restaurant was larger than I thought at first. In the candlelight and gray light from outside, I could see a raised seating area behind sliding doors.

The lights flickered and then returned. Just then, three men in suits ran in from the rain. Vitalik leaped up to greet them warmly and lead them through the sliding doors into an area with several private dining rooms.

Yana suddenly seemed cognizant of the political impression she was making in the interview. "I want to tell you that Uzbeks are very good and a hospitable nation. They are peaceful and hardworking—like Koreans. We have many common points. We both give respect to elders. We both keep the laws of God."

"Are you Christian?" I asked, having seen the large Christian church in town.

"No, but I read the Bible. I was raised by the Soviets not to believe in God, but I am interested." Then out of the blue, she made a statement that seemed to express an oblique criticism of the Uzbek government.

"Americans are patriotic," she observed. "You are proud of your country. Most important is human rights. We are not so proud."

Yana did not let the statement hang in the air for long, following it with criticism of Americans. "But Americans are fat. Actually in Uzbekistan we fear the invasion of the American hot dog."

I laughed and agreed. Karimov's policy of keeping American fast food out was beneficial in some ways, even as it symbolized closed borders. The relative absence of fast food gave more room for Korean restaurants to offer an alternative, and a healthy one at that, to Uzbek food.

The rain had finally let up. Dodging puddles, we waved goodbye. A bag full of dog meat dangled from my arm, a gift of the owners. Muneera summed up one lesson of the day on how food symbolizes differences between ethnic groups:

"Russian Orthodox people don't eat horse. Koreans don't eat sheep. Uzbeks don't eat pork. Mohammed preached about that in the desert. Arabs ate pork, but when they brought it on a journey across the desert and the meat went bad, people got sick. So Muslims don't eat pork."

"And Americans don't eat dog!" I chimed in.

"Some say it will bring you good luck," she said, "and others that it will make your eyes turn upwards."

Here it was again, the split attitude of enjoyment of Korean food, but continued prejudice against Koreans, even from a young woman who lived among Koreans.

Much later that evening, after riding various buses home, I sat the dog meat in front of Clint. He was interested in hearing about my eating it, but he didn't seem too excited to try it. The package of dog meat sat in the refrigerator where no one touched it. I kept telling myself that it was fine to eat, yet somehow once was enough for my food adventure. Even anthropologists have cultural preferences built into their taste buds from their upbringing.

KOREAN ETHNICITY AND FOOD

My interviews had answered some of my questions about Koreans. Food was an important marker of Korean identity in Uzbekistan. It symbolized differences between them and Uzbeks, and it evoked pride in Korean culture rather than shame or inferiority associated with minority status. Their food represented the hard work and purity of their very "souls." They unabashedly loved their food and gathered around it. Although not going so far as to claim its superiority over Uzbek food, they did not hesitate to boast that their particular kind of Korean food was the most pure and authentic Korean food in the world.

Food also helped them celebrate their ethnicity in the eyes of other ethnic groups, even among the dominant Uzbeks who felt that Korean food contributed spice to their diet and richness to life. Since middle-class Uzbeks living in Tashkent were starved of most global food, Korean food was a window into a wider world beyond tightly controlled national borders.

The fact that the government and Uzbeks in general viewed the Koreans as culturally different worked to the Koreans' advantage in the marketplace.

In restaurants and bazaars, Koreans had found a channel to make a living through the commercialization of their food. Such commercialization of ethnic food is an example of using ethnicity as a profit maker. Although commercialization of ethnicity for the sake of tourists or customers can demean ethnicity and sometimes change it for the worse, it can also reinvigorate pride in ethnicity for the people performing it or serving it up (Comaroff and Comaroff 2009).

Ethnic food also has a darker side. Its popularity has skyrocketed in our globalized world, but suspicions of dirtiness often lurk around it, as in the case of the bathtub story above (Cardenas, 2007). Furthermore, Uzbeks viewed Korean dog meat and fat as having medicinal properties and at the same time being subject to a taboo on its consumption. Dominant groups often view ethnic food as a form of powerful magic, stronger than anything possessed by the dominant group, and capable of hurting as well as helping (Winant, 1994). In other words, ethnic food has beneficial qualities that the food of the dominant culture lacks, but it is dangerous.

It is no wonder that Koreans in Uzbekistan are wary of acts of discrimination and attitudes of prejudice. They still lag behind Uzbeks economically and socially due to a history of economic and educational deprivation, although young Koreans strive for education and some excel in the field of information technology. Koreans are still the butt of jokes. The knowledge that they live at the mercy of the Uzbeks and the Uzbek government emerges clearly both in their statements carefully praising Uzbeks, and in their veiled criticism of human rights in Uzbekistan. Some regard escape as an appealing option, either through marrying a South Korean or working in Russia.

Ironically, no matter where they turn, Russian-speaking Koreans would be an anomaly, not quite fitting in. In Uzbekistan, they face a challenge because the government is increasing tracks in schools taught in Uzbek at the expense of tracks taught in Russian. If they go to Russia, their faces and accented Russian bring them discrimination. If they go to South Korea where their faces fit in, they cannot speak Korean.

The Koreans have food sovereignty in terms of access to culturally appropriate food and pride in their food. Their food gives them human dignity, but it also marks them as always being Korean in a primordial sense. No matter how much they adapt and feel Uzbek, they are to some extent forever a different minority within the Uzbek nation. By being marked as different, they serve Karimov's Uzbek nationalism in defining the boundary between those on the inside and those on the outside.

TAJIK ETHNICITY: EBB AND FLOW

No minority group could present a greater contrast to the Koreans in Uzbekistan than the Tajiks. Koreans are viewed as a small, physically distinct minority from the outside, whereas Tajiks are viewed as a large indigenous minority that looks similar to Uzbeks, though often with narrower faces and more chiseled features. Like Uzbeks, they are Muslims.

Ironically, however, while Korean ethnicity is gaining in status, Tajik ethnicity is losing in status. The mystery surrounding Tajiks is this: by government calculations Tajiks constitute a much smaller part of the Uzbek population than by other calculations. Official figures show that Tajiks constitute 5% to 8% of the population of Uzbekistan. The embassy of Tajikistan in Tashkent claims that this figure should be 20% (Yalcin, 2002, p. 108) and Foltz (1996) estimates it to be 25% to 30%. Why does this discrepancy exist?

THE HISTORICAL VIEW OF TAJIKS

Historically, Turkic-speaking Uzbeks were conquering nomads, and Persian-speaking Tajiks were settled people with developed city administration and literature. They lived side-by-side and intermarried for centuries, but their languages, which are from entirely different linguistic families, did not disappear. Instead, people became bilingual. So intermixed were they that in the late 1800s, Russians labeled Uzbeks and Tajiks living together in cities as one ethnic category called "*Sarts*," a term used historically to refer to town dwelling merchants.

Eventually Russian anthropologists, practicing their primordial theory of ethnicity, decided to classify Tajiks and Uzbeks as separate ethnic groups. At the turn of the century Uzbeks themselves began to claim allegiance with Turkish-speaking people in central Asia, a process that also classified Tajiks as a separate ethnic group.

In the 1920s when the USSR created Tajikistan, supposedly for Tajiks, and Uzbekistan, supposedly for Uzbeks, competition was on for two large, ancient, and mostly Tajik cities, Samarkand and Bukhara. If Uzbekistan got them, it would add a huge number of Tajiks to its ethnic mix. Although this would be a victory in population numbers and territory over neighboring Tajikistan, it would challenge the centrality of Uzbek ethnicity to national identity.

The Uzbek government solved this dilemma by using the census as an effective tool in misrepresenting the population of ethnic groups. The 1920 census showed that Samarkand had 44,758 Tajiks and 3,301 Uzbeks. The 1926 census, however, showed a huge turnaround: 43,304 Uzbeks and 10,716 Tajiks (Sengupta, 2003, p. 107). Tajiks were disappearing and Uzbeks increasing. Why?

Census takers and officials convinced Tajiks to register as Uzbeks. Tajiks who were bilingual and had intermarried with Uzbeks had an ambiguous identity anyway (Melvin, 2000, p. 50) and could be easily persuaded to change their ethnicity on the census forms. Officials reportedly threatened recalcitrant Tajiks with exile in the mountains of Tajikistan if they did not register as Uzbeks. Perhaps as much as 50% of the Tajik population reidentified as Uzbek in 1926 (tajikam.com). Quarrels between Uzbekistan and Tajikistan leaders about territory continued for the next several years, but Samarkand and Bukhara became permanent parts of Uzbekistan.

Discrimination against the Tajiks in Uzbekistan heightened under the post-World War II leader, Rashidov. Holding power from 1959 to 1983, he denied Tajik students the right to use the Tajik language in the classroom, especially at universities. More and more Tajiks found it to their benefit to switch their official ethnicity to Uzbek, even though they still maintained their language and customs at home. Having adapted to Uzbek language and culture for centuries, they regarded this as one more adaptation.

When Karimov came to power after independence, he became totally invested in Uzbek ethnic nationalism. Ironically he is part Tajik! He grew up in the culturally Tajik city of Samarkand and married a woman who is part Russian and part Tajik. Both his and his wife's ancestors come from the same area in what is now Tajikistan.

Thus, our story raises another perplexing question: how can Karimov be part Tajik and yet shamelessly promote ethnic nationalism based on Uzbek-ness?

A TAJIK MOVEMENT RISES AND FALLS

After independence, Karimov allowed Tajik associations advocating ethnic freedoms to flourish. For example, the Samarkand Social and Cultural Association worked to restore Tajik language in schools, Tajik newspapers, Tajik arts, and the right for Tajiks to change their passport identification from Uzbek back to Tajik. In 1991, there were 35,000 people in Uzbekistan who registered as Tajiks, and 200 Tajik schools flourished. Even some university courses were taught in the Tajik language (tajikam.com).

The new recognition of Tajik ethnicity was short-lived, however. Karimov began to crack down on Tajiks in Uzbekistan as a civil war raged in neighboring Tajikistan from 1992 to 1997. Karimov feared both democracy and conservative Islamic ideology, as both were popular with different groups in Tajikistan and might spread across the border into Uzbekistan. Karimov moved thousands of Tajiks living too close to Tajikistan into central Uzbekistan, and his security forces arrested the leaders of the Tajik Movement in Uzbekistan, torturing and killing some of them and their relatives (Murray, 2006). Karimov ordered Tajik schools closed and books written in Persian burned. He allowed Tajik newspapers in Tashkent and Samarkand to continue publishing, but only if they printed the news approved by the Uzbek government.

Tajiks in Uzbekistan got the message. Aspiring Tajik scholars who wanted to advocate for Tajik schools, for example, received gentle guidance: "Why would you want to write about that? It's not interesting." Most Tajiks deserted the Tajik ethnicity movement, opting for stability and safety (Roy, 2007). On their passports, some stalwarts kept their Tajik identity, but many others switched to Uzbek.

Thus, Tajiks are fewer in number according to government statistics because government policy builds a pretense that the majority of Tajiks are Uzbeks. Karimov chooses this strategy in order to make Uzbekistan look strong against its neighbors and to promote the idea of an Uzbek nation unified around one ethnicity.

For public consumption, Karimov finds it politically expedient to emphasize his Uzbek ethnicity and ignore his Tajik roots. Behind the scenes, however, he takes advantage of his connections with Tajik politicians. Many of his main government officials and business leaders are fellow Tajiks from Samarkand and Bukhara—officially registered as Uzbeks of course. Thus, while the Tajik people as a separate ethnic group lack rights in Uzbekistan, certain Tajiks have connections to Karimov and exercise considerable political and economic power. The Tajiks as an ethnic group may be slipping from public view, but Tajiks have by no means disappeared.

TAJIK AND UZBEK MIXING

How have Tajiks in Uzbekistan managed to deal with this most recent unspoken policy that they mute their Tajik-ness and become Uzbeks on their passports?

People cope in a variety of ways. The fate of *palov* illustrates one of them. *Palov* is the representative dish of the Uzbeks, but it is Persian (or Tajik) in origin. Turkish nomads who became city dwellers learned to love and respect *palov*. During the Soviet times, *palov* became more accessible to everyone, and Uzbeks claimed it as their own national dish, despite the fact that Tajiks also claimed it. Increasingly since independence *palov* has become Uzbek. In a similar way Tajiks have become Uzbek while maintaining aspects of Tajik-ness in their lives, as we will see below.

In addition to hiding their identity Tajiks have two other coping strategies—one is registering as Uzbek and ignoring one's Tajik heritage in favor of a neutral, international identity and the other is openly committing oneself to Tajik ethnicity while remaining active in Uzbek society.

Generation makes a difference because young people adjust to historical changes. Tajik ethnicity was simpler to practice under the Soviet Union when Tajiks could easily travel from Uzbekistan to Tajikistan to pursue higher education in a Tajik-language university. Young Tajiks in Uzbekistan now cannot achieve the same level of literacy and fluency in the Tajik language as they did in the past. Tajik language instruction survives only in isolated rural villages.

The personal story of a 25-year-old woman named Ziyba provides an example of generational differences in coping strategies, and also indicates that people think differently depending on whether they are purely Tajik or Tajik-Uzbek in heritage.

Ziyba said, "My father is Tajik from Bukhara. He married my mother who is an Uzbek from Tashkent. At first we lived in Bukhara near my father's parents, and I heard them speak Tajik. I lived there until I was twelve. Then my mother wanted to return to Tashkent to be near her mother, so after that I spoke Uzbek with my other grandmother."

"What language did you speak at home?" Ziyba's answer shouldn't have surprised me, but it did.

"Russian." Her parents had chosen to speak the neutral language that they held in common and, not incidentally, the language of status in the USSR that both had learned at school. They each maintained their own languages with their parents, siblings, and friends. But they believed that opportunities for

Ziyba and her siblings were linked to fluency and education in Russian because it is a widely-spoken language with various textbooks in all subjects.[2] Ziyba was part of an educated middle class of Russian speakers created by the Soviets. "I feel most comfortable in Russian," she added. She claimed not to speak Uzbek well and not to understand Tajik at all, but as I spent time with her, I realized that she could speak Uzbek some and understand Tajik when necessary.

"Are you and your father listed as Tajik on your passports?" I asked.

"We're Uzbek. My father changed his ethnicity to Uzbek back in the seventies." Changing to Uzbek had worked to his advantage because he excelled at cooking *palov*. His Tajik know-how in making *palov*, combined with Uzbek ethnicity on his passport, made him an acceptable cook for government functions.

Marriage preferences are often the ultimate proof of the importance of ethnicity in people's lives, so I asked Ziyba about marriage.

"My father always wanted me to marry a Tajik, but I said I wouldn't." She clenched her lips and shook her long black hair vehemently, but then burst into a laugh. "Then I fell in love with a Tajik and married him!"

Her husband's education was also in Russian, and that is the language they speak to each other. Later, when we went to their home for dinner, I noticed that her cooking also reflected a taste for Russian and Russianized French recipes for salads, meats, and desserts. It seemed to be an attempt to go beyond her Uzbek and Tajik backgrounds and enter into a broader world.

"What ethnicity is listed on your husband's passport?" I asked later.

"Tajik." She hesitated, looking into space. "And when we have children ..."

"Yes?" I waited with half a smile because I knew they were trying for children.

"Well, I'd like them to be Uzbek on our passport. They would have more benefits in society. I mentioned it to my husband, but he said emphatically, 'Never. The children will be Tajik.'" She furrowed her brow, but the curve of her lips signaled resignation. Her husband argued that it would be no problem. Tajiks have complete access to education, albeit in Russian or Uzbek, and he himself was climbing the ranks in his profession. However, Ziyba felt nervous because Uzbek ethnicity was the safest route in contemporary Uzbekistan.

INSISTENCE ON TAJIK ETHNICITY

Tajik ethnicity was very important to Ozod, a man in his 30s. I interviewed him in his three-room apartment while his daughters ran in and out. He grew up speaking Tajik. When he served in the Soviet military and met other Tajiks, he became highly aware of his Tajik ethnicity. Now married to a Tajik woman, he lives in the newer area of Tashkent, identified originally with Russian residents.

As we talked, Ozod sat in a chair where he could keep one eye on the soccer game on television. Soon he got up and went to a shelf in the corner to pull off a book and handed it to me. It was a Tajik cookbook.

"The food in here isn't so different from Uzbek food. But it's written in the Tajik language and in little ways, it is different—a lot of dishes use peas (*mosh*);

the *shashlik* or *kebab* has chicken; and little dumplings, called '*chuchuwara*' in Uzbek are called '*tujbera*' in Tajik. I'm not a cook, but I think Tajiks fry them and Uzbeks boil them." I heard it differently later, but the point is that he wanted to emphasize the differences.

As innocent as a cookbook seems, for Ozod it represented a rallying point for Tajik ethnicity. Unlike Korean dishes that contrast sharply with Uzbek national dishes, Tajik dishes are dangerously similar and thus threaten to reveal that Uzbek national cuisine is not so unique in central Asia.

TAJIKS IN SAMARKAND: A GLIMPSE

Despite the official demographic records, Tajiks still represent the cultural majority in Samarkand. The food in many restaurants is Tajik by default because Tajiks do the cooking, though they do not advertise it as Tajik. Since Tajiks are the majority, we often heard their language spoken in public.

We toured Samarkand with two Tajik friends who were citizens of the neighboring country of Tajikistan. They felt right at home, able to speak freely with almost everyone. A friend of one of the Tajiks guided us around. He took us by Karimov's boyhood home. "Karimov was partially raised by his Tajik grandmother!" he exclaimed. "But now he has decided he is Uzbek and does not speak Tajik, at least in public. His Uzbek isn't perfect, but he uses that. He married a Russian woman and he is very good at Russian."

Our guide had both Uzbek and Tajik ancestors. "And what about you," I asked. "If you had to choose, which are you—Uzbek or Tajik?"

"Uzbek, I guess." He identified with his Uzbek grandfather. Furthermore, he was intent on getting ahead in education and politics, and his answer was politically correct for the times.

Most Tajiks we talked with in Samarkand maintained that they felt little discrimination, but one man was willing to speak freely. He curled his lip and said gruffly that Tajiks had lost their schools. He pointed out that only a few elementary schools in outlying villages used Tajik as the language of instruction. He also claimed that Tajiks and Uzbeks are different in character—the Tajiks more volatile and the Uzbeks more passive.

A young Tajik woman who worked with a human rights group in Samarkand made the same point more tactfully, conveying a sense of quiet resistance that persisted among Tajiks despite government pressure to blend in.

"Samarkand is unique. There are many ethnicities. Tajiks number more than others here, but it is Tashkent policy not to support ethnic diversity. Tajiks are oppressed and don't feel at home. There is a debate now as to why everything has to be Uzbek. All the Tajik schools have been closed and all Tajik departments in the university are closed. There is no Tajik mass media."

My head buzzed with the ironies of everyday life. Karimov tried to shape his nation as homogeneous and independent by promoting the use of Uzbek language and by "Uzbekifying" history and food. His policy turned Tajik language and ethnicity into forces representing heterogeneity. In order to accomplish his

A high school English class, taught in Uzbek, in the heavily Tajik city of Bukhara.

goal of homogenization he needed to weed them out, or at least force it underground like roots that travel under the soil. However, it is hard to get rid of weeds in a garden or a nation. Voices of minorities did not remain silent despite Karimov's efforts.

TAJIKS NEAR TASHKENT

In food and family, the Tajik way of life continues to live in Uzbekistan. I interviewed Tajik families who had lived in villages around Tashkent for generations and spoke of their affinity for Tajik dishes, Tajik family, and the nearby country of Tajikistan. Though not in a public way, their lives and histories revealed a strong identification with Tajik ethnicity and strategies to maintain it.

One Sunday in late spring, Clint and I travelled several hours northeast of Tashkent to visit the family of a Tajik friend, Ravshan. His father, mother, aunt and some of their children had gathered at Ravshan's natal home.

We sat at a picnic table, new grape leaves appearing succulent overhead, while our hosts served up *dolma,* a dish made from steaming bundles of rice, onions, and ground mutton wrapped in grape leaves. I never realized how many grape leaves were going to waste in Oregon, where to us grape leaves smelled only of the wine to come! Ravshan's father also had made red wine, and although Ravshan did not think it was so great, its sweet flavor tasted fine to us.

The Tajik dish for the day was one of their favorite treats—bread warm from the oven topped with new garden greens and fried, and the whole thing soaked with warm butter on a wooden dish. Everyone reached with their fingers and tore off the bread. It tasted delicious.

While we licked our fingers, the older generation who had come of age in the 1960s and 1970s told us their life stories, all revealing a strong Tajik identification. The father, mother, and aunt had grown up in small all-Tajik villages north of Tashkent, gone to Tajik language schools and then moved to Dushanbe, the capitol of the Soviet Republic of Tajikistan, to pursue higher education.

Ravshan's mother, now about 60 years of age, told her story. "Dushanbe was only a few hours away, and we could continue our education in Tajik. I went when I was 15 to study medicine. We married other people who had come from the same small villages near Tashkent and were also studying in Tajikistan. The Tajiks would tease us that our Tajik sounded funny. 'It was Uzbekified,' they said. They thought Bukharan Uzbeks spoke better Tajik. But it was easy to get jobs and we stayed there and worked. I was a village doctor, and my sister-in-law was in obstetrics in the city. My husband worked as a scientific researcher. We could go back and forth easily in those days between Uzbekistan and Tajikistan."

Ravshan's aunt chimed in. "It was good living in Dushanbe where everyone spoke Tajik. My husband worked in a meat factory and made good money. But then the war started and life was not safe there. Our parents were still back in Uzbekistan, so we came home. We couldn't find jobs in the little villages where we grew up and our parents still lived, but we set up homes not too far away. I work as a pediatrician in the local hospital. My husband has had a harder time. He drives a taxi when he can."

She went into the house and came out with dishes of boiled calf's leg. She had boiled it for many hours making it into a gelatinous mass. "We could always get parts of the animals from the factory where my husband worked, so I like making things like this." The dish had a very strong cow taste and Clint, not required by his profession to be stoic, ate only a mouthful. I finished my helping, dedicating it to anthropologists all over the world who must eat everything they are served for the sake of demonstrating respect for local culture.

Next came *palov*. "Tajiks like rice," Ravshan's aunt declared, "People in Uzbek villages eat more noodles and dumplings. Uzbeks like their meat fried and Tajiks prefer ours boiled." Little differences in food preferences can be important in marking ethnic differences, I thought.

Then she chuckled. "But there isn't all that much difference! We eat noodles, too!"

We ate the *palov* with our fingers off of a common plate, ignoring the spoons offered to us. This style was not particularly Tajik; we had met it among rural Uzbeks as well. Clint and I weren't too bad at it because we had eaten this way during a previous field trip to India, but picking up rice, shaping it into a bundle, and flicking it quickly into one's mouth without letting anything drop is no mean trick. Laughter, humility, and homemade red wine washed it all down.

Ravshan talked as he stretched back in his chair, full and content. "The situation is entirely different for my generation. We can't easily go back and forth to Tajikistan."

In the 2000s, Karimov had tightened the border with Tajikistan. Although it was within an hour's drive of Tashkent, men could pass across only with difficulty. Karimov might suspect a young man crossing the border of having ties with fundamentalist Muslim groups. Since old women had the best chance to cross the border, elderly mothers visited their sons rather than the other way around.

Our young host continued, referring to this country town several hours northeast of Tashkent. "We went to school here at a really good Russian school with practically all Russian classmates. Their parents had come to build a dam in 1966, and many stayed. The sad thing is that after independence, 90% of them went back to Russia. I have no friends from high school to gather with by the river in summer and make *palov* together. Now I ask my parents why they didn't send me to an Uzbek school!"

His mother shrugged and smiled. Russian had seemed more practical and more acceptable than Uzbek from an ethnic point of view. She had lived long enough to know that times change, and their family's response was to adapt. They all spoke Tajik and Russian, and now her son needed to speak Uzbek. Indeed, she also needed Uzbek in her hospital work in the village. She summed up the strategy in terms of food. "We like both Uzbek and Tajik dishes, and really there isn't much difference between them."

Another strategy, a family rotating credit association (*gyap*), was important to their financial and social survival as an extended family, although it was not unique to them as Tajiks. The mother's face broke into wreaths of wrinkles as she said, "We have a rotating credit association with our relatives where we meet once a month. All the siblings and their spouses come and bring food. Mostly it's for talking, eating, and dancing. We just have fun. But we also bring money, and each time somebody [different] gets to take the money and use it for whatever they want—maybe a wedding, a television, or a car."

Marriage strategies also supported family unity and Tajik ethnicity. Children came home from the city to visit almost every weekend, or at least felt they should. The eldest sons of Ravshan's mother and aunt had married Tajik-speaking wives from this area.

One of Ravshan's cousins had married a Tatar woman whose family had lived in Uzbekistan for several generations after migrating from western Russia under orders from Stalin. I had heard of Tatars mainly through stereotypes, such as Tatar women make delicious baked goods, but are too strong-willed to be obedient wives. It made me identify with them, as American women often suffer from a similar worldwide stereotype—that is, being too strong-willed.

The family's main concern with a Tatar bride, however, was not with gender roles, but with maintaining Tajik ethnicity. Ravshan told us: "There was a quite a rift for awhile, because he is the youngest son and will inherit the house. But his new bride studied Tajik language really hard for about four months, and now she can speak it pretty well. So everything is okay … but they live separately for now."

Ravshan's story reminded me of other stories I had heard indicating that inter-ethnic marriage is not simple. One Tajik-Tatar woman married to an Uzbek man said that when matchmakers of Uzbek descent approached her about prospects for her daughter, they would ask, "Is your blood clean?" implying a desire for pure Uzbek heritage. Furthermore, an Uzbek family we knew gathered together all but one of several siblings and their families for a party. Later, I found that the absent sibling turned out to be married to a Tajik who had tried to become part of the family, but felt subtle discrimination, so now stayed apart.

TAJIK ETHNICITY IN A MOUNTAIN VILLAGE

After our meal, we drove farther, winding up into the mountains north of Tashkent around a large reservoir and across a ravine where goats were tethered on its steep banks. "This is the area where my parents grew up," said Ravshan. "There are three Tajik villages up here. They were actually part of Kazakhstan until the 1950s when land got traded between the nations."

The dam's construction threatened the family unity of these Tajiks. Our friend continued: "Those goats on the hillside over there belong to the villagers. Everyone lost a lot of land when the dam was built, and they got land across the

In the mountainous Tajik village, streets are rough.

river in compensation. The sad thing is that many adult children have moved across to the new land and don't live with their parents now."

We bounced over the narrow, rutted roads, which clearly received no public money for maintenance, to the house of Ravshan's uncle and aunt. His cousin, the youngest son who stood in line to inherit the land, was busy paving the driveway for his mother and father. His 6-year-old twin daughters greeted us with big eyes and nary a smile as they led us across a courtyard and into a small, wooden house where their grandparents awaited. We sat on floor pillows next to the girls. Their grandfather had a rough-hewn, ruddy face with thick eyebrows, hairs sticking out as if to tickle the faces of his granddaughters. Their grandmother was plump in a pillowy sort of way with a ready smile that showed few teeth. Brown eyes watching us, the twins cuddled shyly against their grandmother and grandfather's sides as we talked.

The old man was almost blind, but in short bursts he revealed his thoughts about food while his nephew was translating from Tajik. "Our mountains are rich. All things are here. Apples, cherries, peaches, pears, apricots, walnuts, greens in the spring." And later, he added, "We eat a lot. It's scary!"

His wife gestured towards the homemade cherry jam on the table. "Look at the jam! It will keep you healthy in the spring!" The daughter-in-law said nothing as she brought in fried flat bread (katlava), soon followed by a Tajik dish called guja, a white soup based on yoghurt (katik) made from the milk of their cows with greens picked in the mountains and ground wheat. They grew, threshed, and boiled the wheat. This was really local food. Clint and I spooned some into our mouths. Its base had a strong mutton taste and the strong flavor of unpasteurized yoghurt. We lapped it up, since it was one of the keys to long life, a bragging point for the people living in this area.

The old woman told us that winters were tough here in this isolated area. "We stay in most of the winter by the warm fire, except to feed the cows and sheep. And we go out to use the beehive clay oven (tandoor) to make bread everyday. And now the twins go to school." She showed us the clay oven which opened from the top; she would reach down in to bake the bread. Their garden faced right up to mountains behind their house. The little girls were loosening up now and grinned for the camera as they held their grandmother's hands.

Ravshan told us that these villages still had Tajik language elementary schools. Perhaps they were still allowed, he thought, because the villages were so isolated. No one would expect a political uprising here. Thus, it was only in such small villages as this where Tajik linguistic ethnicity could flourish. Physical survival in this environment, however, was a constant struggle.

The family farmed not only their own household plot, but also about ten hectares across the river used for cows, sheep, wheat, corn and so on. "In the summer, I take the crops my son grows and sell them in the city markets," said the old woman with a sparkle in her eye. "He drives, but I do the selling—otherwise, we get no money!"

Their house had electricity, and they were eager to show us a videotape of the grandfather's birthday party at age sixty-three: "the age of our messenger

The grandmother in a Tajik village hugs her grandchildren to her sides with her garden in the background.

Mohammed when he entered paradise." It was a huge party with far-flung family and neighbors. They sacrificed a sheep and shared the meat along with a lentil-wheat dish (*halim*) they had boiled for 24 hours. "We must have sheep. We sacrifice for our parents who have died. Just recently we sacrificed a sheep and shared it for the safety of these two," the old woman added. On either side of her, she hugged her two granddaughters, spitting images of each other, hair tied up in ponytails with bright ribbons. They were the future of the Tajiks in this area.

TAJIK ETHNICITY AND ASSIMILATION

Tajiks have disappeared in official population statistics but not in the reality of everyday life. They have adapted in various ways to Karimov's political policy of Uzbek-ness in order to survive.

The effects of Karimov's policies run in two directions. On one hand, his policies diminish a sense of Tajik ethnicity as Tajiks concentrate on adapting and merging into the Uzbek nation. On the other hand, they call people's attention to what they cannot have—the full expression of Tajik identity in public life. Tajiks and Uzbeks have lived together for centuries and have the potential to integrate and segregate over time. In 2010, ethnic conflict in Kyrgystan between Kyrgyz and minority Uzbeks shows that ethnic divisions can erupt in violence in central Asia.

Tajiks in Uzbekistan have survived by assimilating into Uzbek ways of life, as each political period requires. Even Karimov, who is part Tajik assimilates. He uses his Uzbek ethnicity to unite his people against the fear of Russian domination and the disorder that might spread from Tajikistan. Yet he turns to his Tajik connections behind the scenes to find trusted political cronies. Ironically, Karimov, who built his nation by establishing a sense of primordial ethnicity for Uzbeks, is himself a perfect example of situational ethnicity, which changes to fit the circumstances.

Do Tajiks have food sovereignty? They can eat their preferred and culturally appropriate foods. Because Tajik foods are very similar to Uzbek foods and have grown out of a shared history, ingredients for making their foods are available. At home, they cook their foods as they choose.

Tajiks hesitate, however, to claim any of their foods as Tajik. Tajik food cannot claim the exotic magic or heightened nutrition of Korean food. Tajik restaurants do not exist because they would only call attention to unwanted differences across a wide swath of the population. National homogeneity depends on Tajiks' acceptance of Uzbek-Tajik foods as Uzbek if Uzbeks say so, no matter what the origin of the foods.

CONCLUSION

These accounts of Tajik and Korean ethnicity in Uzbekistan indicate an important point. Ethnicity is situational, a process and not a fixed attribute. It changes over time as politics, economics, and ideologies shift. Even Koreans, who seem so authentic in their culturally preferred food, speak Russian. In addition, ethnicity changes in relation to other groups. In this case, both Tajiks and Koreans have modified their identity to adjust to the increasing dominance of Uzbek ethnicity in Uzbekistan.

Ethnic groups such as Koreans and Tajiks live on the margins of Uzbek-ness, caught in the pincer of the strong forces of nationalism and the culturally meaningful experiences of the tastes, language, and interaction styles of their own ethnic groups.

I have described two examples of ethnicity in Uzbekistan to show a contrast in the crosscutting currents of ethnicity, food, nationalism, and food sovereignty. Each group shows a different example of how ethnicity forms, ebbs, and flows. In both cases food is central to family and community. However, Tajiks must emphasize the assimilation of their food, whereas Koreans must highlight the uniqueness, and even the magic, of their food in relation to the larger Uzbek community.

Both groups have food sovereignty in terms of eating foods they prefer and consider culturally appropriate. But in terms of human dignity and human rights, neither Koreans nor Tajiks can live completely as they wish with free expression of all aspects of food preferences and ethnic identity in public as well as private life.

Food expresses and marks ethnicity, it can also work across boundaries to shape ethnicity. Whether immigrants from afar or people indigenous to the region, non-Uzbek ethnic groups shape perceptions of their food and their ethnicity around the demands of Karimov's ethnic nationalism. Minority groups make trade-offs. Koreans play up their food in restaurants as a survival strategy, yet they have mostly lost their language. Tajiks have kept their language, yet play down food differences and Tajik-ness so that they can participate in Uzbek society. Their scope for expressing Tajik-ness narrows in the process.

Koreans acknowledge that they are always outside of Uzbek ethnicity. Even as they contribute to the Uzbek economy, their position as outsiders and minorities reinforces the insider identity of Uzbeks. They live on the other side of an ethnic line that Uzbeks can wander across without leaving their own country, for example, in going to Korean restaurants. Such small transgressions help to define by opposition the norms with which Uzbeks live.

Tajiks play down food differences and Tajik-ness so that they can play full roles in Uzbek society. Tajiks who have turned Uzbek or who hide their Tajik-ness swell Uzbekistan's population and economy. Uzbekistan swallows them like an energy drink.

Ultimately, Karimov manipulates ethnic differences to enhance his power, built on ethnic nationalism. Yet the tight borders of Uzbekistan stay intact for all of its ethnic groups. For Tajiks and Koreans, as well as ordinary Uzbeks, the main problem is not the cultural boundaries between them but the national borders that the Uzbek government screws shut ever more tightly to limit citizens' mobility and potential for growth in a global world. Limits in the arena of ethnic food sovereignty are a symptom of a larger deprivation of human rights that I turn to in the next chapter.

ENDNOTES

1. Other major groups are 2% Tatars; 2.2% Karakalpaks in their own autonomous zone in the west; 1.5% Kyrgyz; and .2% Ukranians (Yalcin, 2002, p. 108). The CIA World Factbook reports the 1996 estimate for ethnic populations at: Uzbek 80%, Russian 5.5%, Tajik 5%, Kazakh 3%, Karakalpak 2.5%, Tatar 1.5%, other 2.5%.

2. Education in Russia and Uzbek is available, often in separate tracks at larger public schools and universities, and sometimes in separate high schools. Education in Russia has been considered superior, but as the government pushes the use of Uzbek, education in Uzbek is increasing. The script for education in Uzbek changed from Arabic to Latin in 1929, then to Cyrillic (Russian alphabet) in 1940, but recently is gradually shifting by government decree back to the Latin alphabet.

Chapter 7

Region and Religion: Hunger, Protest, and Violence

This chapter is about the breaking point of ordinary people, pushed to the edge by oppressive political power and lack of economic opportunities. It tells a story of unjust treatment in the fertile Ferghana Valley, home to about a quarter of the population of Uzbekistan. An area with its own strong food traditions, the Ferghana Valley is famous historically as a center of political and religious fervor.

PROTEST AND GOVERNMENT SUPPRESSION
IN THE FERGHANA VALLEY

I strolled to the Institute one morning through the May sunshine, but for some reason, the president's cavalcade did not appear at its scheduled time. I cheerily greeted the graduate students across the hall. They hardly answered before they said, "Did you hear about Andijan?"

"Actually I'm going there this weekend."

"I don't think you are. The whole city is blocked off. No one can leave or enter. There was a protest yesterday, and we heard that a lot of people were killed."

One of the students was from Andijan. "Is your family all right?"

"I'm not sure. No one can call in or out." Her face was white and drawn.

People did not stay around the Institute long that day. The air was thick with worry. Various rumors flew around—businessmen arrested and found guilty, armed insurgents, a jailbreak, thousands of protestors, and killings by Uzbek soldiers.

I headed back home. Clint reported that the university where he was to give a business lecture that morning had cancelled his appearance. The government suspected Americans of working to help the protestors.

We turned on the television set. At first, nothing but songs and dances appeared on the screen, but later a Russian news program aired pictures of dead bodies laid out on the ground. The program also showed a room containing drug debris such as cotton and syringes, as the announcer talked of terrorism.

WHY?

Shahnoza, the woman who was to go with me to Andijan, called that day. She was confused and anxious about her family. "Remember, I was going to take my little nephew home, and now he is stuck here! He is crying for his mother." The next day we took the same 5-year-old nephew to the Tashkent zoo where everything seemed as calm as ever except for the startling cries of the peacock.

"We don't know much," Shahnoza said, as we sat on a bench. "A gang of armed protestors stormed the city prison, killed the guards, and let out the prisoners. They took some city officials hostage the next morning at the city hall. People gathered in the square outside. Thousands of them were there, I guess."

"Is that when people were killed?"

"Yes, I heard that the soldiers just fired into the crowd and killed people—women and children, not just men. A lot, maybe hundreds." She rubbed her nephew's butch-cut hair sadly.

"What were they protesting?" I asked.

"Well, the government says it is religious terrorists trying to take over the government. I don't know. Maybe the people who stormed the prison are like this, but I can't believe all those people in the square were terrorists. I think it's bigger than this. I know that the government isn't paying government salaries and pensions in Andijan, and people are angry. They can't even afford meat."

Andijan is the name of a city and a province of small size geographically in the very east of Uzbekistan. However, it contains 10% of the nation's population. It is also the country's largest producer of cotton, and as we know from Chapter 4, cotton production unfairly burdens both farmers and laborers. Rather than outlying areas cities like Andijan, President Karimov's policies favor Tashkent. Andijanis fill their stomachs with grains rather than meat and milk, which are plentiful in Tashkent. The incidence of food poverty in Andijan province was 31.8% and extreme food poverty 9.1% in 2007. Tashkent's rates were much lower—9.2% and 2.9% respectively. (WFP, 2008, p. 34, 29; Musaev et al, 2010, p. 54).

Shahnoza was angry. "These ordinary people aren't terrorists. Why did the military kill them?"

We sat on a bench in the hot sun feeling dejected. "He is a smart hypocrite," she muttered, referring to Karimov.

"Who are the businessmen that were on trial?"

"The government accused them of religious extremism. Their friends and families were protesting outside the courthouse for a long time. The storming of the prison happened on the night of their conviction, and the rumor is that they got away across the border into Kyrgystan."[1]

"What had they done?"

"It's hard to tell. Some say their businesses were doing well, but they were working outside of the government framework—like not getting government loans and not banking their profits at government banks. The government wanted to take control of them and their money. So the government labeled them radical Muslims trying to overthrow the government."

INSTITUTIONAL RESPONSE

The next day the professors and graduate students reported to the Institute and gathered around the large table with grave faces.

The director wanted detailed schedules from everyone and warned us of the danger—radical Muslims, followers of Akram, were trying to take over the government. The accused leader, Akram, was an activist from Andijan who advocated living by Islamic values. One professor wanted to conduct research on this group; another was wary and mentioned economic reasons for the protests. A graduate student ventured that information was still inadequate to judge anything, and another stated that journalists were reporting conflicting stories. "Don't believe everything that journalists are saying. We are intellectuals, and we have to educate the people on this new radical group," responded the director, who had to abide by the government line.

VISITORS FROM THE UNITED STATES

In the midst of all this turmoil, our daughters, both in their twenties, were scheduled to arrive in Tashkent that very week. Before leaving New York City, they called. "Should we really come?" We checked with the American embassy and they assured us that there seemed to be little danger. When they got to London they saw newspaper pictures of red paint thrown in protest on the Uzbek embassy in London. A more frantic call came: "Is it safe?" Perhaps my daughters were following their anthropologist mother too far this time. They travelled on, unsettled because almost all the passengers debarked in Yerevan in the country of Armenia.

When they had arrived safely, Shahnoza and her nephew came over for dinner. We shared a round loaf of bread to celebrate the arrival of my daughters, made soup, and stuffed ourselves with dumplings (*chuchuwara*).

The conversation turned serious after dinner. More news was seeping out. As her nephew played in the living room, Shahnoza told us what she knew.

"My family, thank God, is fine, but three people on our street were killed. One was a seven-year-old girl shot while fleeing with her father. One was a friend of my brother. The tanks just moved in and shot. Everyone is so upset but they can't say anything. The schools are all closed in the Ferghana Valley. Police and students dressed in blue camouflage are checking at every house in the city and registering everyone. They want to find anyone who participated."

My daughters watched her with saucer-like eyes of horror.

"The students here in Tashkent are talking like wildfire. They weren't so sure about the president before and now they know they can't trust him. The government is checking attendance in every class and making students show their papers." The government was keeping track of young people, watching for signs of resistance.

"But everything seems so quiet here," said Elise, my older daughter.

"The government doesn't want anything to spread to Tashkent. They make sure the markets here are full of food." Shanoza's arm waved towards the left-overs on the table. "People in Tashkent are rich, and so they don't care about a change. Not like in the Ferghana Valley," she said bitterly.

"In Andijan, my mother says it's hard to get food because it's not getting in from the country. Sellers are charging high prices—3000 *sum* ($3.00) for a kilo of potatoes that normally would cost 300 *sum* ($.30). But my mother went out of the house and says things are calm."

FERGHANA VALLEY: POLITICS, RELIGION, AND ECONOMICS

That night, we sat up late with our daughters. Laura, the younger one, was majoring in political science, but seeing a dictatorship up close shocked her. "What is happening here?" she gasped.

We had more questions than answers. We could only offer broad insights from what we had learned about the frustrations of people living in the Ferghana Valley when we had visited there earlier that year. Usman, who had shown us around his hometown of Kokand (1.5 hours from Andijan), was a good guide, sensitive to the political, economic, and religious problems that bedeviled the region. I even consulted my field notes—the log that an anthropologist keeps of ongoing experiences and conversations when she is in her area of study (the field). As we talked, the economic problems and religious oppression we had heard about took on new significance in light of this latest event.

FERGHANA VALLEY: ECONOMIC DEPRIVATIONS

We had headed over the snowy mountains dividing Tashkent from the Ferghana Valley in February. The "taxi" driver was one of many men who used their own cars to transport paying passengers. He told us that he used to work for a state-owned factory in Kokand under the Soviets. Now that almost all the factories had closed, he drove his car back and forth to make a living for his four children, wife, and mother. He seemed to know the police who stopped and checked cars along the windy road. They could close the road instantly if there were trouble in the Ferghana Valley.

Cotton-Picking

As we approached Kokand, we passed through large fields newly planted with cotton. The Ferghana Valley produces more cotton than anywhere in Uzbekistan. Usman pointed out a little school with a small water tower next to the road. "That's where we lived—me and my classmates—when we picked cotton. In rural areas students and even workers live near the cotton fields when they pick the cotton. They don't have to pick cotton in Tashkent. But we had to do it for two-and-a-half months!"

"You mean they just take you out of school?"

"Yes. The principal makes a deal with cotton farmers. The harvest is really important to the country because a lot of the national budget comes from selling cotton."

"What's it like?"

"Well, at first it's fun because you are with your friends—boys and girls together—and you can stay up and talk at night. But it really gets tiring. They gave me a row of cotton to pick, and because I am kind of tall, I had to pick 50 kilos in a day. There was no way I could do it—even when we put some stones in the sack or wet down some of the cotton. So then at the end I had to pay about 9,000 *sum* ($9.00)—a fine for what I couldn't pick! My mother only makes 18,000 *sum* ($18.00) per month and my dad even less!"

The taxi driver was nodding in agreement.

"And the living conditions are really awful. One outhouse for a lot of students and it really gets stinky. And you only get some soup and a round of bread to eat. Some people get sick and have to leave, but then they have to pay a bigger fine at the end."

"Is it required by the government?" Clint asked.

"No. My mother's workplace did it, too, and she had to pick, though she could commute from home."

Cotton-picking by ordinary citizens, including children, was common in rural areas, but Tashkent people were not required to do it. It was a source of political resentment because workplaces and schools were less effective, and the labor was grueling and poorly paid.[2]

Employment Woes

As we rolled into Kokand, potholes and old public buildings contrasted with Tashkent's shiny halls and wide boulevards. We passed one neighborhood of whitewashed walls that looked ordinary, but the taxi driver said that it was known for illegal drugs. A drug route passed through the Ferghana Valley, running from Afghanistan's opium fields up through Kazakhstan into Russia. "More and more people are taking drugs. And some transport them across borders—in the diapers of babies or even in bags swallowed into their stomachs."

"Nasty! Why do they do it?" I asked.

"There are no good jobs. Maybe 60,000 people are unemployed in this city of what—200,000. The drug lords have the money," the taxi driver said.

"People work under the radar, like my friend from high school," added Usman. "He works as a car mechanic, privately for individuals. They go to the bazaar and get the car parts he tells them he needs, and he installs them in the car. He used to work for the South Korean Daewoo factory over in Andijan (115 kilometers to the east), but lost his job. Now he has stomach problems. He has to suck the gas up with his mouth out of the tanks because he doesn't have the machine he needs to do it, and some of it sometimes goes into his stomach."

My daughters, draped sleepily over chairs listening to our stories, groaned when they heard that.

Absent Family Members

Usman's mother, father, and sister-in-law greeted us at his house. We gathered around a low table full of raisins, walnuts, and seeds from inside the apricot pit. "People in the Ferghana Valley always drink green tea," said his mother, as Usman, the youngest, served it to us. Both she and her daughter-in-law wore traditional Uzbek clothing—long sleeves, knee-length dress, and pantaloons underneath—but made from modern fabrics. The daughter-in-law wore a pink scarf tied behind her head, hair showing, and the mother wore a sheer beige scarf draped loosely over her head and tied far below her chin in a fashion I had not seen in Tashkent. I realized that scarves were more than a social norm for women; they were an accessory of beauty.

Usman's nephew, almost two years old, toddled from person to person, but he already knew how to put his hand to his heart and say, "*Olinlar*"—Take! (in a polite form). We laughed. It was remarkable how early children learned the bodily gestures of Uzbek hospitality!

And where was Usman's brother, the father of this little boy, we asked. "Russia, working in a factory." He and others like him wanted opportunities for employment near home, but the unemployed and underemployed people who stay home in areas like Kokand with low employment opportunities have one of the highest food poverty rates in Uzbekistan (WFP, 2008, p. 36). Going to either Kazakhstan or Russia was their best alternative, and Karimov's exit policies were more flexible for this purpose. He was one among a quarter of the local workforce who had migrated to find work, as many as one per family on average in the Ferghana Valley. The payoff was that migrant workers' income sent back to the Ferghana Valley was five-to-ten times higher than family income from local employment. Remittances from abroad were one of the major sources of income for the cash-strapped towns of the Ferghana Valley. Overall, earnings sent home by migrant workers made up 11% of GDP in Uzbekistan in 2007 (Ergashev & Akhmerova, 2010, p. 11, 20).

Usman's brother had gone for the second time not long ago to work in a factory in southern Russia. He hated to leave his wife and child, but he wanted to earn enough money to build a house for his family and did not want his son to be undernourished. More than half of the children in small cities like Kokand are anemic from eating too little meat and too few high-nutrient vegetables

(WFP, 2008, p. 53). Usman's brother's absence was a source of sadness. The family became quiet and changed the topic.

Later Usman told us more. When people leave Uzbekistan, they need to obtain an exit visa from the government—one more method in Karimov's arsenal to keep track of citizens and prevent them from leaving the country if he wished. Usman's brother had to pay a little "extra" last time, a bribe, to get the exit visa. A man who had not done military service might be prevented from leaving the country, even with a bribe, but Usman's brother had already completed several years of service.

Working in Russia had its risks. One night, racist thugs assaulted Usman's brother and his friend. After this incident they ventured out of their apartment as little as possible. When they returned to Uzbekistan between jobs, a Russian customs official demanded that they hand over some of the money they were bringing back. Usman had tried to convince his brother not to go back to Russia because it was too dangerous, and men drank a lot there, but his brother's need to earn an income prevailed.

Later that evening, Usman's father was making *palov* out in the courtyard—a treat for his guests. Usman promised it was the best. His father gave us the cracklings—tasty fat from the fat-tailed Uzbek sheep fried up to perfection. He made *palov* in the typical style of the Ferghana Valley—the mutton, the onions, the yellow carrots, and later the rice, in layers. Midway in the preparation, Usman's father made a hole in the rice and put cumin into it—the magic touch. People in the Ferghana Valley were proud to have the best apricots, the best almonds, and the best *palov*, and they offered them even when they could not afford them. As we sat in the twilight waiting for the *palov*, Usman's mother held her grandson and waved the smoke over him for good luck and good health.

Elise, my older daughter, rolled over, holding her stomach. "I'm so stuffed I can't stand to hear about food. Tell us about the markets. I really want to go and get some of those shoes that are long in front, like Shahnoza had on tonight."[3]

"We'll go tomorrow," I chuckled.

MARKETS: OPPORTUNITIES AND RESTRICTIONS

Clint took this is a cue to talk about markets in Kokand. "The markets are an important part of how people survive in the Ferghana valley. Kokand has one of the biggest markets in Uzbekistan. Usman's sister-in-law's father took us to see it. He had good connections from his days working in the police force. He could drive as fast as he wanted, and the police wouldn't arrest him! Now he's a truck driver and takes goods up into Siberia or drives supplies down to American forces in Afghanistan. The market was huge! It had every imaginable thing—live chickens, furniture, and a huge section of sports clothes and sneakers from China. It had all the latest shoes."

"You could have gotten some deals, Dad!" Laura knew how her father loved running shoes.

"Yes, but they said that Uzbekistan gets the cheaply made stuff from China. The good stuff goes to the United States. Actually, Usman said that his friend gets clothes to sell from a train. They throw off packages to him as they pass through."

"You girls would have loved the dresses that Usman's aunt was selling in her booth. Fancy party clothes," I said. "She goes to Dubai to buy them. She seems to know how to deal with the customs officials. Her booth was shaped like a big container with doors that she could lock at night. It even had a changing room in the back."

Clint broke in. "The truck driver bought us some great pastries, with honey and nuts, like *baklava*. Then in the car he told us they were good because they were made from Kazak wheat that is of better quality than Uzbek wheat. More of it gets smuggled over the border than is brought in legally. The way they do it is to drive at night through farms that straddle the border. They drive into the farm from Kazakhstan and out into Uzbekistan!"

Confronted by severe restrictions, everyone used ingenuity to survive.

Later that afternoon, we met Usman's uncle, a small man who sold nuts in a small, neighborhood bazaar. He was one of Usman's favorite uncles who had gone to Moscow for a few years of university education. But now he was

At a Kokand market a woman vendor of men's hats poses humorously for the camera by putting a hat on top of her scarf. Beside her a woman takes a *kurt* ball of hardened goat's milk out of a bag.

stuck in this last-ditch job. Beside him, stretching in each direction were nut-sellers just like him, each trying to get a small piece of the market. When nuts were ripe in the fall, he made about $5.00 a day, but ordinarily he made about $.50 a day.

Afterwards, we asked Usman why his uncle did not go to Tashkent to try to find work. "You can't live in Tashkent without government permission," he answered.

"Really?" We were startled.

"Ever since the bombings in 1998, you need proof of residence in Tashkent. So people from the regions can only go for a few days and then they have to leave. I have permission to live in Tashkent because I am a student, but I have to leave on vacations." This policy was the crowning touch in the government's strategy to keep areas outside Tashkent weak, and to keep anti-government ideas out of Tashkent.

As a result of the residence permit system, the Ferghana Valley overflows with under-employed people like Usman's uncle. People of working age make up almost 60% of the population in Uzbekistan. Some of these people work illegally in Tashkent, but unlike most of the world, population is growing denser in small and medium-sized cities like Kokand where poverty is much higher than in Tashkent (Ergashev & Akhmerova, 2010, pp. 23–25).

"My uncle is stuck here," Usman said sadly.

We later visited his home—one of several small houses around a courtyard inhabited by the uncle, his mother (Usman's grandmother), his two brothers, and their families. Ironically, households such as this with a number of working-age males are especially associated with food poverty because of chronic underemployment (Musaev et al, 2010, p. 50). After the grandmother's prayer they served us soup and barbequed kebabs. Then, as we stood in the courtyard admiring the furniture built by Usman's brother, his uncle told us of a riot that had occurred a few months earlier in Kokand. Several thousand traders had marched to the district office complaining about new edicts from the government—every market vendor would need a cash register and would have to deposit profits in government banks everyday. "Licenses to trade would cost $68," he said, "more than a month's wage! When tax investigators confiscated goods from vendors and put them into a storage shack, people had reached their limit. The government said their action was to keep prices down, but the people said it was to drive vendors out of business!"

Usman added, "The mayor said that he would put the new laws on hold in Kokand, but he couldn't take them back. People know that in the Ferghana Valley top officials are from the central government. The lower-down regional officials have no influence anymore."

Usman's aunt called to us. "My sister-in-law makes the best cake! You have to have some! Eat, eat, or I will be angry with you!" Usman's young nephew ambled around the table as if half-drunk with sleepiness, and after one bite of cake fell asleep in his mother's lap. Families and food, I thought, the only salve for a very difficult situation.

FERGHANA VALLEY: RELIGIOUS OPPRESSION

I looked at our daughters fast asleep on the floor. They had a very long day. I urged them, "Go to bed. We'll tell you more tomorrow!" But I stayed up reading through my fieldnotes. I could see that economic deprivation was part of the problem that had caused the Andijan massacre, but also, Karimov had cracked down on religion in the Ferghana Valley.

The next morning Usman walked with us past a small neighborhood mosque near his house in Kokand. "I used to go there to learn to read the Qur'an in Arabic," he said. Like most Uzbeks, Usman is a Sunni Muslim who believes that leaders can emerge from the lines of Prophet Muhammad's capable companions, not only from the Prophet's own family line as Shia Muslims believe. "In the 1980s, things loosened up, so a lot of mosques reopened, and new ones were built. But then around 1995 or 1996 many of them were closed down, and so I had to stop going there. Now only older people can go there to study."

"What happened at that time?" I asked.

"There was some trouble in the Ferghana Valley." I did not ask more. These were not topics to be discussed on the streets of Kokand.

Clint and I had read that an upsurge of interest in Islam began in the cities of the Ferghana Valley starting in the 1960s. Missionaries from Saudi Arabia, backed by oil money, found eager acceptance for their message of a purified Islam that returned to the fundamentals of the Qur'an, known as Wahhabism. Wahhabis are "an orthodox group of Sunnis that is dominant in Saudi Arabia. This term was used in the Soviet era as a shorthand for Islamic fundamentalists" (Melvin, 2000, p. 54). Wahhabism goes beyond Sunni teachings to preach specifically against moral and political weakness in modern life. Wahhabi missionaries ask people to purge their Islamic religious practices of impure folk beliefs that have arisen historically.

The Soviet war in Afghanistan in the 1980s ironically resulted in the emergence of another Islamic group in the Ferghana Valley—the Islamic Movement of Uzbekistan. One of its founders, Juma Namangani, fought in the Soviet army and was impressed by the fervor of Islamic fighters in Afghanistan. After Independence, Namangani and a friend led protests against Karimov's refusal to grant a permit for construction of a mosque in his home city of Namangan in the Ferghana Valley. Later they took control putting the city under Islamic law (Daly, 2005). At first Karimov tolerated this insurgence, but in 1992 he took back the city and outlawed Namangani's organization. Namangani and his friend set up bases in Tajikistan, fought in the war there, and established links with al-Qaeda and the Taliban, while at the same time recruiting new followers from the Ferghana Valley. Karimov blames them for the 1999 bombings in Tashkent. Namangani later was killed fighting alongside the Taliban in Afghanistan.

In the late 1990s, an Islamic sect that originated in Palestine, called Hizb Ut-Tahrir, emerged in Uzbekistan, and by the 2000s, the majority of its followers were Uzbek. This sect teaches that all Islamic countries should live in an Islamic way and educate believers so that they will want Islamic leaders. The sect claims to be non-violent, and the United States government has not found them guilty of sponsoring terrorism. Yet members of this group received heavy prison sentences in 1999 and 2000: an average of 50 a month (Global Security, accessed 2010) and in the 2000s Karimov has used their name Hizb Ut-Tahrir as a general label for Uzbek political dissidents.

UZBEK FORM OF ISLAM: POSITIVE APPROACHES

All of these movements, some militant, some peaceful, were threatening to Karimov. He felt this way even though 90% of Uzbeks are Sunni Muslims, and he himself went on the sacred pilgrimage (*hajj*) to Mecca soon after taking office. He wanted to develop "a distinctly Uzbek form of Islam" that would shore up his national ideology against broader Islamic movements. Establishing an Islamic Studies Center to teach Uzbekified Islam, Karimov built an edifice against purist forms of Islam that might link Uzbeks with other nations, promote rule by Islamic law, and give a base for resistance against his rule (Melvin, 2000, p. 53; Yalcin, 2002, p. 98).

The positive side of Karimov's campaign for an Uzbek form of Islam is its encouragement for the Uzbek custom of worshipping at the tombs of local saints

Women walking around a saint's tomb praying and touching each corner as they go.

A young woman passing under the sacred log that was the saint's walking stick as men to her left pick parts of the bark to take home.

(*awliya*), a practice that Islamic purists abhor as idolatry. Performing rituals for family ancestors so that they will bring good fortune, or at least not hurt the living, is another example of Uzbek Islam.

We found our best example of saint worship when visiting the grave of a popular Sufi saint, Bahauddin Naqshband who lived in the 1300s in Bukhara. Sufi is the mystical side of Islam that searches for direct connection with the divine presence through meditation and dance. Islamic purists believe it is suspect.

The refurbished saint's tomb and attached mosque were beautiful and crowded with people on a holiday. Women walked around the brightly tiled tomb with hands together, wiping them over their faces in prayer at each corner. Young men and women crouched low to the ground as they crept under a dead mulberry tree that reportedly was the saint's walking stick. Some picked off bits of the bark to take home as holy relics. At the back of the property, young and old lined up at a spring to drink its sacred water and capture some in old soda bottles to take home.

As we travelled throughout Uzbekistan, we saw similar saints' tombs refurbished by government money. The popularity of these tombs with young and old attests not only to the success of Karimov's campaign for an Uzbek form of Islam, but even more to the cultural strength of this practice. People's continued attraction to the worship of saints shows that purist forms of Islam will not easily take root among the Uzbek population (Zanca, 2004).

UZBEK FORM OF ISLAM: NEGATIVE APPROACHES

A negative side of the campaign for Uzbek Islam also thrives. From the mid-1990s, Karimov started to attack religious activists, linking a return to the fundamentals of Islam with political dissent. His campaign for Uzbekified Islam is what closed the mosque where Usman had been studying the Qur'an.

In 1995, Karimov launched a campaign against independent calls for justice originating from Islamic mosques. His target was the chief Islamic priest (*imam*) in Andijan, the city where the protest and killings had just occurred in 2005. At the Tashkent airport, the imam, Abduvali Mirzayev, boarded a plane for Moscow and was never seen again. The government ignored attempts by Andijanis to discover what had happened. Abduvali had preached for truth and justice. He neither criticized nor praised Karimov, but he wanted to organize Islamic education and community life free from the government's control. The government accused him of being a Wahhabi, but his friends deny it. Not long afterward, every imam had to sit for a government test to be certified. This became the basis for the dismissal of the imam of the leading mosque in Tashkent, who spoke out against Abduvali's disappearance. People were angry about losing their popular imams whose sermons sold well on tapes in the bazaars, but they had to remain quiet or else drugs would mysteriously appear in their pockets, and they would be arrested (Whitlock, 2002, p. 202; Melvin, 2000, p. 55). In 2006, Abduvali's son, himself a religious leader who was searching for his father, was arrested and accused of leading the Andijan protest which is the subject of this chapter. In 2007, he was killed in a mysterious car crash in Saudi Arabia along with his son and mother (uznews.net 2007).

Karimov reacted harshly to another bid for social justice in the Ferghana Valley in 1997. A group of Wahhabi Islamic leaders in Namangan spoke out against the government and began offering their own social services. Although Namangan is home to a Nestles factory, it has an incidence of food poverty of 39.7% and an extreme food poverty rate of 12.2% (WFP, 2008, p. 34). The reputation of the Wahhabi group differed according to perspective—some observers said they were seducing people with free breakfasts, whereas others said that they were relieving people's poverty. Elite troops stormed into the city after radicals in the group killed four policemen and displayed their heads in public. Not only did the troops arrest radical activists, but they also rounded up a huge number of Islamic believers who were not Wahhabis and broke up meetings of veiled women. The arrests spread through the entire Ferghana Valley. Families were frantic to protect their young men who might be identified as too religious because they were praying five times a day or wearing a beard. Fearing international Muslim influence, Karimov also brought home 2000 Uzbek students who had been studying in Turkey and threw many in jail (Melvin, 2000, p. 55). These young men who thought they were furthering their goals in life suddenly were deprived of hope for a better life.

The question to keep in mind is whether the so-called Wahhabi religious activists were mainly expressing political unhappiness with Karimov's policies from which Ferghana Valley people suffered, or whether they were really intent on overthrowing Karimov to establish an Islamic state. This question of intent was at the crux of the 2005 Andijan protest and the massacre that followed.

Uzbeks attracted to purist Islam tend to be "disaffected youth who seek to make a great difference in life ... [and to] alter the course of society for the good of all under God's watchful eye" (Zanca, 2004, pp. 104–105). Most of them are interested in asserting a Muslim identity and in pushing for political reform. Only a small minority of these purists want to take over state activities, but the actions of a few in attempting to regulate dress and behavior, or attack shrines regarded as non-Islamic hurts their cause among Uzbeks who historically are accustomed to tolerance of various practices within Islam. In general youth are not radicalized. A study of 700 university students in Tashkent found that 70% had learned about religion from their parents and grandparents, not from peers or religious specialists (Zanca, 2004, p. 105).

Uzbek people themselves feel confused. They do not want to end up with a strict Islamic government as in Iran or in Taliban-controlled areas of Afghanistan. Yet in the Ferghana Valley, people recognize injustice when they witness indiscriminate arrests of young men in their own neighborhoods.

Karimov links religious practice of any depth, especially in young men, with political dissidence. Thus, protests demanding a more democratic society have become inextricably confused with movements to replace the secular government with a fundamentalist Islamic government. Even now young men draw

A young religious leader prays with a crowd of people near the sacred water at a saint's tomb in Bukhara.

suspicion to themselves with signs of religiosity—if they let their beards grow, frequent the mosque, wear white skullcaps, or even are too serious about Islamic food taboos. Various young men I had met came to mind as possible targets. In one case, the son of a poor woman in a Tashkent neighborhood prayed five times a day and strictly observed the restriction on eating pork, even refusing to eat sausage, though many Uzbeks did. His mother was proud of him, yet a bit worried as well. In another case, an undergraduate male student faithfully carried his prayer rug with him wherever he went and prided himself on drinking no alcohol for the last year. Even when we were eating at a café, he disappeared into a small room to wash and pray at the correct time.

Surveillance is particularly strong in the Ferghana Valley. Shahnoza's male friend had applied to the government to travel to Mecca on the *hajj*—the ultimate Islamic journey to Islam's birthplace. All good Muslims should undertake this journey at least once in their lifetime if it is financially possible. The government denied him a visa. Life in Uzbekistan seemed stable, and yet it was a bit like walking across a minefield.

Although young women attract less government attention than men, they too take political risks if they cover all their hair tightly, and especially if they cover their faces. After the Tashkent bombings in the late 1990s, the government proclaimed that girls attending university classes could not wear headscarves covering their hair and shoulders (*hijab*). A few resisted and got away with it. Nonetheless, the covering of hair and shoulders is increasing rather than decreasing among

Young Uzbek women with various degrees of head covering.

younger women. The reasons point to both religion and fashion. At a neighborhood party in Tashkent we met a young woman, a serious Muslim, who wore a long black scarf over her hair and shoulders. She sat arm in arm with a friend who did not cover her head. Later the mother of the girl wearing the scarf threw up her hands as she told me that she did not wear a headscarf, and her daughter did. Her expression showed both admiration and puzzlement.

More popular than wearing black among younger women is the fashion in the larger Muslim world of wearing outfits of matching blouses, slacks, and headscarves in beautiful patterns and colors. Uzbek women travel to Turkey and bring back these outfits to sell in the market. Uzbek leaders tolerate such dress, and girls feel that it gives them an attractive and virtuous appearance in their neighborhoods where popular Islamic ideas often prohibit girls from flirting outright. Some girls are sincerely interested in modern Islamic movements that make religious practice more available to them. In several instances, young women showed me small copies of the Qur'an, written in Russian or Uzbek, rather than Arabic, that they carried surreptitiously in their purses.

Muslim women's head covering is a focus of policy throughout the world in the 2000s. Muslim countries themselves vary greatly in how they regard this practice. Since Turkey's modernization in the 1920s and 1930s, the secular Turkish government has not permitted women to cover their heads in public schools and offices. However, some women, including the president's wife now wear a scarf, claiming to be exercising their religious rights. In Iran, the government requires that coverings hide the head, wrists, and ankles. Women who push the envelope, which many city women do, get fined.

The head coverings of Muslims living in Western countries sometimes become an issue. The United States allows any head covering on the basis of individual religious freedom, but France forbids religious dress such as Islamic headscarves or *hijab* in schools because it implies inequality between men and women, and because religion and state are supposed to stay strictly separate. Ironically, when young women who wore no head coverings in Uzbekistan move to the United States and Canada, they sometimes decide to adopt headscarves or *hijab* as a mark of their Islamic beliefs and their membership in the Islamic community. The point is that veiling can occur for all kinds of reasons—not only deep-felt religious modesty, but also as an expression of identity, political resistance to Westernization, fashion among peers, or result of male pressure.

AN OFFICIAL NEIGHBORHOOD MOSQUE
IN KOKAND

Usman, Clint, and I walked farther through the dusty streets of Kokand on this early spring day as the sun was shining brightly through new green leaves. White and pink blossoms bedecked an almond tree in front of a neighborhood mosque that was still open for worshippers. Since 1997, mosques like this one with more than 100 devotees had to be officially registered (Melvin, 2000).

Usman introduced us to the imam as we stood in the dirt courtyard. He was a small, clean-shaven man about 40 years of age, wearing a suit and black hat with white embroidery like most men in the city. He spoke with no special emotion but wanted to tell us the dramatic story of his neighborhood mosque. "During the Soviet era, there was a hole in the ground near this tree in the courtyard, and people would hide there when the Communist Party members came to check the mosque," he said, and then gestured towards a windowed office. "Later the Soviets turned those buildings into a café—anything to get minds off of Islam. Of course they didn't really succeed. People would meet in their homes." Communists destroyed twenty thousand mosques in the late 1920s, turning them into hospitals or storage sheds (Yalcin, 2002, p. 98).

The men took off their shoes to go into the carpeted area where they would kneel in prayer on Fridays and listen to the imam. I hesitated. "Is it okay if a woman comes in?" I asked. "Yes, yes. Women can come in, but they just don't usually." I refrained from commenting. Women I knew stated it differently; they did not feel welcome because of social norms even if there was no official ban on their presence. He went on with his political story.

"In the 1980s, the Soviets allowed revival of religion, and we refitted this mosque." At the front, a small set of stairs led up to a wooden lectern for Friday sermons.

"Now so many men come on Fridays [for the main prayers of the week] that we are building a new section. We grew the trees for its construction because there aren't many trees anymore." Most trees were cut for firewood and expansion of cotton fields.

Adjacent to the mosque was a concrete area as big as the carpeted room, but with no walls and a roof held up by handsome, varnished wooden posts. I imagined the men standing shoulder to shoulder, hands together in prayer, as I had seen them in Tashkent.

As we left, Usman added more current political history that the imam had omitted from his story. Official government certification was necessary for the mosque to exist and to expand. The priest had to have government certification to be an imam and his weekly sermons required government approval to make sure he was not inciting people against the government, but rather praising Karimov's policies. Karimov regarded Friday noon services as risky times when many men gathered together and bared their souls, especially in times of crisis. Although the constitution guarantees religious freedom, and mosques increased in number from 80 to 5000 in the 1990s (Melvin, 2000, p. 53), the government circumscribes religious freedom with state power.

A CLOSED MOSQUE-MADRASSA IN KOKAND

Across the city, the Djami Mosque was like stepping into another world. We went from the din of traffic on the busy streets to utter silence merely by walking through a huge brick gate with Arabic from the Qur'an engraved in blue tile above the entrance. The shaded courtyard was as big as a football field, and

The inner courtyard of the deserted Djami mosque.

in the middle stood a brick minaret about 70 feet high. From here, calls to prayer used to echo—from the early 1800s when it was built until the 1920s when they ceased under communism, and then again in the 1980s and the early years after Independence. In the late 1990s, Karimov banned the five daily calls to prayer that punctuated life in most Islamic cities. By that time, however, Karimov's government had already closed this mosque as part of its crackdown on Islam in the Ferghana Valley.

Now no one but us walked through the forest of "stone trees"—98 wooden posts made of elms brought all the way from India to hold up a geometrically carved ceiling on one side of the courtyard. On the other side we peeked into narrow rooms where students from outside Kokand had lived while they studied at the mosque. You could see where a fire had burned to warm the room and a loft above where they slept.

It was hard to imagine this as a bustling school, but later Usman showed us another mosque—full of the life that once inhabited the Djami Mosque. The Narbutabey Madrassa was one of the few functioning religious schools for boys in Uzbekistan. The courtyard hummed with young voices as elementary-age boys kneeled at little wooden stands holding Qur'ans and recited their lessons. Usman escorted us inside. We stood there for a few minutes and then we left. The mosque was closely watched by government security, and we did not want our visit to bring unwanted attention.

ANDIJAN: AMERICANS BECOME SUSPECT

Back in Tashkent, four months after our trip to the Ferghana Valley, our daughters awoke slowly, still jet lagged. I went off to the Institute, while Clint took them to the museum devoted to Karimov, a visit that could not help but be colored by Karimov's recent military moves in Andijan. I was to meet them later in front of a market. I waited for 30 minutes. Finally they walked up with excited faces. "We were walking down into the Metro, and a policeman took Dad off down a hall!"

"They kept asking, 'Narco, narco?'" Clint said, "and made me take everything out of my pockets and put it on a table. They asked where I had been recently, and I said just Tashkent. They just yelled at me for about five minutes and then let me go." He made light of it, covering any fear.

Soon after, Clint and Laura attended a town meeting of people connected with the American embassy. The Web was abuzz with threats to foreigners, and the American government advised non-essential personnel to leave. Was this Web noise originating from the threat of insurgents or from government officials trying to get rid of foreigners? No one really knew.

The city was abuzz with rumors about what had happened in Andijan and everyone had an opinion. A taxi driver was careful at first but could not hold back his anger. "People's frustration is boiling over! It's all about power. Just like the streets here in Tashkent that he changed into parks." We had heard that this policy was intended to make the route to government buildings difficult in case of attack, but it complicated life for taxi drivers. A Russian woman worried about the fundamentalists and the influence from neighboring Kyrgystan and its recent revolution. A bank manager was angry that money was scarce now because the government was finally paying salaries and pensions in Andijan, and there was not enough left over in Tashkent.

ANDIJAN: THE INSIDE SCOOP

The next Sunday afternoon, Laura and I went out to meet a friend named Nargiza, her husband and 18-month-old daughter from Andijan. We sat in a rarely frequented snack bar next to a broad square in front of the Tashkent circus building. It was a fitting place to meet, I thought, when the government was trying to keep people in Tashkent well fed and happy.

Nargiza's daughter did not want to sit on her mother's lap and talk; she toddled off across the plaza, and her mother ran after her. It turned out that Nargiza's husband had a story to tell us that he obviously wanted people from abroad to hear.

"It's hard to digest what has happened," he said, his voice catching. "I drove with my friend the other day to a conference in Samarkand, and in the car, he told me what happened. He was there."

We all knew what he was talking about—the Andijan massacre.

"There were 4000 to 5000 people in the square that morning. Some came because they wanted policy to change. People don't have money, jobs, and food. Others came just because they were curious—grandmas and grandpas, mothers and children. The rumor was that Karimov himself might come to talk to them. The tanks came in and surrounded them on three sides. Perhaps people thought the tanks were for protection. Some negotiating between people holding hostages and the military was going on, but it failed. The military started taking sniper shots into the crowd, but for some reason people still thought it was okay and stayed. Finally they opened up fire. They shot so many people. They just kept shooting with big bullets." He held up his hand, his thumb and forefinger two or three inches apart to illustrate the size. "They killed so many people— women and babies, too." He stared at us over his Coke, horror in his eyes.

"Part of the crowd started up a street out of the square towards a big theater. The soldiers fired at the marchers from the sides and from the roofs above them. Hostages walked in front of the marchers and the soldiers even killed them. People ran into doorways to get away, and soldiers followed them in and shot them. My friend went to an apartment of a friend, and he was so lucky. They didn't find him there. They followed one man into his neighborhood and questioned his father about where he was hiding. When the father said he didn't know, they killed him. Later they found the son and killed him too."

"My friend was watching from the windows and later he saw things. He saw the police get out of their tanks and find people hiding under dead bodies and shoot them. He thought 1500 or 2000 people had been killed. During the night, trucks came in, and all night the soldiers were packing up bodies. Other people saw them burying bodies in mass graves in parks around the city. They marked some graves of the men they say were terrorists. History will tell the story."

"Would the soldiers do this?"

"These weren't regular soldiers. They were in the division controlled by the Security Forces, probably trained by the Americans at their base! Some say the soldiers were drunk. Otherwise I don't think they would have done it."

RUMBLINGS AND SOCCER IN TASHKENT

Later that week, we all went to a soccer game—Uzbekistan against South Korea. My daughters had both played soccer, but we were among the few women in an ocean of black-jacketed Uzbek men filling the big stadium. Above and below the seats stood rings of Uzbek soldiers, watching for any trouble. Uzbekistan lost as South Korea scored a winning goal at the last minute. The crowd was tense and unhappy as it exited the stadium and streamed down the broad expanse of Navoi Street in the dark.

As we walked, stones hit a police truck parked along the street. The crowd started to run, and policemen lining the streets shouted and waved to people to walk calmly. "Don't run, just walk fast," Clint said. We were more nervous now than we had been on the day of the Andijan massacre.

We kept walking and heard the sound of more rocks bouncing off of vehicles, but the crowd and the policemen remained calm. Karimov did not want trouble in Tashkent.

We turned off into the alley running up to our apartment complex, and an older Uzbek woman asked us who won. "South Korea," we told her in dejected tones, "but Uzbekistan played hard." Hearing our accents, she asked if we were from Poland. "No, the United States."

"Have you tried this restaurant?" she asked, referring to a cafeteria on the corner of the alley and the big street. "It has wonderful Uzbek food."

Her spontaneous remark was a fitting close to our stay that would soon come to an end. Struggling between newly found independence and an authoritarian government, she represented Uzbeks who delight in their nation and want to share their culture with the world. Despite harsh political tactics, or perhaps because of them, Uzbeks focus on points of pride, such as the national cuisine. They can enjoy it and share it proudly even in times of crisis.

SUMMARY

The protest in Andijan was a result of repression and resistance on many levels—economic, political, and religious. Lack of food security and of food sovereignty over agricultural land contributed directly to the problems that led up to the Andijan revolt and massacre. In 2007, the Ferghana Valley, including Andijan, experienced protests once again because the price of bread had recently risen 50 to 100%, and the price of flour from Kazakhstan had doubled. The price of one kilogram of meat was up from $3.75 to $6.00. The protests were small this time and ended in a whimper (IRIN, 2007). People had learned that they had no power to express their socioeconomic grievances.

Other political reasons for the Andijan protest are less clear. Was this a militant religious group leading the charge, or citizens brought to the boiling point over intolerable socioeconomic conditions? Perhaps both. Political repression and economic hardship motivated citizens and provided fodder to radical Muslims (Ozbek, 2007).

The businessmen accused of being religious radicals, 23 of them altogether, were certainly guilty of going beyond tight government restrictions on economic activity (Gomart, 2003). They were devout Muslims, but whether they were connected with a radical religious group is unclear. Many of their families had suffered persecution after the 1999 Tashkent bombings, and as a result they had to depend on each other for loans rather than on official banks. Karimov liked neither their actions outside of the state's financial web nor their competition against state monopolies. What is more, they earned the loyalty of thousands of workers by paying them more than government-mandated wages and giving them health benefits (Rotar, 2005). As community leaders following the Muslim call to community charity, they gave money to hospitals, orphanages, and schools. In a city like Andijan where many people are underemployed and food insecure, their aid gained them popularity. They also had good connections with the regional leader of Andijan, who perhaps became too powerful for Karimov's tastes.

The Uzbek government was at fault for shooting innocent civilians. Certainly the military killed more people than the 187 officially claimed by the Uzbek government. Exactly how many is unclear. One doctor reported that he saw 500 dead bodies at a school. Human Rights Watch reported 700 dead, while a Security Service defector later reported 1500 (Human Rights Watch, 2005).

Local insurgents also contributed to provoking the violence. An organized group of men, approximately 50 in number, had freed the 23 businessmen from prison, commandeered military vehicles and machine guns, killed four guards, and took local government officials as hostages, using them as shields. Local scholars think that these men may have been Akramists, followers of the local activist, Akram Yuldashev, who preached a return to Islamic fundamentalism. One of the group's demands to the government was to release Akram Yuldashev from prison. A refugee from this group reported later, however, that they had no desire to establish Islamic rule in Uzbekistan; they only wanted justice. Neither, he said, did they anticipate that most of the hostages would be killed by Uzbek troops (Daly, 2005, p.5).

INTERNATIONAL REACTIONS

Karimov claims that he did not order the shooting. He lives in an age when nations are supposed to find more subtle ways to control their populations than by the spectacle of massacre. He would rather have people internalize his volumes of ideological writings, and become distracted by soccer, food, and weddings.

The reactions of other countries reflect Uzbekistan's precarious position in the world community, and the gamble Karimov took in waging an attack on his own citizens. Karimov received support from Russia, China, and Egypt. These countries were the exceptions, finding common ground with Karimov in their fear of Islamic terrorists, and not wanting to ruin their chances to procure Uzbek natural gas. In contrast the European Union, particularly Britain, criticized Karimov's violation of human rights, demanded an international inquiry, and applied economic sanctions. Karimov never allowed such an independent inquiry, and instead sent neighborhood leaders door to door in Andijan to tell residents not to speak to journalists or foreigners (Freedom House 2007).

America's reaction was conflicted. Only a few years before, the United States had joined forces with Uzbekistan in the 'war on terror.' At first the official response from Washington was muted. In 2002, George W. Bush had struck a deal with Uzbekistan. In exchange for rent and aid, the Americans could use the Karshi-Khanabad military base in southern Uzbekistan. It was located only 144 kilometers from Afghanistan, ideal for deployment, intelligence, reconnaissance, and logistics (Freedom House 2007). In return, the unspoken agreement was that Americans would mute their criticism of Karimov's human rights record. When the Andijan massacre occurred, the base housed 1800 American soldiers and the United States paid $15 million yearly for its use, while $51 million more went to Uzbekistan for aid, including law enforcement. Karimov wanted money and Bush wanted access to Uzbek facilities (Daly 2007:8).

The war on terror already had compromised the United States' historical leadership on human rights. As for Uzbekistan, it had become a pawn in American political maneuvering. Meanwhile, Russia was only too ready to resume its political influence in the region.

Shortly after the Andijan massacre, several United States senators went to Uzbekistan on a self-appointed fact-finding mission (Daly, 2005, p. 9). Ultimately, the United States feared the spread of violence and recommended American personnel such as Peace Corps volunteers leave Uzbekistan. The United States then criticized Karimov for human rights abuses, and two months after the Andijan massacre, Uzbekistan gave the United States six months to move out of its rented military base (Freedom House, 2007). As of 2010, the United States has no military base in Uzbekistan.

THE AFTERMATH

Inside Uzbekistan, political, religious, and economic repression has continued. Karimov has closed down more than 300 non-governmental organizations, particularly those concerned with human rights and supported by international funds. The government blocks international news Websites. The police have arrested journalists and artists, and those who are still free, censor themselves or leave the country (Zilberman, 2010; Freedom House, 2007).

State control over preaching and all religious gatherings has widened. Pentecostals, Baptists and Jehovah Witnesses active in Uzbekistan have received fines and prison terms. Muslims continue to face harassment in the name of fighting terrorism, as local neighborhood officials scrutinize religious activities in Andijan and elsewhere. The National Security Service also spies on religious leaders and their communities. No new Islamic organization, no matter what its stance, can grow, and imams must condemn any Muslims who practice their faith outside of government control (Corley, 2007). Just at the time when Muslims everywhere struggle to deal with a changing world, Islam in Uzbekistan cannot move.

Furthermore, in the Ferghana Valley and elsewhere, the government discourages individuals from worshipping. Neighborhood leaders tell young men that they do not "need" to go to mosque on Fridays to worship. Without completely banning their presence, the government also discourages women from attending prayers at the mosque.

Karimov has his eye particularly on children. "Children belong to the president not to the religious leaders," the authorities tell imams (Bayram, 2009). They say that children should not come to night prayers during the month of Islamic fasting known as Ramadan, particularly in the Ferghana Valley. As a normal practice they do not allow children in the mosque during school time, and in addition police instruct imams during weekly meetings to keep children out of the mosques, even after school.

CONCLUSION

The Andijan massacre is one particularly violent event in a string of injustices. It represents a culmination of economic deprivation, politico-religious repression, and a search for justice linked with religious seeking and activism. Such events occur all over Uzbekistan, but nowhere more than in the Ferghana Valley. The region is proud of its history and its food, but it is also aware that Karimov keeps them poor and weak—cotton pickers for the national economy.

The situation in Uzbekistan is similar to that in many countries fallen victim to inequalities among nations in the nineteenth and twentieth centuries. Like all so-called "less-developed" countries, Uzbekistan has been and continues to be a reservoir of agricultural goods and natural resources for the industrialized world. The lack of popular control over land use, and thus food, in these countries is one of their root problems. Much of this book has put the blame on Karimov, and he, like many leaders of poor countries, holds his citizens hostage to enhance his own power and wealth. Yet, the injustices internal to poor countries such as Uzbekistan are also related to a larger pattern of world inequality.

ENDNOTES

1. See the YouTube video by British journalist Monica Whitlock, "Uzbekistan: People Ready for Change."

2. See the YouTube video by the Environmental Justice Foundation entitled "White Gold: The True Cost of Cotton" which describes child labor and environmental degradation in Uzbekistan. The Foundation published a 2005 report by the same name.

3. Traditional women's shoes in this area extended far out in front of the toes into a small squared-off end. One style of contemporary shoes copied this older style.

Chapter 8

Low Income, Food Security, and Food Sovereignty in America

After returning from Uzbekistan to the United States, I marveled at the freedom of speech and movement, the ability to trust banks, and stores full of global goods. But studying food in America also reveals inequalities and lack of control over the food system. Even in this land of plenty, we experience food insecurity and lack of food sovereignty, but it smells and tastes different than in Uzbekistan.

Manipulation of the food system in the United States operates more subtly than in Uzbekistan. Rather than the power of a dictator and his political machine, the market is the main arbiter, full of opportunities and risks, either to make money or to fail, permitting some to buy anything they want while others can afford little. Government and non-profit organizations provide some safety nets, but the market led by large corporations largely determines the way food relates to our everyday lives—what we buy and eat, what our farmers grow and how they grow it, and even what is leftover for emergency food boxes.

HUNGER IN OREGON

My interest in food originated in doing applied anthropology work in Oregon. An applied anthropologist investigates problems and tries to work towards solutions on the ground with local people.

My work in Oregon has focused first on food insecurity and low-income consumers, and second on the development of a local food system that connects with low-income people. These are the themes of this chapter. I also explain the American food system that accounts for the American type of food insecurity and limited food sovereignty at the community level.

In 2000, Oregon was number one in hunger in the United States. Joan Gross, my colleague, and I helped a local task force on hunger to investigate food insecurity in two rural towns: Mountville, located in the coastal mountains 19 miles west of Corvallis; and Fountain, located in the Willamette Valley 9 miles north of Corvallis, the county seat and home of Oregon State University where we teach. We interviewed 79 rural, low-income people about food security, food habits, their use of government food programs, and household expenses. Our goal was to develop a broad picture of food in the full context of their lives.

THE FOOD LIVES OF LOW-INCOME PEOPLE

For contemporary Americans, nutritious food is far down on a list of items such as cars, houses, computers, and sneakers that people feel they must purchase to be like normal, middle-class consumers. We assume that food is cheap, a place in our budget that we can squeeze if necessary. However, in the United States in 2008, 6% of households experienced very low food security, in which their eating patterns were disrupted and diet reduced; 9% of American households experienced low food security, in which households' eating patterns are not disrupted, but they eat a diet based on cheap foods, participate in federal food assistance programs, or receive emergency food from community food pantries (ERS, 2008). In Oregon, 5.5% of the population experienced very low food security, and 12% experienced low food security between 2005 and 2007 (Oregon, 2008).

As in Uzbekistan, rural poverty in America exceeds urban poverty. In 2006, rural poverty stood at 15% while urban poverty was 12% (Reuters, 2007). Rural people face particular problems as rural towns lose farms, businesses, and people. They lose neighbors as only 21% of Americans still live in rural areas, down from 36% in 1953 (Tarmann, 2003). Rural towns appear to offer cheaper housing, bounty of the land, and more community. Yet, because they are distant from cities, buying food and connecting with public services is difficult, and access to land and community is not guaranteed.

Two examples of low-income rural people interviewed in our study help to bring the problems of food insecurity in America alive. On the face of it, both said they had enough food, but as the details of their lives emerged, we began to see that their food security hung on slender threads and that they rated low in food security. Susan, a single mother with children, represents the kind of household that is more likely to be at risk, as 37% of households with children headed by a single mother are food insecure (ERS, 2008).

SUSAN: A SINGLE MOTHER IN MOUNTVILLE

Susan lives in a small house in Mountville that she and her husband converted from a shack. She is now divorced and in her mid-40s, a single mother of six children, ranging from 15 to 23 years of age. So far all of the older children have graduated from high school, and she herself has a GED.

Although Susan says "hi" to everyone, she depends mainly on her children and herself, and not on neighbors or friends. She feels that after twenty years in this rural community, she is still treated as a newcomer. "I got used to not having friends, because people would move in and move away. And the people that were already here will not let you in."

Susan and her children depend instead on government assistance.[1] Without food stamps, she is food insecure, but with food stamps she can buy enough food for all of her children. In 2006, with four children qualifying as minors, she received $700 per month in food stamps. Only she and one younger son had health insurance coverage under the Oregon Health Plan targeting low-income people. Her two older sons had just returned from Arizona putting more pressure on her food budget, and prompting her to re-join the local gleaning group, a volunteer organization that 'gleans' most of their food from leftovers at grocery stores and a local emergency food center connected with the Oregon Food Bank. Volunteers collect and divide the food and members volunteer four hours per week per family. People bump heads in the process. Susan had dropped out of the gleaners group in the past following accusations that she did not help enough with the work. She had only recently rejoined in order to provide her children with a "more balanced diet," but she had complaints. "It's a lot of work ... You have to take as much food as they put in your box whether you need it or not, and then you have too much of whatever. Then you get in trouble from the neighbors for putting it in the compost pile."

Susan's annual income exceeds $10,000 only if combined with her TANF (Temporary Assistance for Needy Families) and proceeds from a small plant business. To qualify for TANF, she must work 20 hours a week at the library as part of a welfare-to-work program. Susan spoke of it sarcastically as "slave labor." Susan sells plants and seeds locally in front of her house and over the Web. She set up a computer with Internet access in 2004, to sell her products online; by 2006, the computer was broken. She did not have the money to fix it and was in debt for office supplies.

Were Susan's children helping? Susan's daughter cared for an elderly person in town, and contributed some of her earnings to the family. Her two older sons, who had just returned home, were looking for jobs. They had several strikes against them in addition to the lack of jobs in this rural town—they had no computer, no cell phone, and, the ultimate barrier, no car.

Having a car to drive was absolutely necessary to live in this town. Susan's family owned three cars, but when we interviewed her in 2006, none of them was working. That day her son was out hunting for car parts. Furthermore, it was impossible to keep up on car insurance. She chose to let that go and hoped that she would not get caught for violating state law. Sometimes she and her children could catch a ride with a neighbor, or hitchhike into town. In short, job hunting was difficult and food shopping was expensive and time-consuming.

Mountville has a rural grocery store, an amenity many rural towns have lost. But citizens felt that the food sold there was expensive and sometimes out of date. Choice was limited and fresh vegetables few. Furthermore, the store did not take food stamps. In 2004, Susan went to the town of Corvallis once a week to shop. By 2006, she was only going once a month and spending more of her food dollars at the local store.

Rural living has its advantages, however. In the summer, Susan grows vegetables such as tomatoes, squash, and onions in the adjacent lot that neighbors let her use. She loves the taste of the fresh food and shares what she cannot use. Her sons helped by hunting elk and gathering wild mushrooms in the fall and spring.

On a typical day, family members each prepare their own breakfast of cereal or potatoes, and their own lunch of sandwiches and canned soup. Susan makes salads for dinner, or sometimes mashed potatoes, gravy, and a vegetable. She rarely cooks beef, not only because it is expensive, but also because her teeth are bad, and it is hard to chew. She quotes her high school age son as saying, "You know what, Mom? I don't even miss beef."

Although Susan seemed to have enough food for her and her children, the underpinnings of her food security were fragile and the way towards more stability was not clear. She summed it up: "As long as I do my slave labor and get food stamps, I have enough to eat."

KEITH: WORKING POOR IN FOUNTAIN

Keith is a 38-year-old man who rents half of a duplex with his 33-year-old wife Sarah in Fountain. They had moved to Fountain in 2004, so that he could begin college while she started her nursing career. Because she worked nights, he took most of the responsibility for feeding their two children: a girl ten years of age and a boy age eight. Keith's wife's income is right around $30,000. They are part of the so-called working poor who have a hard time qualifying for food stamps or the free school lunch program (Berg, 2008). Households of working poor people with low food security are proportionately higher in Oregon than in other states (Edwards et al, 2007).

Keith and his family appeared to be food secure. "We always worry, but I don't necessarily worry about starving I guess." The food they bought did not run out, he insisted, except for only a "few times" during the last year. Yet he added, "A lot of times I will do my mom's old trick. I will eat a little bit, and then I will make sure everybody eats, and if there is anything left over, I will eat it."

Keith thinks that their problem is lack of nutrition. Because his wife sleeps during the day, he has to make the children's meals. "We don't eat a whole lot of balanced meals ... I don't like nasty food, but I don't care so much about quality. I am more concerned about getting enough." He blamed himself. He grew up poor, sometimes stealing tomatoes from fields when there was nothing else to eat. Mentioning ramen and macaroni and cheese, he said, "You get so programmed" relying on low-cost foods. In addition, he had never really learned how to cook. "If I went in the kitchen my mom said, 'Get out, I don't want you to bother me.'"

Keith gets up earlier than the children to pack lunches with a sandwich, little pudding snacks or Jell-o, chips or pretzels, and Capri Sun drinks. Breakfast consists of cereal or frozen waffles as he rushes to get the children and himself out the door. They all return home around 3:30 in the afternoon, and he tries to have dinner ready by 6:00 that evening. "A lot of times I ... pull things out of the freezer, and I'll make it that night, or other times I'll just say, 'What do you guys want,' and we'll have something like macaroni and cheese because we don't feel like making anything. I don't feel like preparing a three-hour meal, you know."

Most of all, he thought that time and fatigue caused his problems in preparing food. He always had "his head in a book" trying to do well in his classes at the community college, but it turned out that he had an underlying problem. Just recently he found that he has type II diabetes. "It makes a lot of sense, because a lot of times I would have days when I didn't feel like doing nothing for no apparent reason ... I probably did it to myself because I was not the most nutritious person ... I didn't know."

Keith was trying to change his diet, but it was hard. He claims that he likes vegetables and meat, but must be careful financially. "We'll get a lot of meat once a month ... and in theory it lasts a month." However, old habits die hard. "There's a reason why stuff tastes good. It's sweet. If it wasn't like that people wouldn't eat it."

The price of Keith's medications for diabetes as well as for his son's medicine for hyperactivity complicated their ability to be fully food secure. His wife's job offered health insurance at a cost of $600 a month for the family, but they figured it would save money just to pay out of pocket. The trade-off is that Keith takes only one of the medications that his doctor prescribes. Faced with two alternatives, they chose the cheaper medication for their son, which has the side effect of suppressing his appetite. This medication creates dramas around food, because their son loves starchy foods and hates meat. "I don't like it, but you're faced with either a kid not eating or you catering to him."

The family's food security was also threatened by debt. They could only afford one car, a "gas guzzler" with lots of room, and they still owed money on it. "The gas is killing us." Keith had to drive 80 miles up and back to Portland twice every other weekend to transport his son from his first marriage for parental visits; and he had to pay child support. Keith and Sarah were also in debt for doctor's bills, moving expenses, and past utility bills. They had chosen to live in an older duplex in the country for its low deposit and cheaper rent, but worried about paying for its expensive electric heat.

When we asked about clothes and school supplies, Keith said, "I probably shouldn't be telling you guys this, but we had some credit cards so we put a little bit of the expense on them." His wife did not want to use the credit cards, but he felt good that "we didn't have to be so skimpy when we bought them their clothes ... especially our girl ... she needs that sort of thing ... You want your kids to be happy. You want them to wear good clothes."

Keith and his wife were trying hard to become middle-class people who could engage in consumption as his image of regular Americans required, and he was self-conscious when his family seemed different. He feared the car repair place would think he was not "normal" because he absolutely could not do without his one car. He felt that he "got funny looks" from other people when a few years earlier they had stopped sending their preschool children to daycare. He disclosed this information near the end of the interview when he also admitted that he was the children's stepfather.

Keith and his family have the quantity of food they need, but are not food secure. They are part of a large group of working poor that does not receive adequate nutrition, suffers from mounting medical bills, and cannot afford health insurance. They cut corners by purchasing and eating cheap, processed food, which only makes their situation worse in the long run.

THE MEANING OF THESE LIVES
ON A BROADER SCALE

Keith and Susan's lives illustrate the nature of food insecurity in America (Gross and Rosenberger, 2004; Gross and Rosenberger, 2009). If food security means access not only to enough food, but also to nutritious and culturally appropriate food, then by definition, Americans live in a conundrum because many of the foods that they are culturally drawn to by habit and by advertising are high in carbohydrates (starches and sugars), animal fats, and salt.

In our study we asked people to name their favorite foods; four-fifths of adults cited high carbohydrate foods such as pasta, macaroni and cheese, tacos, pizza, rice, potatoes, bread, pastries, chips, and soda. Meat was the second favorite, mentioned by about half, and vegetables the third, just behind meat. However, people talked of eating "a lot of meatless meals" or "a week of just beans." They mentioned price as the primary barrier to buying meat, fresh fruits and vegetables, and secondarily the inability to get to the store often due to work schedules and distance in rural communities (Rosenberger et al, 2006).

Several adults we interviewed identified themselves as ethnic minorities. One Mexican family was able to acquire Mexican cooking ingredients from local Mexican grocery stores and by mail directly from Mexico. A native woman from Alaska loved walrus fat, but she could acquire it only by visiting her relatives in Alaska.

Even if adults prefer nutritious food, their children's preferences push them towards purchasing food high in carbohydrates and fats. According to parents, their children all preferred foods such as macaroni and cheese, pizza, spaghetti, noodles, and peanut butter and jelly sandwiches. A mother of three remarked that she is busy and pizza is cheap. "I don't care for pizza, but we get a heck of a lot of pizza!"

Half of parents said that their children like meat, but often in less healthy dishes. As one mother said, "I want to try healthier recipes that are low fat … [but] my son likes fried chicken—anything with batter."

Keith was not alone in being too tired to make a good meal. Low-income work is often long and tiring, and in the case of the mother above, having only one car meant extra travel to pick up her husband and children after work. She said, "I don't enjoy the make-your-own dinner nights when there's nothing to cook or we are too tired to eat. I just don't eat. The kids are hungry, and they'll eat peanut butter and jelly or cereal."

OBESITY AND DIABETES

Obesity often leading to diabetes typifies the nature of food insecurity in America, as food habits from childhood intersect with the availability of cheap foods loaded with carbohydrates and fats. Even the salt in processed foods exacerbates high blood pressure in people with diabetes more than in non-diabetic people (Feldstein, 2002). A Fountain woman in her sixties reported that her husband was diabetic and had just lost his job. "He used to think macaroni and cheese was the only food. He shouldn't be eating pasta. It's hard though when you are trying to stretch money; you buy pasta instead of meat." She feared that he would lose his legs or go blind.

All diabetic people we interviewed knew that they should cut down on carbohydrates and fats, but it was a constant battle for them to do so. A diabetic Fountain man in his forties talked proudly of counting the grams of fat and carbohydrates on packages and switching to turkey hot dogs. Yet price discounts still led him to buy Hamburger Helper, which is no more than pasta with seasoning.

Obesity and diabetes are debilitating not only to people's bodies, but also to their chances for success. Keith needs steady medication and a good diet in order to have enough energy to succeed at school and care for his children. One very obese woman living in Fountain could not pass a simple physical test necessary to become a medical worker—she could not squat and stand up again.

The food that disadvantaged people receive from food pantries or gleaning groups represents the remains of the industrial food system, full of carbohydrates, fats, and salt. As Susan's words indicate, they are supposed to be grateful for whatever they receive and eat everything. The Food Bank of Oregon, connected with the nation's largest hunger-relief charity now called "Feeding America", survives on leftovers from food corporations and government surpluses of food commodities. If the bank's food supply lacks protein, they try to compensate by adding tuna or peanut butter through private donations. Locally, gleaning groups also pick up out-of-date merchandise from local grocery stores.

A young mother commented on foods she gets in the winter from Gleaners. "You can only eat so many kidney beans!" She laughed and then noted that she also receives frozen vegetables, pizza pockets, individual servings of rice, and broccoli and cheese in a box. "We get donuts, pies, cake, and cases of half-and-half creamers." The food is substantial and some of it healthy, but is often processed, not fresh and heavy with carbohydrates and fats. The volunteer-recipients in Gleaners consider health needs when they divide the food, trying to remember who is dieting or who is diabetic, but recipients still complain. "We get a variety of things. We get chips and cookies, whether we need them or not.

My husband eats lots of desserts…Whatever foods we get from the Gleaners, he eats them at night and watches TV."

Most emergency food resembles what is consumed in the mainstream American diet, containing carbohydrates, fats, and salt in most abundance. The quantity of the food is sufficient, but too much of it is the wrong kind of food.

LIVING IN A RURAL AREA

Some expenses such as rent may be lower in rural areas, but car trips are longer, and most rural communities no longer have nearby grocery stores. The stores that still exist charge more because of low sales volume and because wholesalers are not willing to deliver to them. According to David Proctor at Kansas State University, many store owners do not accept food stamps (now called SNAP, Supplemental Nutrition Assistance Program) because they think local patrons will feel stigmatized. As a result, rural people do most of their grocery shopping in town.

One advantage in gaining access to healthy food is that gardening is more possible in rural areas. Middle-aged and older people in Mountville and Fountain are accustomed to cultivating gardens and preserving food by canning and freezing. They have the knowledge they need to carry out these tasks, as long as they can maintain their bodily strength and have space for a garden. However, we found that younger people usually do not have gardening and food preservation skills. In Mountville one young adult told us, "We were going to plant in the back yard, but Mom, she didn't have enough time to do it … I don't know how to do a garden … I've helped people but never had my own garden." Another young woman said that her husband wants her to learn how to do canning: "This summer my grandmother's going to teach me how."

Hunting and fishing is also popular in rural areas, and in the fall several residents of Mountville reported that their freezers were "completely full with fish and venison." In contrast, one couple, having moved to Mountville hoping to live off the land, found that they were too poor to buy fishing and hunting licenses, and that the grocery store was too expensive.

SOCIAL NETWORKS

Social networks are an important part of food security in the United States, just as they are in Uzbekistan. Susan is a prime example of someone who lacks a social network, as she lives in a community dominated by an in-group mentality based on class and the status of old, pioneer families. She is angry with the school board for not voting to redo the kitchen and provide the federal program with free or low-cost lunches. In her opinion this vote shows the community's do-it-yourself attitude and disdain for people on welfare. Keith also lacks friends, relatives, or church connections.

Results from a short, additional survey of twenty households in Fountain shows that food insecurity was most prevalent among newcomers. Not only do they have moving expenses, but also they lack social networks. Newcomers lack information about local sources of food aid and inexpensive places to shop. They also have no means to exchange rides, meals, or childcare.

Social networks can pull people through times of crisis. Marsha, who came to Mountville thirty years ago as a bride, lost her low-wage job after hospitalization for knee surgery. Friends pitched in to feed her dearly-loved horses. Pets seem like a luxury, yet for Marsha, getting back on her horse was a huge motivation to recover from her operation. A local church built a ramp for her wheelchair. The daughter of her ex-husband drove her to town to buy food and visit the doctor. Later, caught in a spiral of alcohol abuse, she lost her house, but again a distant relative bailed her out by allowing her to move into a hunting shed.

Several low-income people had moved to Fountain in order to be near a sibling or parent, with whom they shared meals. One woman's extended family rescued her and her family; her father sent fish from the coast; her cousin sent elk from the mountains; and her aunt sent commodity foods such as butter and flour that she received regularly as a low-income Native American living on an Indian reservation.[2]

Social networks are also valuable for personal enjoyment and relief of stress. When asked about their favorite meals, almost everyone talked first about meals in the company of people they enjoyed, and only secondly about the food. Keith was an exception. His best meals were those when he had plenty to eat.

CONSUMING TO BE NORMAL AND UNEXPECTED EXPENSES

Another important aspect of food insecurity in the United States is the pressure to consume the goods that low-income people believe give them the appearance of normality among mainstream middle-class Americans. Although we do not like to admit that class differences exist in the United States, we immediately recognize them through personal appearance, speech, and consumer habits. Susan's bad teeth and Keith's grammar, for example, would give them away.

Keith is in competition to "keep up with the Joneses" as he prepares his children's lunches, purchases his daughter's clothes, and pursues a college education in which he already feels "behind." His wife and he hardly see each other, working on opposite shifts to avoid daycare costs. Susan, on the other hand, cannot keep up, and this sets her and her sons even further back because they need cars, computers, and cell phones for business and job searches.

The high expenses of health care and housing in American life also contribute to food insecurity. Keith and his wife are taking a gamble by not carrying health insurance; a hospitalization for either of them could be devastating financially. One mother in Fountain did not heat her bedrooms in winter and was behind on rent in order to pay a collection agency for her daughter's dental bills. Housing expenses often leave low-income people too little money to buy food. Susan's house is paid off, but that keeps her from moving elsewhere because paying for rent or a mortgage would be prohibitively expensive. Another woman was paying more than 50% of her income on mortgage payments in Fountain, while trying to save enough money for gas to visit her husband who had been sent to jail in eastern Oregon.

In light of all these expenses, low-income people in the United States tend to regard food expenses as a place where they can cut corners because our food system has produced such inexpensive food. Inequalities around food security exist in America as surely as in Uzbekistan.

But what about control over food in the United States where people have far more freedom to acquire information and engage in consumption than in Uzbekistan? In the next section, I turn to questions of food sovereignty in relation to the American food system at both national and community levels, particularly in Oregon.

FOOD SOVEREIGNTY AND THE AMERICAN FOOD SYSTEM

The United States is seemingly high in food sovereignty—the control we have over the food we eat. Our self-sufficiency ratio in calories, measured by comparing the per capita daily calorie supply of food from domestically produced food, to the per capita daily calorie supply available overall in the country, is 128% (Nagata, 2008), implying that our domestic food production is greater than the food we have available to consume domestically. Our food corporations export huge quantities of soybeans, corn, wheat, beef, and chicken. We also import a huge diversity of food products from all over the globe.

Let's review the definition of food sovereignty by Via Campesina, as it pertains to control over food from the point of view of people and communities (Family Farm Defenders, 2005). Food sovereignty highlights agriculture and trade as important areas in which people need to have control. "Food is first and foremost a source of nutrition and only secondarily an item of trade," states the Via Campesina declaration. Furthermore, "Food sovereignty entails the sustainable care and use of natural resources, especially land, water, and seeds and livestock breeds." Lastly, food sovereignty guarantees "democratic control" by smallholder farmers and consumers. Such democratic control would give food security at the community level, which can be defined as the ability of a community to cope successfully when facing economic changes that influence parts of its food system (Maxwell, 1996). In short, food sovereignty means that agriculture should be sustainable for the earth and provide nutritious food for people, in a food system over which people and communities have somewhat equal control. Do we have that?

FOOD SOVEREIGNTY AT THE COMMUNITY LEVEL

At the community level, American people do not experience food sovereignty. Rather than communities controlling food, large, transnational, corporations monopolize our food chain—with the help of government policies. This shift from communities to corporations started in the 1930s, and has gained momentum since the 1970s, continuing at a breakneck pace into the twenty-first century. It has resulted from a combination of corporate pressure to increase profits and government encouragement of industrialized agriculture to supply cheap food at home and expand export markets abroad.

"The greater efficiency, specialization, and scale of agriculture and food product manufacture have led to one of the great unspoken secrets about the American food system: overabundance" (Nestle, 2002, p. 13). Soon after World War II, the government made a deal with farmers in the Agricultural Act of 1947. It would guarantee a market and a price for corn, soybeans, and wheat, and promote beef exports, but in return farmers had to increase their production and standardize their quality. The government would even compensate the farmer if the price went down. Some of these products, now called "commodities" and traded on the stock market, left the country as food aid or export crops. This act is the source of the commanding role of the United States in world agricultural markets. Yet the largest portion of food production stayed in the country and provided cheap food for workers during the period of the most rapid economic growth in American history.

OVERABUNDANCE: WANING FARMERS

On the path to a cheap, overabundant food supply, farms grew larger because it was the only way they could survive. Between 1960 and the end of the century, the average size of farms rose by 40% and productivity by 82% (Nestle, 2002, p. 11). However, two-thirds of family farmers lost their land between 1940 and the mid-1980s (Villianatos, 2006, p. 54), and the farm population in the United States shrank from 11.5% in 1953 to 1% in 2000 (Tarmann, 2003).

Farms gave up diverse crops and livestock to concentrate on one or two commodities such as chickens or cows, or a rotation of corn and soybeans. In California, the mono-crop might be nuts, milk, or garlic, but the output is huge in order to satisfy the corporate contract that guarantees their market. Farmers have had to turn to the tools of industrialized agriculture to survive, depending on expensive machinery and high levels of fertilizer and pesticide application. Production costs a lot of money, and without high productivity, farmers cannot even get loans to stay in business.

When labor is needed for non-mechanized farm jobs such as harvesting vegetables or unpleasant jobs such as slaughtering cows, farmers turn to cheap, immigrant labor, usually Mexicans, who are willing to work for a small wage because it is more than they can make at home. Legally, farm workers must be paid at least the federal minimum wage, which was $7.25 per hour in 2009, but an estimated 60% of farm labor consists of illegal Mexican workers who receive less than that amount.[3] Mostly, the government has not enforced the laws. The essential role of illegal immigrant labor is one paradoxical secret behind America's cheap, abundant food.

In the case of crops such as corn or soybeans, farmers receive government subsidies to compensate for dips in price. The larger the farm, the more money it receives. Ironically, the average farm subsidy is $7,501 per annum, whereas the average yearly benefit from food stamps for poor families is only $1,148 (Berg, 2008, p. 149). However, from the farmers' points of view, they struggle even while receiving government subsidies. On average farmers only receive back 20% of the retail cost of the food they grow, the rest going to packaging, labor, advertising and corporate profits; many small farmers do not even make production costs (Nestle, 2002, p. 17).

OVERABUNDANCE: CORPORATE CONTROL

Another effect of a food system based on overabundance is the penetration of corporations throughout the food chain. Food corporations have grown and multiplied to bring this huge flow of food to market in a form that whets American appetites and fattens our bellies.

Agriculture is now vertically integrated from field to shelf. For example, two huge agribusinesses—Archer Midlands Daniel (AMD) and Cargill (the largest privately held corporation in America)—buy one third of all corn grown in America. They buy up corn at cheap prices kept low by government subsidies to farmers. Meanwhile they sell pesticide and fertilizer to farmers to increase the yield of corn, and operate big grain elevators to store the corn. They mill corn in huge quantities in order to make high-fructose corn syrup sold inexpensively as the sweetener for Oreo cookies and Coca-Cola. Their corn also goes into a mush to feed cows in the feedlots owned by Cargill and AMD, who then sell the corn-fattened animals to supply our steak dinners and Burger King Whoppers (Pollan, 2006, p. 63).

One support for these huge food companies is the export market which the American government has encouraged since the 1950s as a destination for surplus food. Cargill and AMD ship out grain exports to other countries such as Mexico. Huge slaughter companies like Tyson buy up chicken from contract farmers cheaply to sell not only in America but also in countries such as Russia and Uzbekistan. Thus, American food comes into poorer countries both in raw and processed forms, and because it is cheaper than domestically-grown food, threatens the livelihoods of farmers in poorer countries. Farmers turn away from growing subsistence crops for food to cash crops for money, but then are at the mercy of international markets. For example, when cheap American corn came into Mexico after the North American Free Trade Agreement started in 1994, farmers give up growing corn and sent family members to work in the United

States! In Uzbekistan, we saw cheap chicken parts from the United States, which Uzbeks called "Bush legs," a name that Russians have used derisively since the early 1990s for imported American poultry. Price competition from Bush legs made it harder for Uzbek poultry farmers to make money. In 2010, Russia banned the import of American chickens ostensibly because American processors bathe slaughtered chickens in chlorine to cleanse them. The Russians were also glad to rid themselves of the humiliation of depending on American food imports and supply their own chickens.

In the United States, corporate control of our food system extends into processing, which makes a difference in the community of Corvallis, Oregon, as we will see. Eleven large firms control food processing in the United States. Four companies that slaughter and pack beef dominate 84% of the market. Only three companies do 55% of the flour milling. (Hendrickson & Heffernan, 2005). These big firms have also influenced government standards for certification so that the standards are easy for them to meet, but make it very difficult for smaller processors to comply.

Corporations have also cornered the seed market, selling to farmers who used to save their own seed and use it the next year. Six companies, led by Monsanto, hold 75% of all United States patents in the seed sector (Sell, 2009, p. 189). Corn seeds sold by Monsanto, for example, are genetically modified to withstand Roundup, the pesticide sold by Monsanto. Farmers can spray Roundup from the air onto corn and weeds alike, killing the weeds but not the corn. The process is convenient and fast, but the seeds are expensive. The astounding thing is that these are terminal seeds—they cannot be used the next year. The farmer has to buy them repeatedly. This requirement is expensive for farmers in the United States, and debilitating for farmers in poor countries (Shiva, 1997).

On the consumer end of the American food system, overabundance of production has fed the expansion of food and beverage companies. For example, the cereal industry has flourished and diversified based on cheap grains, bringing us Cornflakes, Fruit Loops, Kashi Go-Lean, and my favorite mini-innovation for profit, chocolate Cheerios. Kraft General Foods, known for selling Macaroni and Cheese, Oreos and Cheez Whiz, was the largest American food company in 2007, and is the second largest food and beverage company in the world after Nestlé. McDonald's is the highest selling food service chain, twice the size of its nearest competitor in 2007. Everyone's familiarity with Ronald McDonald is proof of the lavish spending by these food companies on advertising to encourage us to buy their ever-burgeoning products.

Large corporations also sell us the food for our tables at home. Mom-and-pop stores have given way to large self-service stores that appeal to consumers because they are cheap, convenient, and clean. In 2006, big supermarkets, led by Walmart, Kroger, and Safeway, controlled about 60% of the retail food market in the United States (Supermarket Consolidation, 2006). Prices are low because these stores buy huge amounts of food. In the case of Walmart, its large volume of purchases can even bring down the price they pay to wholesalers who in turn pressure farmers for lower prices.

In our system of industrialized agriculture, the main motivation is profit achieved through high volume production and ever-growing sales. The final retail product is appealing to the eyes, stomachs, and pocketbooks of American citizens and people around the world. Individuals and communities exercise food sovereignty only by buying or not buying. As Heffernan writes, "The centralized food system was never voted on" (Villianatos, 2006, p. 62).

LOSS OF LOCAL FOOD ECONOMY

A quick overview of the history of the farming area around Corvallis, Oregon, will illustrate the local effects of this historical loss of food sovereignty. In the late 1800s and early 1900s, small farmers grew wheat, hops, beans, livestock, and all sorts of vegetables and fruits in the Willamette River Valley. Nearby mills ground the wheat, canneries canned vegetables and fruit, and local butchers slaughtered chickens, pigs, and cows. The area was virtually self-sufficient, except for imports of coffee, tea, sugar, and oranges.

Commercialization came to farmers in this area as early as 1868 when they began to export wheat to China. However, with the coming of the railroad to Oregon in 1883, eastern Oregon wheat farmers started to dominate the market. Beginning in the 1930s, local farmers turned to the grass seed industry to supply an upsurge of dairy farms around the state. Mild, wet winters and hot, dry summers proved to be ideal for raising grass. During World War II the Willamette Valley supplied the military with fiber for ropes, parachutes, and tents. In the 1950s, this area became number one in the nation for the production of grass seed headed for pastures, and increasingly for golf courses and parks (Malone, 2010).

Along with the grass seed industry came industrial agriculture. Farmers produced for a globalized commodity market and either grew bigger or went out of business. The use of chemical fertilizers and pesticides soared to meet production standards. Although wheat was still a commercial crop in the 1960s, by the 1980s, farmers lived by grass seed alone. Not surprisingly, small storage and processing plants for wheat and other grains disappeared (Malone 2010). I visited the shell of one abandoned plant from which wheat had gone to China, its giant wheel still turning and siphoning off water from a local river.

During the sudden economic downturn in the fall of 2008, family farmers who had hung on by contracting for grass seed faced extinction because prices fell steeply as demand plummeted. Grass seed piled up in silos. Some farmers turned to growing wheat again, but places to store wheat, much less to mill it, had virtually disappeared from the area. Some farms held on, supported by the non-farm employment of family members, but the average age of farmers in Oregon now is 58, and families often have to give up the farm when inheritance taxes come due or because younger family members see no future in farming.[4]

The economy of the Willamette Valley has suffered from the loss of many small farmers since the 1950s, as well as the loss of jobs in food processing and food selling. As local farm food decreased in volume and diversity, Corvallis lost family-run grocery stores that were replaced by corporate food chains. When my family moved to Corvallis in 1988, several medium-sized stores run by local families still existed. They brought in wholesale food, but they also were free to buy fruits and vegetables from local farmers, and one of the stores ran its own farm to supply local food. In 2010, the last of these family-run stores closed.

The landscape of grocery stores in Corvallis reflects the national story of increased corporate control of the food system. When we first arrived in 1988, Albertson's, Safeway, and Fred Meyers, a northwest chain, each had one store that sold groceries. The number of Safeway stores in Corvallis has increased from one to three, reflecting Safeway's growth nationally. It now controls 9% of the national market. Fred Meyers is larger now, and features self-swipe check out counters. Although the company name is still Fred Meyers, it was taken over by Kroger, a chain controlling 13% of the national market (Supermarket Consolidation, 2006). Walmart tried to come into Corvallis, but public pressure from relatively prosperous citizens concerned with preserving local businesses kept it out.

In Corvallis, rural, low-income people shop mostly at Winco, a northwestern discount chain.[5] They complained bitterly a few years ago when richer people successfully moved to keep Walmart and its low prices out of Corvallis. They must drive sixteen miles east of Corvallis to find a Walmart. New specialty stores coming into Corvallis do not help low-income shoppers either. Trader Joe's is the latest addition, reflecting the fast-growing niche market for healthy, partially prepared food among upscale customers. The wealth gap leads us to the next part of the story about food in Corvallis: the production and sale of local food is dependent on elite consumers and excludes low-income people.

But first, we must ask: What, if anything, is wrong with the American food system being dominated by corporations? Our food system gives us huge selection, low prices, global food in all seasons, and elite food for those who can afford it.

WHAT IS WRONG WITH THIS PICTURE?

Industrialized agriculture has a huge carbon footprint—a measure of the amount of carbon dioxide produced by human actions. Our food travels thousands of miles, using oil and filling the atmosphere with carbon dioxide. Huge feedlots for cattle and frequent plowing emit still more carbon dioxide, as does huge machinery used for harvesting crops.

Profit-oriented agriculture is inexpensive because it does not pay for the externalities that it causes. Externalities are the side effects of industrialized processes, particularly environmental side effects that corporations never pay for; taxpayers either cover the cost of mitigation or the problems simply grow worse. Synthetic fertilizers put phosphorus, nitrogen, and potassium into the soil. Pesticides kill both good and bad insects, upsetting their balance. Both fertilizers and pesticides enter our domestic water supply, and pollute the ocean causing dead spots with no sea life in the Gulf of Mexico and off the coast of

Oregon. Large-scale meat production requires huge amounts of water. It also pumps antibiotics into cows sickened by the corn force-fed to them. Cows evolved biologically to eat grass.

Industrialized agriculture also threatens biodiversity. Out of 500,000 plant species on this earth, only four are responsible for 60% of the world's food (Villianatos, 2006, p. 60). If farmers want to diversify, they have no access to seeds because corporations have acquired patents on thousands of seeds primarily for the purpose of restricting their use.

"The hidden hunger of industrialized agriculture is invisible" (Villianatos, 2006, p. 58). Our nutrition suffers because chemically based farming produces rice, wheat, and corn deficient in basic micronutrients that our bodies need, such as iodine, zinc, and chromium. Increased carbon dioxide causes plants to absorb less water and nutrients from the land and air. Beef and milk contain growth hormones and antibiotics. Many manufactured foods advertise on the basis of added vitamins or minerals, but this ploy does not make up for missing micronutrients such as omega-3 in seeds and fish (Pollan, 2008).

Our form of hunger is not starvation but overeating of the wrong things because they are cheap. While the average intake of calories in Uzbekistan in 2003 was 2312 per person per day, in America the figure now is 2700 calories, and the food supply offers us 3800 calories per person per day (WFP, 2008; Nestle, 2002, p. 13). Big food processors use cheap high-fructose corn syrup and cheap, crushed soybeans to sweeten and thicken our manufactured foods. Corporations want us to keep buying more, and as humans who have made the nutritional transition out of traditional plant-based diets to meat and processed foods, we have been seduced into liking energy-dense foods with sugars, fats, and salt. Corporations take advantage of the food addictions they have created to keep us buying and eating more. If people only consume the amount of calories they need, the profit in selling food is limited. If people eat more than they need and keep increasing their consumption, then profit is unlimited.

I have puzzled over why processed food seems cheaper to low-income people, because fresh fruits and vegetables appear cheaper to me. The answer is that calories are cheaper in manufactured food. Consumers take in more calories in the form of sugars and fats if they buy soda, pastries, or pasta than if they buy carrots or tomatoes. A dollar can buy 1200 calories of chips and cookies compared to only 250 calories of carrots (Pollan, 2006, p. 107). For the same reason Coke is less expensive than milk (Berg, 2008, p. 119). The result is that low-income people spend their scarce funds on processed foods high in sugar and fat to get enough calories to feel full.

Increased rates of obesity and diabetes are linked to the consumption of cheap calories. Taking Oregon as a typical example, in 2005, 60% of adult Oregonians were either obese or overweight. One quarter of Oregon eighth graders were overweight. Among this group, 82% had diabetes. Several studies have shown that obesity is linked with poverty and food insecurity, particularly in women and children (Berg, p. 123). What is amazing is how quickly this has happened. In both Oregon and America as a whole, in 1990, obesity stood at around 11%, but by 2005, the statistic was 24% (Ngo & Leman, 2007).

As in Keith's case, diabetes costs people money since they must pay for drugs and eventually hospitalizations. Diabetes increases depression and causes death sooner. In 2008, one in fifteen adult Oregonians had diabetes, a slightly higher rate than for the United States as a whole. Even worse, poor Oregonians are 1.5 times more likely to have diabetes than those who are wealthier. Whereas 10% of Latinos and 13% of African-Americans in Oregon had diabetes, only 6% of non-Latino whites had the disease in 2005 because of socioeconomic inequalities related to ethnicity as it overlaps with class (Lockwood, 2008).

Thus, the industrialized food system causes serious nutritional, health, and environmental problems from which lower-income people suffer more than others. Another adverse result is that it deprives communities of food security. Corvallis and the Willamette Valley would be hard-put to survive in an economic crisis or natural disaster that disrupted the flow of food in the industrial distribution system.

We have lost social empowerment as passive consumers in a food chain designed to support the profits of multi-national food corporations. Furthermore, this system creates social inequities. Poor people suffer more than the wealthy because the food that is least expensive for them to buy soon ruins their health.

THE LOCAL FOOD MOVEMENT

The local food movement in the United States is a reaction to people's sense that they have increasingly lost control over their food through the last half of the twentieth century. Americans do not know where their food comes from, who grows it, or how it grows. Local food is transparent. By eating locally, people eat more nutritious food, grown and delivered in a more environmentally sustainable way. Local food builds a thriving local food economy and strengthens community as people from different walks of life meet in farmers' markets.

Corvallis is the center of a vibrant local food movement. Small farms have started to flourish again in this new niche of local, often organic, food in the Willamette Valley. In season, vegetables from local organic farms—Denison, Deep Roots, Gathering Together, Spring Hill—fill the produce aisle at the First Alternative Coop, a members-owned store that has been organic since its beginnings in 1970, but in the last five years, also endeavors to be local. The same farms also sell at two Corvallis farmers' markets and several Portland markets, while supplying restaurants in the area.

Each farm has its own member organization of consumers called community-supported agriculture (CSA).[6] My family pays several hundred dollars in the spring, and then from June to October, we receive a weekly box of vegetables—lettuce, cucumbers, and tomatoes—tasty and smelling fresh from Gathering Together Farm. Furthermore, an online marketplace called Corvallis Local Foods features not only vegetables and fruits, but also direct-sale meats and processed foods.

This local food economy represents only a small percentage of food eaten in Corvallis, but it is growing. Farmers and their customers are active participants in moving towards an alternative to industrialized agriculture by building "food-sheds" defined as:

> self-reliant, locally or regionally based food systems comprised of diversified farms using sustainable practices to supply fresher, more nutritious foodstuffs to small-scale processors and consumers to whom producers are linked by the bonds of community as well as economy (Woodin & Lucas, 2004, p. 161).

Foodsheds are flexible and can expand to meet growing demand. They will never become global, but as the demand for local food increases, the Corvallis foodshed, for example, might extend itself to Oregon as a whole or even to the Pacific Northwest region including parts of northern California. Local foodsheds will never completely replace global food, but they have potential to greatly lessen corporate control over our food.

LOW-INCOME PEOPLE IN LOCAL FOODSHEDS

The local and largely organic food economy has thrived in Corvallis because its consumers tend to be professional people with decent incomes. Local food, especially organic local food, is a privilege afforded primarily by upscale consumers who have decent salaries and health insurance. Prices are often one-and-a-half or two times the price of conventional vegetables in the grocery stores. Despite my conviction that we are paying the true price of sustainable food, Clint has taken a while to be convinced—not of the taste or the ethics, but of the price tag. Given the choice, he saves money by buying conventional vegetables at a family-owned grocery store that sometimes sells local food. We refrain from commenting to each other about our different buying habits, and dinnertime is peaceful. However, Clint's favorite store is closing soon, and sparks may fly about where to buy food.

Ours is a small problem compared with that facing Keith and Susan. Although in our interviews many people expressed concern for eating well to be healthy, the ability of low-income people to take part in the local, fresh food economy is severely limited. An important question emerges: How do we develop sustainable, local food economies and include low-income people in them? This question has led me and other anthropologists to take action in the local food arena.

WORKING ON MAKING MORE LOCAL FOOD

Eating is more fun than being an anthropologist, but doing applied anthropology is one of the most interesting aspects of being an anthropologist. Joan Gross and I are both founding members and serve on the Board of the Ten Rivers Food Web. Based in Corvallis, this organization advocates for the production, distribution, and consumption of local food in a tri-county area.

The organization has done various projects that fulfill its mission to increase the availability and consumption of local food. Some members have facilitated neighborhood meetings to exchange garden produce and initiate fresh-food buying clubs. Farmers in the organization work on persuading other local farmers, both conventional and organic, to consider growing crops for local consumption, especially grains and beans (rather than grass), that local people can actually eat. Given the plunge in grass seed prices, farmers are open to change, but problems are rife: "Where are we going to store and grind the wheat now that small mills are gone?" Currently, we are applying for grants to facilitate new construction of a mill and storage facility, and private donors are also stepping forward to contribute. Accomplishing this goal is not easy because we are trying to rebuild what we once had in a new form in the midst of plentiful global food.

As an anthropologist, my main concern is with the question of how to get local food into the hands of low-income people. It is a major challenge to the local food movement to extend the experiences of taste, nutrition, and the security of knowing where your food comes to economically disadvantaged neighbors (Winne, 2008).

Even before the severe recession in 2008, the rich were getting richer and the poor staying poor in the United States (Berg, 2008, p. 128). Although the situation is better than in 2000 when Oregon was first in hunger in the United States, in 2010, the unemployment rate in Oregon is over 10% and distribution of emergency food boxes rose by 14% in 2009 (ODA, 2010).

The Ten Rivers Food Web, along with other agencies in Corvallis, run a variety of programs to provide nutritious local food to low-income people.[7] Local, organic food makes its way into the emergency food system through deliveries of leftovers from booths at farmers' markets to food pantries and gleaners. Several community gardens also donate their harvests to food pantries. In 2009, the supply of local food in the pantries increased so much that the problem became one of overflow and the need for better coordination! In 2010, local farmers are starting small farmers' markets in low-income apartment complexes in town. On the state level, Farmers Ending Hunger is a group that donates Oregon farm produce to the Oregon Food Bank to make up for the decrease in federal food (ODA, 2010).

Local farmers' markets also now have a machine that enables electronic transfer of food stamps so that low-income people can take advantage of new federal guidelines that allow them to use food stamps in farmers' markets and roadside farm stands.

Ecumenical Ministries of Oregon sells packets of coupons for $20 that buyers can use as currency with participating farmers at farmers' markets. The buyer receives only $18 of food value in the coupons while $2 goes to support coupons donated to low-income people to spend at the market.

Several organizations, including the Ten Rivers Food Web, have started community gardens for low-income people who receive training in gardening, cooking, and preserving food. One of my favorite examples is a garden where low-income youth learn jobs skills. The emphasis in this program is on the marketable skills of selling and cooking food; the trainees also learn skills that they might someday use in managing their own gardens or food businesses. Other workshops directly teach low-income people about opening food-related businesses. One of our anthropology graduates who received this training opened a mustard business.

Several of the organic, community supported farms in town have income-adjusted memberships for low-income people. One of the paradoxes of growing local food and serving the poor is that these farmers are trying to make a living by running businesses. They work hard and live close to the margin financially, taking advantage of a myriad of marketing opportunities to survive. It is only when they really get on their feet financially that they can reach out to low-income people.

IS THIS THE SOLUTION?

Do all these strategies solve the problems of food insecurity, or of the industrialized food system? No. What I have described are social movements, directionally important in shaping the future because they are happening all over the country. They offer foodways that are alternative to the global market and more embedded in the local community (Allen 2004).

The United States Department of Agriculture still spends billions of dollars for subsidies to industrialized farmers, but they are also funding community efforts to develop local economies and make links between disadvantaged people and local food (Allen 2004).

Food insecurity in the United States continues to worsen in 2010 as we recover from a prolonged economic recession. Emergency food, whether it comes locally or nationally, does not solve the basic problems of poor people (Poppendeick, 1998). Fundamental is the need for jobs—everywhere—but particularly in rural communities. Susan's sons need jobs. Susan also needs help to pay for car repairs and car insurance; alternatively public transportation would open up opportunities for her. Keith needs financial aid to continue to study for his college degree. Keith and his wife need help to pay for their utilities. Perhaps the Health Reform Act of 2010 will help them obtain health insurance and pay for the medications they need.

Food stamps and the emergency food system do not solve the "paradox of plenty" caused by the industrialized food system; instead, they perpetuate it (Winne, 2008). The search for profits and the lure of advertising drive our food system into overabundance of sugars and fats. Joel Berg (2008) even questions whether it is ethical to advertise food that is not nutritious to children and people who can ill afford empty calories financially or physically.

Although Americans enjoy broad freedoms compared with Uzbek citizens, our eating is largely dictated by a corporatized market system that most people only hazily understand. Yet, discontent with the food system is growing, particularly as obesity and diabetes epidemics surge. Changing any large system is extremely difficult, but anthropologists' voices and actions are part of the social movement towards a revitalized local food economy that includes low-income people.

ENDNOTES

1. The poverty line for a family of four in 2008 was $21,834, but people could access a food bank if their incomes were 185% of the poverty and join gleaning groups if their incomes were 200% of the poverty level. Eligibility for food stamps measures income and assets.

2. This aid is called the Food Distribution Program on Indian Reservations (FDPIR). The federal government distributes surplus food commodities to elderly and low-income Native Americans living on or near Reservations.

3. See the website of the Federation for American Immigration Reform for more details.

4. See the website of the Friends of Family Farmers who are working on transferring farmland in Oregon to young, interested farmers and on improving state policy to preserve small, family farms.

5. Winco owned 43 box stores in 2003 throughout the Northwest and into California. Formerly Waremart, it has low prices because it buys in bulk from distributors, but shoppers do not have to become members as they do at Costco. See the Winco website.

6. Community-supported agriculture or CSA is a direct-market partnership between a farm and a local consumer, in which the participants pay up front for their yearly share of food from a given farm, and the producer commits to providing a weekly assortment of food grown on their farm (Hinrichs, 2003).

7. Other active participants are Ecumenical Ministries of Oregon, Linn-Benton Food Share of the Oregon Food Bank, Community Services Consortium, and the Corvallis Environmental Center.

Chapter 9

Conclusion

Grown, sold, bought, eaten and shared, food unites our bodies and souls, yet ignites jealousies and anger. National cuisine simultaneously solidifies patriotism and highlights economic and social inequalities.

This book recounts differences of class, gender, ethnicity, and urban-rural residency that national foods bring to light in Uzbekistan and focuses on inequities of class that food reveals in the United States. The lens of food rights—food sovereignty and food security—expose the nuances of inequalities at personal, household, community, and national levels.

The comparison of food rights between Uzbekistan and the United States shows both stark contrast and surprising similarities. Uzbekistan's post-Soviet authoritarian government frames food rights in government control of agricultural land to ensure cotton for export revenues and wheat for minimal self-sufficiency in food. Household plots are small, but vital to producing vegetables, fruit, and livestock grown for households and the domestic market. The emphasis in the United States on democracy, free trade, and corporate-centered capitalism results in food rights characterized by corporate monopolies of all aspects of the food chain from field to table. A movement towards local food signals a shift to a more democratic agricultural system. While the United States could benefit from more local food systems, Uzbekistan would benefit from more inclusion in world trade.

Despite their contrasting systems, both Uzbekistan and the United States are self-sufficient in food; that is, they both grow enough to feed their populations. However, both populations are divided between rich and poor, with varying degrees of control over their food consumption. The degree of inequality in the distribution of family incomes as measured by the Gini coefficient is higher in the United States (45) than in Uzbekistan (36.8), with zero being equal (CIA, 2008). The poor suffer from food insecurity in both countries, but Uzbekistan's rate is about twice that of the United States.

The nature of food insecurity differs greatly between the two countries. While food insecure people in Uzbekistan lack enough calories, the food insecure in America have too many. In both cases, the calories that food insecure people consume are lacking in vital nutrients. In Uzbekistan the diet of the poor is poor in protein, with barely enough carbohydrates. In the United States, the diet of the poor is overabundant with carbohydrates including sugars, fats, and salt. While Uzbek children suffer from stunting, American children suffer from obesity and diabetes.

This book has shown that food rights such as food sovereignty and food security require detailed investigation with observation and interviews before they can be understood in the context of daily life for communities, households, and individuals. My hope is that this book encourages readers to extend a questioning gaze into the food system that affects your communities, family, and friends. Ask questions such as where your food comes from, who controls it, and who eats what and why. Reach out and help to democratize the food system in whatever way you can.

References

Ali, K., & Leaman, O. (2008). *Islam: The key concepts.* New York: Routledge.

Allen, P. (2004). *Together at the table: Sustainability and sustenance in the American agrifood system.* University Park: Pennsylvania State University.

Anderson, B. (1991). *Imagined communities: Reflections on the origin and spread of nationalism.* London: Verso.

Bayram, M. (2009, September 17). Uzbekistan: Muslim and Christian worship attacked. *Forum 18 News.*

Berg, J. (2008). *All you can eat: How hungry is America?* New York: Seven Stories Press.

Bhabha, H. (1994). *The location of culture.* London: Routledge.

Billig, M. (1995) *Banal nationalism.* Thousand Oaks, CA: Sage.

Bourdieu, P. (1984). *Distinction: a social critique of the judgment of taste.* Cambridge, MA: Harvard University Press.

Bourdieu, P. (2001). *Masculine domination.* Stanford: Stanford University Press.

Butler, J. (1999). *Gender trouble: Feminism and the subversion of identity.* New York: Routledge.

Cardenas, N. (2006). Decolonizing representation: Mexican American food interpretations of identity in San Antonio, Texas. Doctoral Dissertation, University of Texas at San Antonio.

Central Intelligence Agency. (2008). *The world factbook country comparison: Distribution of family income-gini index.* http://www.cia.gov/library/publications/the-world-factbook-rankorder-2172rank.html (Accessed 7/28/10).

Central Intelligence Agency. (2010). *The world factbook: Uzbekistan.* http://www.cia.gov/library/publications/the-world-factbook/geos/uz.html (Accessed 7/26/10).

Comaroff, J., & Comaroff, J. (2009). *Ethnicities, Inc.* Chicago: University of Chicago Press.

Corley, F. (2007, May 21). Uzbekistan: Government issues orders to religious communities. *Forum 18 News.*

Daly, John C. K. (2005, June 8). Events in Andijan anything but black and white. *ISN Security Watch.* http://www.isn.ethz.ch/news/details.cfm?ID=12067 (Accessed 7/15/10).

de la Vaissiere, E. (2004, December 1). Sogdian trade. *Encyclopaedia Iranica*. *Declaration of the Forum for Food Sovereignty*, Nyéléni 2007, Sélingué, Mali. 49_Declaration_of_Nyeleni.pdf

Edwards, M., Bernell, S., & Weber, B. (2007). Identifying factors that influence state-specific hunger rates in the U.S.: A simple analytic method for understanding a persistent problem. *Social Indicators Research, 81*, 579–595.

Ergashev, B., & Akhmerova, A. (2010). *Addressing urban poverty in Uzbekistan in the context of the economic crisis.* Tashkent: Center for Economic Research and United Nations Development Programme.

ERS (Economic Research Service). (2008). *Food security status of United States households 2008.* http://www.ers.usda.gov/Briefing/FoodSecurity/Householdswithstats_graphs.htm#food_secure (Accessed 7/27/10).

Eurasianet.org. (2005). *Andijan massacre linked to local power struggle – Source.* http://www.eurasianet.org/departments/insight/articles/eav092905.shtml (Accessed 9/28/10).

Family Farm Defenders. (2005). *Via Campesina's seven principles of food sovereignty.* http://familyfarmdefenders.org/index.php/Food Sovereignty/ViaCampesinasSeven Principles of Food Sovereignty (Accessed 7/26/10).

Feldstein, C. (2002). Salt Intake, hypertension and diabetes mellitus. *Journal of Human Hypertension, 16* (Supplement 1), 48–51.

Fenton, S. (2003). *Ethnicity.* Cambridge: Fenton Press.

Foltz, R. (1996). The Tajiks of Uzbekistan. *Central Asia Survey 15* (2), 213–216.

Foster, J. (1939). *The church of the Tang Dynasty.* New York: Macmillan.

Freedom House. (2007). *Profile on Uzbekistan.* http://www.freedomhouse.org (Accessed 7/2/10).

Gomart, E. (2003). Standing on a knife's edge: Doing business in Uzbekistan. In N. Dudwick, E. Gomart, & M. Alexandre (Eds.), *When things fall apart: Qualitative studies of poverty in the former Soviet Union* (pp. 95–111). Washington DC: The World Bank.

Gross, J., & Rosenberger, N. (2006). Food insecurity in rural Benton County: An ethnographic study. Working Paper, Rural Studies, Oregon State University.

Gross, J., & Rosenberger, N. (2009). The Double binds of getting food among the poor in rural Oregon. *Food, Culture and Society, 12* (4), 47–70.

Hendrickson, M., & Heffernan, W. (2005). Concentration of agricultural markets, Department of Rural Sociology, University of Missouri, January.

Hinrichs, C. (2003). The practice and politics of food system localization. *Journal of Rural Studies, 19*, 33–45.

Human Rights Watch. (2001). Sacrificing women to save the family? Domestic violence in Uzbekistan. *Uzbekistan, 13* (4) (D). New York: Human Rights Watch.

Human Rights Watch. (2003). From house to house: Abuses by Mahalla committees. *Uzbekistan, 15* (7) (D). New York: Human Rights Watch.

Human Rights Watch. (2005). Bullets were falling like rain: The Andijan massacre. *Uzbekistan, 17* (5) (D). New York: Human Rights Watch.

Index Mundi Uzbekistan. Indexmundi.com/Uzbekistan/gdp_real_growth_rate.html, (Accessed 7/22/10).

IRIN. (2007, September 4). *Uzbekistan: Food price rises spark sporadic protests.* http://www.irinnews.org/Report.aspx?Reportid=74097 (Accessed 7/28/10).

Ismalov, E. (2004). Uzbekistan's corruption-ridden educational system seen as source of frustration, April 28. *http://www.eurasianet.org/departments/insight/articles/eav042904* (Accessed 12/5/10).

Kamp, M. (2006). *The new woman in Uzbekistan: Islam, modernization, and unveiling under Communism.* Seattle: University of Washington Press.

Kamp, M., & Zanca, R. (2008). *Writing the history of collectivization in Uzbekistan: Oral narratives.* National Council for Eurasia and East European Research.

Kandyoti, D. (1988). Bargaining with Patriarchy. *Gender and Society, 2* (3), 274–290.

Keane, W. (2003). Semiotics and the social analysis of material things. *Words and Beyond: Linguistic and Semiotic Studies of Sociocultural Order,* (July-Oct), 409–425.

Khan, V. (1998). The Korean minority in central Asia: National revival and problem of identity international. *Journal of Central Asian Studies, 3,* 66–77. Seoul: Institute of Asian Culture and Development.

Levi-Strauss, C. (1963). *Totemism.* Boston: Beacon Press.

Lockwood, C. (2008). *The burden of diabetes in Oregon: Surveillance report.* Portland: Oregon Department of Human Services, Public Health Division.

Mack, G., & Surina, A. (2005). *Food culture in Russia and central Asia.* Westport, Conn: Greenwood Press.

MacLoed, C., & Mathew, B. (1999). *Uzbekistan: Golden road to Samarkand.* Hong Kong: Odyssey.

Mahmood, S. (2001). Feminist theory, embodiment and the docile agent: Some reflections on the Egyptian Islamic revival, *Cultural Anthropology, 16* (2), 202–236.

Malikov, A. (2005). Some observations on the identity of the rural Uzbeks of the Bukhara Province of Uzbekistan in the 20th Century. Paper presented at the 6th annual Central Eurasian Studies Society Conference. Boston, October 1.

Malone, C. (2010). Returning grain to the lower-Willamette Valley: Prospects and barriers for local food security. MA thesis, Department of Geosciences, Oregon State University.

Maxwell, S. (1996). Food security: A postmodern perspective. *Food Policy, 21* (2), 155–171.

Melvin, N. (2000). *Uzbekistan: Transition to authoritarianism on the silk road.* Singapore: Harwood Publishers.

Mernissi, F. (1985). *Beyond the veil: Male-female dynamics in modern Muslim society.* London: Alsaqi Books.

Murray, C. (2006). *Murder in Samarkand.* Edinburgh: Mainstream Press.

Musaev, D., Yakhshilikov, Y., & Yusupov, K. (2010). *Food security in Uzbekistan.* Tashkent: United Nations Development Program.

Nagata, K. (2008, February 26). Japan needs imports to keep itself fed. *Japan Times,* English edition.

Nestle, M. (2002). *Food politics: How the food industry influences nutrition and health.* Berkeley: University of California Press.

Ngo, D., & Leman, R. (2007). *Oregon overweight, obesity, physical activity, and nutrition facts.* Portland: Oregon Department of Human Services.

Northrop, D. (2004). *Veiled empire.* Ithaca: Cornell University Press.

Nuttal, C. (2009). GM Uzbekistan looks to domestic demand to survive crisis. *Business News Europe,* April 24. http://www.businessneweurope.eu/story1573/ (Accessed 7/26/10).

ODA (Oregon Department of Agriculture). (2010, January 27). *Household food security drops in Oregon and the US.* http://Oregon.gov/ODA/news/

100127food_security.shtml (Accessed 7/27/10).

Oregon. (2008). *Oregon statistics from household food security in the US.* http://www.frac.org/State_of_States/2008/states/OR.pdf (Accessed 7/27/10).

Ozbek, B. B. (2007). The Andijon events: Demand for more development or threat to stability? *Perspectives,* Winter.

Pollan, M. (2006). *The omnivore's dilemma: A natural history of four meals.* New York: Penguin Press.

Pollan, M. (2006). *In defense of food: An eater's manifesto.* New York: Penguin Books.

Poppendieck, J. (1998). *Sweet charity: Emergency food and the end of entitlement.* New York: Penguin Books.

Reuters News Service. (2007, August 28). *US rural poverty rate unchanged despite farm boom.*

Rosenberger, N. (2001). *Gambling with virtue: Japanese women and the search for self in a changing nation.* Honolulu: University of Hawaii Press.

Rosenberger, N. (2007). Patriotic appetites and gnawing hungers: Food and the paradox of nation-building in Uzbekistan. *Ethnos, 72* (3), 339–360.

Rosenberger, N., Richards, L., Gifford, L., & Gossen, K. (2006). *From our own soil: A community food assessment of Benton County, Oregon, and its foodshed.* Ecumenical Ministries of Oregon. http://www.emoregon.org (Accessed 7/28/10).

Rotar, I. (2005, June 16). Uzbekistan: What is known about Akramia and the uprising? *Forum 18 News.*

Roy, O. (2007). *The new central Asia: Geopolitics and the creation of nations.* New York: New York University Press.

Sell, S. (2009). Corporations, seeds, and intellectual property rights governance. In J. Clapp & D. Fuchs (Eds.), *Corporate power in global agrifood governance* (pp. 187–223). Cambridge, Mass: MIT Press.

Sen, A. (1990). Food entitlements and economic chains. In L. Newman (Ed.), *Hunger in History* (pp. 374–386). Oxford: Basil Blackwell.

Shiva, V. (1997). *Biopiracy: The plunder of nature and knowledge.* Boston: South End Press.

Spoor, M. (2006). Agriculture reform policies in Uzbekistan. In S. C. Babu & S. Djalalov (Eds.), *Policy reforms and agriculture development in central Asia* (pp. 181–203). New York: Springer Publishing House.

Suleimenov, M., Iniguez, L., & Musayeva, M. (2006). Policy reforms and livestock in central Asia. In S. C. Babu & S. Djalalov (Eds.), *Policy reforms and agriculture development in central Asia* (pp. 285–293). New York: Springer Publishing House.

Supermarket consolidation. (2006). http:///www.wikinvest.com/concept/supermarket_consolidation (Accessed 7/26/10).

Tajikam Worldwide Community of Tajiks. *Tajiks in Uzbekistan.* http://www.tajikam.com/index.php?option=com_content&task=view&id=68&Itemid=36 (Accessed 6/30/10).

Tarmann, A. (2003). *Fifty years of demographic change in rural America.* Population Reference Bureau, http://www.prb.org/articles/2003/fiftyyearsofdemographicchangeinruralamerica (Accessed 7/25/10).

Tokhtakhodzhaeva, M. (1995). *The re-Islamization of society and the position of women in post-Soviet Uzbekistan.* Tashkent University: Global Oriental Publications.

UNDP (United Nations Development Program). (2005). *Development of the education system in Uzbekistan 00-04: Statistical bulletin.* Tashkent: State Committee of the Republic of

Uzbekistan on Statistics. http://www.statistics.uz/sources/i/education.en.pdf (Accessed 7/17/10).

UNICEF. (2010). *Uzbekistan: Statistics.* http://www.unicef.org/infobycountry/uzbekistan_statistics.html (Accessed on 7/22/10).

U.S. Census Bureau. (2009). *United States: Age and sex.* American Community Survey and Population Estimates Program. (Accessed 7/23/10).

U.S. Department of Agriculture. (2003). *Agricultural fact book 2001-2002.* http://usda.gov/factbook/Chapter2.pdf (Accessed 7/20/10). Uznews 2007 http://www.uznews.net/news_single.php?lng=en&sub=&cid=3&nid=926. Sept 28. (Accessed 1/2/11).

Villianatos, E. (2006). *This land is their land: How corporate farms threaten the world.* Monroe, Maine: Common Courage Press.

Welfare improvement strategy paper of the Republic of Uzbekistan for 2005-2010: Interim PRSP document (I-WISP). (2007). Tashkent: Government of the Republic of Uzbekistan.

WFP (World Food Programme). (2008). *Poverty and food insecurity in Uzbekistan.* http://wfp.org/stellent/groups/public/documents/ena/wfp179011.pdf (Accessed 5/15/10).

Whitlock, M. (2002). *Land beyond the river: The untold story of central Asia.* New York: St. Martin's Press.

Winant, H. (1994). Racial formation and hegemony: Global and local developments. In I. A. Rattansi & S. Westwood (Eds.), *Racism, modernity and identity* (pp. 266–289).

Winne, M. (2008). *Closing the food gap.* Boston: Beacon Press.

Wood, F. (2004). *The silk road: Two thousand years in the heart of Asia.* Berkeley: University of California Press.

Woodin, M., & Lucas, C. (2004). *Green alternatives to globalisation: A manifesto.* London: Pluto Press.

Workman, D. (2007, September 7). *Top ten cotton countries.* http://internationaltrade.suite101.com/article.cfm/top_ten_cotton_countries (Accessed 8/6/10).

Yalcin, R. (1999). Ethnic minorities in Uzbekistan: The case of Koreans. *International Journal of Central Asian Studies, 4.*

Yalcin, R. (1999). *Uzbekistan: Golden road to Samarkand.* Hong Kong: Odyssey Press.

Yalcin, R. (2002). *The rebirth of Uzbekistan: Politics, economy and society in the post-Soviet era.* Ithaca: Cornell University Press.

Yanagisako, S., & Delaney, C. (1995). Naturalizing Power. In S. Yanagisako & C. Delaney (Eds.), *Naturalizing power: Essays in feminist cultural analysis* (pp. 1–22). London: Routledge Press.

Zanca, R. (2003). "Take! Take! Take!" Host–guest relations and all that food: Uzbek hospitality past and present. *Anthropology of East Europe Review, 21* (1).

Zilberman, S. (2010, April 15). Uzbekistan's threaten cultural legacy. *The Guardian.*

Zuzunova, G. (2002). Ritual Uzbek food. *International Journal of Central Asian Studies, 7,* 109–118.